The Letters of
Geerhardus Vos

THE LETTERS OF
GEERHARDUS VOS

EDITED WITH AN INTRODUCTION BY

JAMES T. DENNISON JR.

P&R
PUBLISHING
P.O. BOX 817 • PHILLIPSBURG • NEW JERSEY 08865

© 2005 by James T. Dennison Jr.

All rights reserved. No part of this book may be reproduced, stored in a retrieval system, or transmitted in any form or by any means—electronic, mechanical, photocopy, recording, or otherwise—except for brief quotations for the purpose of review or comment, without the prior permission of the publisher, P&R Publishing Company, P.O. Box 817, Phillipsburg, New Jersey 08865-0817.

The original copies of the letters printed in this volume are located in the following repositories:

Archive of the Free University of Amsterdam, The Netherlands: Letters to Abraham Kuyper, Herman Bavinck, Cornelis van Felderen, Albertus Eekhof, F. W. Grosheide.

Archive of Princeton Theological Seminary, Princeton, New Jersey: Letters to William Henry Roberts, B. B. Warfield, Sylvester Beach, Frank Stevenson.

Archive of Rutgers State University, New Brunswick, New Jersey: Letters to William Elliot Griffis.

Heritage Hall Archive, Calvin College, Grand Rapids, Michigan: Letters to Henry Beets.

The Presbyterian Historical Society, Philadelphia, Pennsylvania: Letters to Donald MacKenzie.

Westminster Theological Seminary, Philadelphia, Pennsylvania: Letters to J. Gresham Machen, Paul Woolley, Arthur Machen, Ned Stonehouse, Edwards Elliott.

I want to express my thanks to Baker Publishing Group for granting permission to incorporate into this work material which earlier appeared in *Bible Interpreters of the Twentieth Century: A Selection of Evangelical Voices*, ed. Walter A. Elwell and J. D. Weaver (Grand Rapids: Baker Book House Company, 1999), 82–92.

Page design and typesetting by Lakeside Design Plus

Printed in the United States of America

Library of Congress Cataloging-in-Publication Data

Vos, Geerhardus, 1862–1949.
 The letters of Geerhardus Vos / edited with an introduction by James T. Dennison, Jr.
   p. cm.
 Includes bibliographical references and index.
 ISBN-10: 0-87552-187-8 (cloth)
 ISBN-13: 978-0-87552-187-9 (cloth)
  1. Vos, Geerhardus, 1962–1949—Correspondence. 2. Reformed (Reformed Church)—Correspondence. 3. Theologians—Correspondence. I. Dennison, James T., 1943– II. Title.

BX9419.V67A4 2005
284'.2092—dc22
[B]
                                                                                                2005053549

To those who love the Lord Jesus Christ in sincerity
To those who love the beloved Father of the beloved Son
To those who love because of the beloved Spirit of the Father and the Son

To those who love the Word of God, breathed out from the loving mouth of God the Father, God the Son, and God the Holy Spirit

To those who love the Reformed confessions, especially the crown of Calvinism, the Westminster Confession and Catechisms

To those who love the testimony of an unassuming servant of the triune God, Geerhardus Vos—lover of the Reformed confessions, lover of the Word of God, lover of the Father, Son, and Holy Spirit: Creator, Redeemer, Consummator

To those first loved by the Lord Jesus Christ

יְהוָה ׀ אוֹרִי וְיִשְׁעִי יִצְפְּנֵנִי ׀ בְּסֻכֹּה
(Psalm 27:1, 5)

θεὸς . . . καὶ ὄντας ἡμᾶς νεκροὺς τοῖς παραπτώμασιν συνεζωοποίησεν τῷ Χριστῷ—χάριτί ἐστε σεσῳσμένοι—καὶ συνήγειρεν καὶ συνεκάθισεν ἐν τοῖς ἐπουρανίοις ἐν Χριστῷ Ἰησοῦ.
(Ephesians 2:5–6)

Vita vestra est abscondita cum Christo in Deo.
(Colossians 3:3)

Never commit the foolishness of exchanging the gospel full of Christ—the Lord of Glory! O the pity and shame that preachers sometimes exchange this glorious Christ for a Jesus after the flesh, a religious genius, a product of evolution, stripped of the supernatural power to save. (Geerhardus Vos, October 14, 1914)

CONTENTS

Preface   11
Introduction: The Life of Geerhardus Vos   13
The Writings of Geerhardus Vos: A Bibliography   87
Letters of Geerhardus Vos
    To W. H. Roberts (August 17, 1883)   115
    To Abraham Kuyper (May 28, 1886)   116
    To Abraham Kuyper (June 7, 1886)   118
    To J. W. Felix (September 4, 1886)   119
    To Abraham Kuyper (October 7, 1886)   120
    To Herman Bavinck (June 16, 1887)   122
    To B. B. Warfield (February 2, 1889)   128
    To B. B. Warfield (October 22, 1889)   129
    To Herman Bavinck (February 1, 1890)   131
    To Abraham Kuyper (February 1, 1890)   133
    To Herman Bavinck (March 4, 1890)   136
    To B. B. Warfield (April 9, 1890)   138
    To B. B. Warfield (June 13, 1890)   139
    To B. B. Warfield (July 2, 1890)   140
    To Abraham Kuyper (July 12, 1890)   140
    To B. B. Warfield (August 5, 1890)   143
    To Abraham Kuyper (October 27, 1890)   144
    To B. B. Warfield (January 31, 1891)   145
    To B. B. Warfield (February 12, 1891)   147
    To Abraham Kuyper (February 21, 1891)   148
    To B. B. Warfield (March 12, 1891)   151

To Herman Bavinck (May 13, 1891)   153
To Herman Bavinck (June 30, 1891)   158
To B. B. Warfield (July 7, 1891)   160
To Abraham Kuyper (July 30, 1891)   164
To B. B. Warfield (August 29, 1891)   166
To B. B. Warfield (September 8, 1891)   167
To B. B. Warfield (September 28, 1891)   168
To B. B. Warfield (March 18, 1892)   170
To Abraham Kuyper (May 11, 1893)   172
To Herman Bavinck (July 3, 1893)   174
To Abraham Kuyper (July 3, 1893)   177
To Herman Bavinck (October 20, 1893)   178
To Herman Bavinck (November 21, 1893)   180
To Herman Bavinck (February 1, 1894)   182
To Abraham Kuyper (February 26, 1894)   183
To Herman Bavinck (March 28, 1894)   185
To Herman Bavinck (December 22, 1894)   187
To Herman Bavinck (July 6, 1895)   189
To Abraham Kuyper (April 30, 1896)   191
To Abraham Kuyper (June 10, 1896)   193
To Abraham Kuyper (July 11, 1896)   194
To Abraham Kuyper (October 7, 1896)   195
To Abraham Kuyper (November 11, 1896)   197
To Abraham Kuyper (March 6, 1897)   198
To Abraham Kuyper (June 15, 1897)   199
To Abraham Kuyper (October 11, 1897)   200
To William Elliot Griffis (December 15, 1898)   201
To Herman Bavinck (April 29, 1899)   202
To William Elliot Griffis (January 13, 1902)   204
To Herman Bavinck (May 17, 1905)   205
To Herman Bavinck (February 21, 1906)   206
To Herman Bavinck (January 7, 1909)   208
To J. Gresham Machen (January 26, 1909)   210
To Henry Beets (March 16, 1912)   211
To Henry Beets (October 4, 1915)   212
To Cornelis van Felderen (September 5, 1921)   213
To Directors (August 11, 1926)   214
To Sylvester Beach (July 13, 1928)   215
To Frank Stevenson (December 19, 1928)   217

To J. Gresham Machen (? 1930)   218
To J. Gresham Machen (March 31, 1930)   218
To J. Gresham Machen (May 1, 1930)   220
To F. W. Grosheide (February 19, 1932)   221
To J. Gresham Machen (April 28, 1932)   223
To Paul Woolley (September 9, 1932)   224
To Albertus Eekhof (October 28, 1932)   225
To Donald MacKenzie (February 26, 1935)   229
To Donald MacKenzie (March 20, 1935)   231
To Paul Woolley (January 27, 1936)   232
To Paul Woolley (January 29, 1936)   233
To Paul Woolley (February 22, 1936)   234
To J. Gresham Machen (May 7, 1936)   236
To Arthur Machen (January 5, 1937)   238
To Ned Stonehouse (December 15, 1938)   239
To Ned Stonehouse (May 18, 1940)   240
To Henry Beets (October 16, 1940)   241
To Henry Beets (January ?, 1941)   242
To Henry Beets (January 9, 1941)   244
To Henry Beets (February 12, 1941)   244
To Ned Stonehouse (July 21, 1944)   245
To Ned Stonehouse (January 11, 1945)   246
To Edwards Elliott (January 25, 1946)   247

Poetry of Geerhardus Vos
  The Sword   251
  A Song of the Nativity   252
  Kerstfeest-Gebed   255
  The Magnificat   256

Index of Scripture   259

Index of Subjects and Names   261

Preface

This volume contains the most thorough account of the life of Geerhardus Vos published to date. Previous work on his life and career must now be checked against this essay. Even my former work has been enlarged, revised, and corrected by this version. Undoubtedly, many rabbit trails remain, which will yet yield tidbits of information about the mysterious premier Reformed biblical theologian of the twentieth century. Thus, even this edition of the story of Geerhardus Vos is open to further enlargement, revision, and correction.

This volume is the result of the combined efforts of many years and many helping hands. First, the archives of Calvin College (Heritage Hall), the Free University of Amsterdam, Princeton Theological Seminary, Westminster Theological Seminary, and the Presbyterian Historical Society have provided the raw data for this volume. Second, since my native tongue is not Dutch (nor have I learned it), many Dutch readers and translators have given of their time to make this volume readable to the English-speaking audience. The Rev. Fritz Harms and his wife Brenda, Nicholaas Van Dam, David Harrell, Mrs. Don (Shirley) Harrell, Sandra Fokkema, Derk Bergsma, and especially Ed M. van der Maas have moved words from one world to another. Mrs. Newman (Lena) Lee and her daughter, Mrs. David (Ling) Harrell, did most of the typing; they were assisted by Mr. Jack Dundas. My brothers, the late Rev. Charles G. Dennison and Dr. William D. Dennison, have provided materials and encouragement. The Rev. William Harris and Mr. Richard Harms have generously provided archival materials and expert counsel. The Rev. Brian Vos has excavated several primary documents by tediously turning page after page. Mrs. Barbara Lerch of P&R Publishing has always been an encouragement. Special mention should be made of Shirley De Boer, Alice Hamstra, John Shaffer, Stephen Lambers, and Raymond Cannata. Other librarians, archivists, and research assistants too numerous to mention have been involved. My thanks to you all!

The late Mrs. William (Marianne) Radius, only daughter of Geerhardus Vos, was the wonderful promoter of her father's work and labored heroically to recover the remains of his papers in 1975 and 1976. Without her involvement, this volume (and my interest in her father) would never have come to print. My conversations with her and our correspondence were a source of insight, direction, and discovery.

Dr. George Harinck of the Free University of Amsterdam has given unselfishly of his broad expertise in Dutch-American relations in the late nineteenth and early twentieth centuries. Many of the explanatory footnotes to the Dutch letters have been formulated from information provided by him. *Vriendelijk bedankt voor U help met de vertaling van de brieven.*

But there is one person who deserves the supreme honor in this section. This "elect lady" is Miss Grace Mullen of the Westminster Theological Seminary library in Philadelphia, Pennsylvania. Gracie has plundered the files, driven many miles, written many letters, and provided many phone conversation reports on rabbit trails and serendipitous discoveries. It has been a joy to work with an unassuming daughter of the Lord Jesus Christ. Gracie, *gratias tibi ago, in novissimo agno!*

INTRODUCTION
The Life of Geerhardus Vos

The letters, which follow, are the epistolary remains of that remarkable Christian, scholar, Calvinist, biblical-theologian—Geerhardus Vos. The missives span his unspectacular life from before matriculation at Princeton Theological Seminary to before his eschatological emancipation. His 87-year career, begun in obscurity in Friesland, ends in obscurity in Michigan. From his tedious prize-winner (*The Mosaic Origin of the Pentateuchal Codes*) to his magnum opus, *The Pauline Eschatology*, shafts of heavenly light erupt from the pages of divine revelation and, concatenated in organic continuity, enlighten every man and woman and child born from above.

And yet the author of these letters was never well known, even in Reformed circles. This mystery haunted Cornelius Van Til, as it perplexed Clarence Bouma,[1] John Jansen,[2] and Peter De Jong.[3] Even in his lifetime, Vos appears to have been unrecognized beyond the tiny

---

1. Clarence Bouma, "Geerhardus Vos and Biblical Theology," *Calvin Forum* 9/1–2 (August–September 1943): 5.
2. John Jansen, "The Biblical Theology of Geerhardus Vos," *Princeton Seminary Bulletin* 66/2 (Summer 1974): 23.
3. Peter De Jong, "The Vos Legacy," *Torch and Trumpet* 29 (December 1979): 13.

Princeton and Christian Reformed circles.[4] Was Vos handicapped by his own self-effacing personality? In evading the spotlight, did he succeed in evading all notice entirely?[5] B. B. Warfield regarded him as "probably the greatest exegete Princeton ever had."[6] But beyond Warfield, who but a handful of students even knew of his existence? There is an intangible elusiveness about Geerhardus Vos—almost as if he wanted it that way. It seems as if he wanted to remain back in the shadows as an enigma, an obscure mystery.

The Netherlands

The mystery opened on March 14, 1862. Geerhardus Vos greeted the world that day in Heerenveen, Friesland, the Netherlands. He was the oldest of four children, all of whom were born in Holland. His siblings were Anna (1864–1955),[7] Bert John (1867–1945),[8] and Gertrude (1870–1962).[9] The Vos parents, Rev. Jan Hendrick and Aaltje Beuker Vos, came from the region of Bentheim and had German roots.[10] Even

---

4. I have been able to locate only a few comments on his work made during his lifetime in journals or other literature.

5. "At times he styled himself a mystic, and his aversion to publicity must perhaps in part be ascribed to the mystic strain in him. Perhaps he nursed this trait to the point of weakness; at least, there were not a few who thought so. If there was one trait closely related to his diffidence, it was his reticence, by which a part of his inner life was kept a closed domain and curiosity mongers were repelled." Jacob G. Vanden Bosch, "Geerhardus Vos," *Reformed Journal* 4/10 (November 1954): 13.

6. Louis Berkhof to Ned Stonehouse, December 21, 1954. Stonehouse Papers, Westminster Theological Seminary, Philadelphia, Pennsylvania. The statement also appears in Berkhof's review of *The Pauline Eschatology* in *The Banner* 87 (October 24, 1952): 1299.

7. She married Marinus Van Vessem, a minister in the Christian Reformed Church from 1887 to 1938. His pastorates were chiefly in Michigan. Interestingly, on October 21, 1883, he made a profession of faith when J. H. Vos was pastor of Spring Street Christian Reformed Church; in 1890, he married Vos's daughter. See Henry Beets, "Rev. Marinus Van Vessem: His Life and Labors," *The Banner* 80 (December 14, 1945): 1234.

8. He was the distinguished professor of German languages and literature at Johns Hopkins University, Baltimore, Maryland (1892–1908), and Indiana University, Bloomington (1908–1937).

9. She never married. She kept house for her mother and father after they retired to Graafschap, Michigan, and then spent her remaining years in the Grand Rapids area.

10. The German ancestry of his parents was noted by Geerhardus Vos in the U.S. Census form for 1900; see New Jersey, Mercer County, Princeton Township/Borough. The notion that his ancestors bore the French Huguenot name Vossé and had immigrated to Germany following the revocation of the Edict of Nantes (1685) cannot be confirmed from any primary docu-

at birth, our subject was part of multiple worlds: Frisian by birth to parents German by birth. He was destined to become proficient in the language proper to each: Dutch and German, to which he later added French and English—not to mention Latin, Greek, Hebrew, Syriac, and Arabic.

Jan Vos came from German Old Reformed pietism and felt the impact of the *Afscheiding* when he completed his seminary education at the Secession Theologische Universiteit in Kampen.[11] His first pastorate (1858–60) was in the church of his youth, the German Old Reformed congregation of Ulzen (Ulsen) in Bentheim.[12] His next five churches were Christelijke Gereformeerde Kerken, Heerenveen (1860–65), Katwyk an Zee (1865–70), Lutten (1870–74), Pernis, on the island of IJselmonde (1874–78), and Ommen (1878–81). Did the frequent changes in pastorates make the move to the United States but one more change? Jan Vos had no long-term pastorate until he immigrated to Grand Rapids. A place to stay, a place to remain—the father of the man who would make this concept the keystone of his biblical theology found a place to rest in the New World, at last!

Geerhardus began his education in the public schools of Katwyk, Lutten, and Pernis. He was then enrolled in the Fransche School ("French School") in Schiedam (no doubt while his father was pastor at nearby Pernis). Next, he was tutored privately and lived in the Spijknisse home of Rev. C. J. I. Engelbrecht, who had taught in South Africa and thus was able to increase Vos's proficiency in French and

---

ment. It first appears in William Henry Green's introduction to Geerhardus Vos, *The Mosaic Origin of the Pentateuchal Codes* (New York: A. C. Armstrong & Son, 1886), iii. Vos himself never documents this tradition, though his fondness for Green suggests that the beloved Old Testament professor did not invent the tale.

For more on the German Reformed background of Vos's parents, see Gerrit Jan Beuker, "German Oldreformed Emigration: Catastrophe or Blessing?" in *Breaches and Bridges: Reformed Subcultures in the Netherlands, Germany, and the United States*, ed. George Harinck and Hans Krabbendam (Amsterdam: VU Uitgeverij, 2001), 101–13, especially p. 104, where Beuker mentions J. H. Vos. Cf. Wayne Brouwer, "The German Element in the CRC: European Background," *The Banner* 115 (April 11, 1980): 10–12.

11. For the career of Vos's father, see Joh. de Haas, *Gedenkt uw voorgangers* (Haarlem: Vijbrief, 1980), 275, and the brief obituary in *De Bazuin,* March 14, 1913. Cf. Henry Beets, "Rev. J. H. Vos Called Home," *The Banner* 48 (February 20, 1913): 122; J. W. Brink, "Personal Reminiscences of the Late Rev. J. H. Vos," *The Banner* 48 (March 6, 1913): 155.

12. In connection with this location, Geerhardus Vos notes his "last act of piety" for his father (Vos to Henry Beets, January 9, 1941, and February 12, 1941).

English. Finally, Vos entered the Gymnasium in Amsterdam in 1877, just before his family moved on to Ommen. Geerhardus remained behind, boarding in "Uncle Beuker's" home, so as to continue his studies.[13] On July 16, 1881, he graduated with honors from the Gymnasium. Within a month, he was transported from the old to the new world of Grand Rapids, Michigan.

In the only known autobiographical sketch of his life,[14] Vos recounts some of the educational influences that shaped his early and teenage years. Surprisingly, the individuals named are all poets. Or perhaps we should say *not* surprisingly, because Geerhardus Vos was a poet in his own right, working with line and verse nearly to the time of his death.[15]

---

13. Hendericus Beuker (1834–1900) was pastor of the Christelijke Gereformeerde Kerk in Amsterdam from 1873 to 1881. Ironically, after a brief pastorate in Muskegon, Michigan (1893–94), he arrived in Grand Rapids in the fall of 1894 to assume his nephew's former teaching position at the Theologische School (see Vos to Herman Bavinck, March 28, 1894).

George Harinck suggests that it was during the Amsterdam years that Vos became aware of Abraham Kuyper and his newly formed Vrije Universiteit (founded in October 1880). See Harinck, "Geerhardus Vos as Introducer of Kuyper in America," in *The Dutch-American Experience: Essays in Honor of Robert P. Swierenga*, ed. Hans Krabbendam and Larry J. Wagenaar (Amsterdam: VU Uitgeverij, 2000), 245. For more on Beuker, see Haas, *Gedenkt uw voorgangers*, 35–36; *De Bazuin*, October 12, 1894; *De Heraut*, June 10, 1900; "Prof. H. Beuker, D.D.," *De Wachter*, May 30, 1900.

14. "Autobiographische aanteekeningen," *Neerlandia* 37 (January 1933): 9–10. An English translation of this sketch by Ed M. van der Maas was published in *Kerux: The Journal of Northwest Theological Seminary* 19/3 (December 2004): 6–10. I am indebted to Brian Vos of Byron Center, Michigan, for the discovery of this sketch.

15. Seven small volumes of his poetry appeared from 1922 to 1936: *Spiegel der genade* (Mirror of Grace) (1922), *Spiegel der natuur en lyra Anglica* (Mirror of Nature and English Verse) (1927), *Charis, English Verses* (1931), *Spiegel des doods* (Mirror of Death) (1932), *Western Rhymes* (1934), and *Zeis en garve* (Scythe and Sheaf) (1934). The second edition of *Spiegel des doods* (1936) contains a revised version of the poem entitled "Habakuks visioen" (Habakkuk's Vision). An eighth volume (undated) by "Desiderius" (Latin for "most desired" or "most yearned for"), entitled *Rhymes Old and New*, has been passed on to me by Eric Watkins of Oviedo, Florida. The verse in this volume is definitely Vos's—in fact, many of the poems are reprints of pieces from other volumes of his verse. The inside front cover is inscribed "Verses of my father" and is signed "Jerry Vos" (Geerhardus's youngest son).

In addition, miscellaneous poems appeared in scattered publications from 1942 to 1949. Some of these appear at the end of this volume.

Vos's daughter, Marianne Radius, has reflected on her father's delight in "playing" with words for poetical purposes. He enjoyed rhyming stanzas in English, Dutch, German, and French, as well as translating verse from one language to the other. Some of his poetry represented his Christmas gift to students and friends, as the dates and labels indicate. A thorough analysis of Vos's poetry is warranted (and needed) by a qualified scholar. While it is not great poetry, it is biographical (note *Western Rhymes* especially) and evocative. There are additional clues to the man in these lines, as Vos himself seems to indicate in his preoccupation with poetry in the *Neerlandia* sketch.

The list of Vos's favorite poetic paragons includes W. Hofdijk, J. L. L. ten Kate, Jan Luyken, Isaac de Costa, Joost Van den Vondel, Willem Bilderdijk, Gottfried Keller, Conrad F. Meier, Rupert Hammerling, Ralph Waldo Emerson, Henry Wadsworth Longfellow, Alfred Lord Tennyson, and Algernon Charles Swinburne (the last two of whom Vos labeled "ideal British poets").

But why was the family patriarch eager to quit the Netherlands for the New World? Is there ever so subtle a suggestion that his repeated short pastorates were indicative of restlessness or disappointment? Was the New World (a fresh start, a new land, an eager Dutch immigrant community) itself the inducement? Or is the family tradition to be credited—that Jan Vos was induced, in part, to immigrate to the western hemisphere because of the agitation generated by Bismarck's late nineteenth-century German nationalism?[16]

Whatever the precise motivation, the family crossed the Atlantic in the summer of 1881. Jan Vos preached his last sermon in Holland on July 27, embarked with his family at Antwerp about August 1 on board the S.S. Belgenland I, disembarked in Philadelphia, and traveled overland by train to Grand Rapids, Michigan, arriving before August 24.[17] The congregation at Spring Street numbered 1,700 souls at Vos's installation. He was to labor happily in this New World parish for nearly

---

16. Otto von Bismarck's *Kulturkampf* of 1870 led to the Franco-Prussian War of 1870–71. The Congress of Berlin in 1878 made him the dominant power broker in European politics. The following year, he concluded an alliance with Austria-Hungary.

Perhaps the memory of persecution for members of the Old Reformed Church in Bentheim was also still fresh in Jan Vos's mind (compare Geerhardus's allusion to German harassment in "Autobiographische aanteekeningen," 9–10; E.T., *Kerux* 19/3:6). Nationalism, intolerance, poverty, and unstable churches may have combined to motivate Jan Vos to look to the New World. Cf. Beuker, "German Oldreformed Emigration," 103. Grand Rapids was well isolated from German imperialism, sword rattling, and prejudice. On the other side of the world, Jan's two sons were far removed from conscription by Holland or Germany.

17. See Harinck, "Geerhardus Vos," 244–46. The records of the Spring Street Christian Reformed Church (now First CRC) indicate that Vos appeared at his first meeting with the consistory on August 24, 1881. See *One Hundredth Anniversary, 1857–1957* (Grand Rapids: First Christian Reformed Church, 1957), 31. The Minutes of the Curatorium (i.e., trustees or directors) of the Theologische School (now Calvin Theological Seminary) for June 23, 1881, indicate that Vos was "expected in August" (see art. 11, in the Dutch-English transcript housed in the Heritage Hall Archive at Calvin College). The website Emigrants to North America from Grafschaft Bentheim, Germany, suggests that they arrived in Kent County, Michigan, on August 15, 1881 (www.dialogos-studies.com/BIS-emigrants.html).

Introduction

twenty years.[18] Crossing the Atlantic was as apparently providential for the father as it was to prove to be for the son.

The New World

The world of Geerhardus Vos was unalterably changed by this transition to America. Still, for many years he maintained a keen interest in the old world Dutch culture that he had left behind as a teenager. In his old age, he acknowledged that he still counted *een-twee-drie*.[19] He even suggested "something Freudian" in all this. In fact, some of the shyness or reticence in Vos may be due to this dual citizenship nationality. He was never really at home in America, though he spent the bulk of his life on her soil. One can take the man out of the Netherlands, but (especially in Vos's case) one cannot entirely take the Netherlands out of the man.[20]

Geerhardus was soon immersed in study once more. He matriculated in the Theologische School in September 1881 and quickly demonstrated his more than ordinary gifts. By March of the following year, the Curatorium was promoting him as "instructional assistant" to Docent Boer.[21] The appointment was ratified, effective for "the period of one year" on June 29, 1882. In the meantime, Vos had been examined at the June 28 session of the Curatorium,[22] and was

---

18. He petitioned for emeritus status in 1900 and was granted his request on November 1 at the age of 74. He retired to Graafschap, Michigan, and lived there until he died on February 17, 1913. His wife preceded him in death on May 22, 1910 (*De Wachter*, June 1, 1910). Most members of the Christian Reformed Church in Graafschap had German Old Reformed roots in the Bentheim region. Jan H. Vos had been born in that region; his first pastorate had been the Old Reformed Church in Ulzen (1858–60) in graafschap ("region") Bentheim. See Beuker, "German Oldreformed Emigration," 103.

19. Vos to Albertus Eekhof, October 28, 1932.

20. For the contacts with Holland, see George Harinck, "A Triumphal Procession? The Reception of Kuyper in the USA (1900–1940)," in *Kuyper Reconsidered: Aspects of His Life and Work*, ed. Cornelis vander Kooi and Jan de Bruijn (Amsterdam: VU Uitgeverij, 1999), 273–82.

21. Cf. Minutes of the Curatorium, March 22, 1882, art. 5. Geert Egbert Boer (1832–1908) was the sole professor at the seminary from his appointment in 1876 until 1883. See *Semi-Centennial Volume: Theological School and Calvin College, 1876–1926* (Grand Rapids: Semi-Centennial Comt., 1926), 93–96.

22. The exams listed include Hebrew, biblical history, natural theology, introduction to religion, biblical geography, Hebrew antiquities, and hermeneutics. See Minutes of the Curatorium, June 28, 1882, art. 7–8.

granted a "diploma" and advanced to "higher studies in Theology" (an apparent reference to taking a second year at the School).

Vos was obviously remarkably advanced as a scholar to be considered an assistant professor at the age of 20. A note in the Minutes of the Curatorium for December 12, 1882, indicates that he was in "the third year" of study, which suggests that in a year and a half Vos had demonstrated a mastery of more than two years of the curriculum.[23] In that second full year in Grand Rapids, Geerhardus taught half-time and took courses half-time.

In May 1883, the Curatorium proposed that Vos become "regular docent." Geerhardus appeared at the August 8, 1883, meeting of the Curatorium in order to decline the offer; he had been accepted for further study at Princeton Theological Seminary, Princeton, New Jersey. As he left that meeting with his face toward New Jersey, the Curatorium noted that he had completed all the required preliminaries for endorsement to the pastoral ministry. Vos would never actually be the pastor of a church; his world was to be the study, the classroom, and (on occasion) the seminary chapel.[24]

Apparently, after settling in at Princeton in 1893, he spoke outside the campus setting only once, giving an address on the "Organic Unity of the Bible" at Wylie Memorial Church, PCUSA, in Philadelphia on Sunday, March 11, 1894. The reporter on that occasion noted that the lecture "was manifestly the work of a scholar, and an expert in the biblical questions

---

23. The earliest extant letter of Vos, dated August 17, 1883, is addressed to William Henry Roberts, registrar at Princeton Theological Seminary, Princeton, New Jersey. In it, Vos confirms elements of this remarkable academic performance (even mentioning the "diploma") in an appeal to skip the first year of the Princeton curriculum and be admitted as a middler, i.e., a second-year theological student. His wish was granted.

24. Following his 1893 arrival at Princeton, Vos appears never to have preached outside the seminary chapel. His personal sermon notebook (deposited in the Heritage Hall Archive at Calvin College) records the dates on which he delivered most of the sermons ("Conference Sundays") printed in *Grace and Glory* (Edinburgh: Banner of Truth Trust, 1994). The dates on the original handwritten versions range from 1902 to 1914. Several of these sermons were preached more than once, revealing that Vos, although an academic, knew the value of the "preacher's barrel." His appointment as professor of dogmatic theology at the Theologische School of Grand Rapids in 1886 included the provision that he "preach on Sundays in English at least once in Grand Rapids, or now and then elsewhere" (Minutes of the Curatorium, August 24, 1886).

now under discussion."[25] The modern student will notice the characteristically Vosian biblical-theological flavor of that address—perhaps a semipopular prelude to his Princeton inaugural two months later. All of this tends to confirm the comments of his daughter that he was "retiring and modest,"[26] "never an activist in church affairs, but always a scholar and a student."[27] Vos himself characterized his aversion to the spotlight as follows:

> I have always been more averse to, rather than a friend of, a personal "stepping into the limelight." This is perhaps a residue of the somewhat world-repudiating spirit of the Old Seceder pietism in which my parents lived and in which I grew up. And you know yourself that the terrible advertising mania that dominates the "New World" is not conducive to moderating such an inherited aversion.[28]

Seminary at Princeton

Vos arrived at Princeton sometime before September 20, 1883.[29] His two years as a student there were spent at the feet of such worthies as William Henry Green (Old Testament), A. A. Hodge (systematic theology), C. W. Hodge (New Testament), and Frances Landy Patton (apologetics). At his graduation in 1885, his superior scholarship was recognized in the Hebrew fellowship award—a purse for future doctoral studies.[30] Vos's defense of the Mosaic origin of the Pentateuch

---

25. *The Presbyterian* 64 (March 14, 1894): 5.
26. Marianne Radius to the author, November 29, 1975.
27. Marianne Radius to the author, June 26, 1976. The one exception appears to be Vos's signature on a protest signed by thirty-nine members of the Presbytery of New Brunswick, PCUSA, on April 25, 1925. These presbyters were objecting to the Presbytery's endorsement of Professor C. R. Erdman as a candidate for moderator of the General Assembly of the denomination in that year. See *A Statement concerning a Pamphlet Entitled "The Presbytery of New Brunswick to the Church at Large,"* April 25, 1925. Vos joined those who were opposed to the progressive evangelicalism of Erdman—a progressivism that, along with that of President J. Ross Stevenson of Princeton Seminary, would lead to the polarization over J. Gresham Machen and the reorganization of the Seminary in 1929.
28. Vos to Albertus Eekhof, October 28, 1932.
29. See Vos to William Henry Roberts, August 17, 1883.
30. William Henry Green recommended Vos for the award, commending his manuscript entitled "The Mosaic Origin of the Pentateuchal Codes." (He called it "masterly" in the *New*

was anchored in the progress of the history of redemption. The prophetic era was, he argued, retrospective of the administration of the Law and prospective of the eschatological thrust of a "better era," advanced first by the Law and subsequently by the Prophets. But such biblical-theological fidelity was antithetical to the idealistic, Hegelian, and Darwinian reconstruction animating not only higher critical approaches to the Pentateuch, but also critical assaults on the entire canon—Old Testament and New Testament alike.[31] In critical fundamentalist circles, the whole Bible became a foil for (post-)Enlightenment nineteenth-century German philosophy and ethics.[32]

Germany

Vos now prepared to step back into the Old World—the world he had left behind when he arrived in Grand Rapids in 1881. In 1885,

---

York Observer, May 23, 1885). The work was a detailed critique of Wellhausenism, Deuteronomism, the Documentary Hypothesis, and the paradigmatic reversal, common to the philosophically driven higher criticism of the Pentateuch, which conceived of law coming after prophecy (as the legalistic Exilic era was subsequent to the free and charismatic—even democratic!—era of the seers and nebiim). Green undoubtedly helped promote the manuscript for publication; it was printed by A. C. Armstrong & Son in 1886, with Green's introduction.

31. Vos wrote, "The critics . . . lay down the principle that in Israel's history all phenomena are to be explained according to the law of natural causation. On the other hand believing critics necessarily deal with the history of Israel and the origin of Scriptures from the point of view of supernatural revelation, and will be led at each step by considerations ultimately rooted in this idea. [The critics] candidly admit that there is an antithesis between naturalism and supernaturalism, not merely in the results, but likewise in the principle of investigation" (*Presbyterian and Reformed Review* 8 [1897]: 107; hereafter *PRR*).

32. "By true faith in the Biblical sense is meant faith in the manifestation of God in history, faith in the interference of God in the world for the salvation of humanity, faith in the living word of the prophets. This, we are told, is the unalterable element in the Bible, which historical study cannot shake. Is it really so? It would seem to us that the whole tenor of Piepenbring's book is remarkably well adapted to drive out this last remnant of supernaturalism, diluted as it is. The only thing on which the author bases his right to retain it, is that in the elite of the Israelitish nation we meet with a superior ethical life. . . . We might ask the author how high a degree of ethical life he thinks the natural development of humanity sufficient to produce, and where is the exact point where the supernatural must be called in to explain the ethical phenomena. The old supernaturalism of the Church, of which the author speaks so deprecatingly, had at least something more tangible and convincing to offer in the line of evidence, for miracles are facts which no process of natural development will account for. It is not so with the ethical life of a class of men, who on the author's own premises, can perhaps not be entirely acquitted of the charge of untruthfulness." Vos, review of *Theology of the Old Testament*, by Ch. Piepenbring, *PRR* 6 (1895): 151–52.

Geerhardus Vos enrolled at the University of Berlin, planning to pursue a Ph.D. in Old Testament studies. He took courses in the winter and summer semesters of 1885–86, enrolling on October 20, 1885, and concluding his second semester on August 9, 1886.[33] Vos sat at the feet of major critical scholars, including C. F. A. Dillmann (Introduction to the Old Testament), C. P. Bernhard Weiss (Epistle of Galatians), and the legendary Hermann Strack (Book of Proverbs). He also took Assyrian/Akkadian and Arabic—the latter of significance for his future Ph.D. dissertation. Significantly, he also scheduled two philosophy courses (History of Philosophy and Introduction to Philosophy).

In the spring of 1886, Vos was contacted by Abraham Kuyper of the Free University of Amsterdam. Kuyper was seeking a professor of Old Testament.[34] Vos was his choice. Geerhardus was caught in a dilemma: employment at the Free University would "replant [him] into the old native soil," but it would also sever his ties from "that which is dear to me." The last remark is a veiled reference to his parents; it is our first recorded instance of his filiopiety.[35] It would not be the last.[36]

---

33. Archives of Humboldt-Universität zu Berlin; Letter of Dr. Kossack to the author, dated March 16, 1984.

34. Harinck notes that Vos was not the first professor of Old Testament at the Free University. F. W. J. Dilloo had resigned the chair in 1885 in order to return to the pastorate. "Geerhardus Vos," 247.

35. Vos to Kuyper, May 28, 1886.

36. Perhaps in an effort to augment his family and New World affinities, the Curatorium of the Theologische School in Grand Rapids sent Vos a letter calling him as "third docent." See Minutes, June 22 and August 24, 1886. The call urged the necessity of teaching English (as well as teaching *in* English) and modeling preaching in English in the churches of Grand Rapids.

The irony here is the controversy over "Americanization" in Dutch Reformed circles. In 1882, a group of congregations that had seceded from the Reformed Church in America (RCA) swelled the ranks of the smaller Christian Reformed Church (CRC). L. J. Hulst was their leader; see Henry Beets, "Rev. L. J. Hulst," *The Banner* 40 (December 22, 1905): 537–39. Beets gives the date of the formal secession from the RCA as September 8, 1881. (It no doubt took a few months to formalize their reception by the CRC.) Although the specific issue was Freemasonry and its tolerance in officeholders of the RCA, the broader context was "accommodation to the American scene" (Robert P. Swierenga and Elton J. Bruins, *Family Quarrels in Dutch Reformed Churches in the Nineteenth Century* [Grand Rapids: Wm. B. Eerdmans Publishing Co., 1999], 133). Remarks in several of Vos's letters indicate his belief that Americanization meant a decline in orthodoxy. For example, he wrote, "There is nothing that I consider more harmful for our little church there than to introduce English ideas" (Vos to Bavinck, June 16, 1887). The non-Dutch speakers (and readers) among us have come to thank God for "forcing" Vos to communicate in English!

Cf. also Henry Zwaanstra, *Reformed Thought and Experience in a New World: A Study of the Christian Reformed Church and Its American Environment, 1890–1918* (Kampen: J. H.

In addition, Vos's second letter to Kuyper (June 7, 1886) indicated that he suffered from some health problems: "I cannot make long journeys without harmful consequences to my system."[37] IBS (irritable bowel syndrome) would match the high energy of his mental processes ("nervous tension"?), strained and stressed by the slightest metabolic or physiological upset.

Vos declined the appointment,[38] but not before he met the "Curatorium" of the Free University at the home of Rev. J. W. Felix in Utrecht during the fall of 1886.[39] This meeting was scheduled for the interim between Vos's departure from Berlin and his enrollment at the University of Strassburg on October 27, 1886.[40] His letter to Kuyper, dated October 7, 1886, rehearses the now-famous reason for his demur: parental disapproval ("I would bring grief to them").

Taking rooms at 29 rue des Bateliers in Strassburg, Vos resumed his Ph.D. studies. But once more his health would delay his progress: "More and more I realize that my health has definitely broken. . . . [O]n doctor's orders I have had to reduce my work-hours by half."[41] The situation is confirmed by a note recorded in the Minutes of the Curatorium for the Theologische School in Grand Rapids for August 3, 1887: Vos "has not been able to pursue his studies in Germany as rapidly as he had wishes [sic] because of illness."

Vos studied in the Department of Philosophy, majoring in Semitic languages. This strange combination only accentuates once more Vos's

---

Kok, 1973); Jan Veenhof, "A History of Theology and Spirituality in the Dutch Reformed Churches (Gereformeerde Kerken), 1892–1992," *Calvin Theological Journal* 28 (1993): 166–97.

37. Vos's ecclesiastical reticence and retiring nature may perhaps be explained by his physical constitution, as much as by his Old Seceder pietism. The way in which he refers to his "nerves" suggests that he may have suffered from what is currently called IBS (irritable bowel syndrome). It is significant that he nearly died of bleeding hemorrhoids and impacted teeth in 1932, as indicated by a letter from Catherine Vos to J. Gresham Machen, in the Machen Papers, Westminster Theological Seminary, Philadelphia, Pennsylvania. Although her letter is undated, the scenario matches Vos's descriptions of his convalescence in the spring and summer of 1932 (see his letters from that period).

38. Proffered September 15, 1886. See Harinck, "Geerhardus Vos," 248.

39. Vos to Felix, September 4, 1886.

40. The date of enrollment is noted in a letter from J. d'Orleans of the Archives of the Région Alsace, Strasbourg, to the author, August 28, 1984.

41. Vos to Bavinck, June 16, 1887.

keen interest in philosophy, in addition to biblical languages. For the latter, he had Theodore Nöldeke as his advisor and Arabic expert. For the former, he sat in on courses taught by the renowned Wilhelm Windelband. It was at Strassburg that he also encountered H. J. Holtzmann, a famous advocate of Markan priority and Q, i.e., the two-source theory of the origin of the Synoptic Gospels.[42] In a letter to Herman Bavinck, Vos lamented not having chosen Strassburg over Berlin from the start: "It would have been desirable for me if I had chosen Strassburg right away and had not visited Berlin."[43] Strassburg was smaller, the library was more accessible, and the professors more approachable.

Vos returned to Grand Rapids in the summer of 1887.[44] The delay in his progress toward a Ph.D. constituted a concomitant delay in his appointment to the faculty of the Theologische School.[45] Returning to Strassburg, Vos completed his work and was awarded the Ph.D. on April 26, 1888. The dissertation was an exercise in Arabic textual criticism.[46] If Vos was seeking a "safe" dissertation topic, he succeeded.

---

42. Holtzmann labeled the second document L (for Logia, "sayings"). Modern scholars call it Q (for the German *Quelle*, "source"). He was probably the most famous higher critical New Testament scholar of the day. His approach to the gospel of Paul was to align it with Greek thought, arguing that Paul's theology was Hellenized on account of his dependence on Alexandrian or Philonic Judaism. Vos appears to have been unaffected by Holtzmann. His courses on Pauline theology emphasize not only the Old Testament (Hebrew) roots of Paul's gospel, but concrete supernatural revelation as well. Thus, the risen Christ actually *appears* to Paul on the road to Damascus. As for Q, Vos would have echoed the late William Farmer's dismissal of "hypothetical Q." Cf. "The Case for the Two-Gospel Hypothesis," in *Rethinking the Synoptic Problem*, ed. David A. Black and David R. Beck (Grand Rapids: Baker, 2001), 97–135.

43. Vos to Bavinck, June 16, 1887.

44. Harinck notes that Vos preached in Leiden to a "*dolerende* congregation" in August 1887 ("Geerhardus Vos," 259, n. 14). Perhaps he paused there to preach on his way to embarking for the States. Harinck opines that he is not sure that Vos preached anywhere else. In view of the condition of his appointment in Grand Rapids, however, it is likely that he did. "When I was in my teens I occasionally heard him preach," writes Jacob G. Vanden Bosch (1875–1970) in "Geerhardus Vos," *Reformed Journal* 4/10 (November 1954): 11. A note in *De Hope*, June 20, 1888, indicates that Vos had preached the previous Sunday, i.e., already fulfilling the mandate of his appointment!

45. See the note in the Minutes of the Curatorium, August 3, 1887.

46. *Die Kämpf und Streitigkeiten zwischen den Banū 'Umajja und den Banū Hāšim. Von Takijj ad-dīn Al-Makrīzijj* (The Struggle and Quarrel between the Umajads and the Hashimites. By Taqi ad-Din Ahmad al-Maqrizi). The work (published by Brill of Leiden in 1888) is a record of the strife between two Islamic factions written in the fifteenth century by al-Maqrizi (1364–1442).

The work is not only noncontroversial, but inert. A proposed translation with an introduction never followed[47]—as forgotten as the work itself.

On May 19, 1888, Geerhardus Vos left the Old World for the last time.[48] On June 12, 1888, he appeared before the Curatorium in Grand Rapids in order to request a postponement until the fall to the start of his appointment as docent. He also asked that the requirement that he preach each Sunday be waived. No doubt both of these requests were prompted by the state of his health.

Professor in Grand Rapids

The Spring Street CRC was the site of Vos's installation as professor of didactic and exegetical theology on the morning of September 4, 1888.[49] In his home church, with his family gathered around, Vos was charged by his father from 2 Timothy 2:15: "Study to show thyself approved unto God, a workman that needeth not to be ashamed, rightly dividing the word of truth."[50] For forty-four years, Geerhardus Vos would not only rightly divide the Word of God, but do so with virtually unmatched profundity. On the evening of the same day, it was the son's turn.[51] He delivered an inaugural (or acceptance) address entitled "De uitsichten der Amerika theologie" (The Prospects of American Theology).[52] The reporter for *De Wachter* summarized the address

---

47. Noted by John F. Jansen in "The Biblical Theology of Geerhardus Vos," *Princeton Seminary Bulletin* 66/2 (summer 1974): 23, n. 2.
48. Once more, he embarked in Holland. See Harinck, "Geerhardus Vos," 249.
49. See "Installatie van Dr. Gerhardus [sic] Vos," *De Wachter*, September 12, 1888.
50. See Minutes of the Curatorium, September 4, 1888, art. 1.
51. Ibid., art. 12.
52. This characteristically future-oriented address is preserved in two handwritten versions. The first contains two signatures and two dates. The first date, followed by the signature "G. Vos," is August 29, 1888—likely the date on which Vos finished composing the piece. The second date is May 7, 1889. Above this date is the name J. B. Hoekstra of Pella, Iowa, and the word *overgeschreven* ("copied"). The second handwritten copy is seventy-two pages long. It too is signed by J. B. Hoekstra and dated May 7, 1889. Did Hoekstra come into possession of Vos's original in 1889 and recopy it? Or was he present at the inaugural in 1888 and copy down the lecture in shorthand? Or did he hear the address in 1889 and make his own copy? And, if the latter, did Vos give this lecture elsewhere? These small mysteries may be unsolvable.

Introduction

in three points: (1) the difficulties which impede its development, (2) the advantages which favor the same, and (3) the requirements which, as a consequence, it must presuppose.[53]

And then the work began. And what a workload it was! The Minutes of the Curatorium for July 26, 1893, suggest that Vos was responsible for twenty-three hours of instruction at the Theologische School. The written materials produced by Vos during this period confirm the laborious schedule. He wrote *Dogmatiek*, a work in five volumes, consisting of 1,892 handwritten pages (there is also a three-volume version). He added "Systematische theologie: compendium" as a summary of the content of the course in dogmatics. In addition, he taught Philosophy and Idololatrie (i.e., non-Christian religions), not to mention the "exegetical" sciences.

In 1889, contacts with Princeton Theological Seminary resumed. B. B. Warfield, coeditor of the *Presbyterian Review*, asked Vos to review some Dutch theological titles.[54] Thus, in the last year of its publica-

---

An English translation of this address was made by Ed M. van der Maas, "The Prospects of American Theology," *Kerux: The Journal of Northwest Theological Seminary* 20/1(May 2005): 14–52. The original documents are in the Heritage Hall Archive at Calvin College.

53. *De Wachter* 21/27 (September 12, 1888): [3].

54. The *Review* had been launched in 1880 in an ultimately futile attempt to keep the progressive and orthodox wings of the Presbyterian Church, USA from polarization and rupture. Charles Augustus Briggs of Union Theological Seminary in New York was the emerging poster boy of the liberal-critical wing of the denomination. He assumed coeditorship with A. A. Hodge of Princeton. A skirmish soon developed over the inspiration of Scripture. Hodge, with B. B. Warfield (then of Western Theological Seminary in Allegheny/Pittsburgh, Pennsylvania), affirmed verbal inspiration of the Scriptures as the historic doctrine of the church. Briggs countered with his infamous "limited inspiration" view, as well as his concomitant attack on "scholastic Calvinism" (arguing that seventeenth-century Reformed orthodoxy, exemplified by Francis Turretin, was responsible for the primitive and retrograde doctrine of the inerrancy of Scripture). Briggs unfurled his critical-philosophical (i.e., Enlightenment and post-Enlightenment) presuppositions in a presentation of the prevailing spirit of the age. Old Princeton's doctrine of Scripture may have been that of the historic church, but Briggs spoke to the contemporary "broadening church." His view would triumph in the church at large.

Vos anticipated the relationship of the "plenary inspiration" of the Bible to the biblical-theological nature of the "organic unity" of Scripture. If one is jettisoned, so is the other; defense of one is defense of the other (see his review of *Leesboek over de Gereformeerde geloofsleer*, by H. E. Gravemeijer, in *PRR* 1 [1890]: 147). However, the specific rift that scuttled the *Review* in 1889 was the call for revision of the Westminster Confession of Faith. Briggs led the charge for the progressive forces of revisionism. Warfield, who became coeditor in 1888, resisted the move to alter the system of doctrine in the Confession.

After the demise of the *Review*, the conservative Old School men launched a new journal, *The Presbyterian and Reformed Review*, which lasted from 1890 to 1902 (see Lefferts Loetscher,

tion, Vos was enlisted to keep American readers aware of "Old World" theological trends. It was the beginning of more than one hundred reviews that Vos would contribute to the *Review* and its successors.[55] For thirty years, Vos wrote penetrating synopses of biblical and theological titles. Most of the titles hailed from Dutch and German authors. Several of these reviews are devastating critiques of liberal-critical fundamentalists.[56] This is particularly evident in his review of Albert Schweitzer's *The Quest of the Historical Jesus*[57] and Wilhelm Bousset's *Kyrios Christos*.[58] Both of these reviews are masterpieces of orthodox biblical-theological antithesis. Unlike modern evangelical and Reformed progressives, there is no capitulation in Vos to critical, enlightenment, modernist presuppositions.

The pattern is consistent. Vos moves in two worlds: the world of liberal higher criticism and the world of orthodox supernaturalism; the world of Dutch Americans and the world of Holland Nederlanders; the world of Grand Rapids and the world of Princeton; the world of human weakness and frailty and the world of divine and heavenly sufficiency. This fluidity—indeed, this impermanence—powerfully accentuates the eschatological element in his thinking.[59] And the eschato-

---

The Broadening Church: A Study of Theological Issues in the Presbyterian Church since 1869 [Philadelphia: University of Pennsylvania Press, 1957], 29–39).

Vos reflects on the termination of the *Review* and the inauguration of *PRR* in his letter to Bavinck, February 1, 1890. The "Revision Movement," he says, was the *casus belli*.

55. After *PRR* ceased publication in 1902, the Princeton faculty launched the *Princeton Theological Review* (1903–1929); hereafter *PTR*. It was in this journal that Vos's last known book review appeared in 1919. Although the journal survived for ten more years, Vos contributed no more reviews. Was he tired? Was he no longer reading new works at age 57? (This hardly seems likely.) Was he no longer welcome as a reviewer? These are intriguing, if unanswerable, questions. For Vos's reviews, see the Internet site www.biblicaltheology.org.

56. I am using the term *fundamentalist* intentionally to describe the mind-set of the (biblical and theological) higher critical establishment—the "high priests" of liberalism. Fundamentalism, i.e., closed-mindedness and intolerance, is not peculiar to conservative Christianity. It is equally vicious on the left side of the theological spectrum.

57. Reprinted in *Redemptive History and Biblical Interpretation: The Shorter Writings of Geerhardus Vos*, ed. Richard B. Gaffin Jr. (Phillipsburg, NJ: Presbyterian and Reformed, 1980), 517–25 (hereafter *RHBI*).

58. Ibid., 534–43.

59. Note his famous comment: "Eschatology is the mother of theology." Compare his lecture notes on "The Pauline Teaching in Survey" (1916), p. 6, in the Heritage Hall Archive at Calvin College. "The eschatological element in our Lord's teaching is but another name for the supernatural" (review of *The Eschatology of Jesus*, by Lewis A. Muirhead, *PTR* 4 [1906]: 126).

logical?—that is the permanent, the abiding, the eternal. And the eschatological is reached through *unio cum Christo* ("union with Christ"). In that mystical union—"in Christ"—Vos found another world, a better world. Like Abraham, he confessed that he desired a heavenly country (Heb. 11:16).

In 1891, Vos was named rector of the Theologische School and delivered an address commemorating the occasion. "De verbondsleer in de Gereformeerde theologie"[60] was delivered on September 2, 1891, to the assembled students, the members of the Curatorium, and the Grand Rapids Christian Reformed community. This address remains a masterful summary of the history of Reformed covenant theology. It also expresses his views on election and covenant, as his letter to B. B. Warfield on July 7, 1891, indicates.

The world of Geerhardus Vos was ever in a state of flux. He lamented the Confessional Revision movement in the PCUSA as an "Arminianizing" of the denomination.[61] In this, he was prescient. Then Abraham Kuyper's concept of "presumptive regeneration" caused Vos to raise questions with B. B. Warfield as to whether this was "the proper Calvinistic view."[62] Kuyper's dogmatic idiosyncrasy was creating a reaction in Vos and his Dutch world. At the same time, his comfortable Dutch Grand Rapids world was challenged because of his alleged supralapsarianism[63]—a position rendered even more complex by his views on the covenant—all of which, ironically, turned him back to Kuyper.[64] In

60. Translated as "The Doctrine of the Covenant in Reformed Theology," in *RHBI*, 234–67.
61. Vos to Bavinck, February 1, 1890.
62. Vos to Warfield, February 12, 1891.
63. We catch a glimpse of Vos's position in his review of A. G. Honig's *Alexander Comrie*: "Predestination, originally and anterior to the decree of permitting sin, had reference to the elevation of definite persons to a supernatural state of glory in union with the Theanthropos, and correspondingly reprobation consisted in the decree to leave certain persons in their natural state, without sin, without glory, and without union to Christ. Thereupon the decree to permit sin follows and makes out of this supralapsarian predestination an infralapsarian decree to save from sin in Christ, and to leave in sin" (*PRR* 5 [1894]: 334). Compare his comments in his review of *Gereformeerde dogmatiek*, vol. 2, by Herman Bavinck, *PRR* 10 (1899): 697–98. Vos's "middle view" on the infra/supra question is unsatisfactory, as Francis Turretin's exquisite exegesis of Romans 9:11–24 demonstrates. See Francis Turretin, *Institutes of Elenctic Theology*, ed. James T. Dennison Jr. (Phillipsburg, NJ: P&R Publishing, 1992), 1:345–47.
64. Vos to Kuyper, February 21, 1891.

a subsequent letter to Warfield (March 12, 1891), he admitted "great difficulties on every side" of these issues. His rectoral address must be considered in its broader context.

Indicative of Vos's perplexity in sorting out these matters is his mention of L. J. Hulst in the letter of March 12 to Warfield. Hulst was the prominent editor of the Dutch newspaper *De Wachter*. Firmly anti-Kuyperian (on baptism and the divine decrees), Hulst identified the young seminary professor with his counterpart across the Atlantic. Lumping Vos and Kuyper together, Hulst accused the former of teaching supralapsarianism, contrary to the infralapsarianism of the Canons of Dort.[65] Vos was obviously irritated by the tiff.[66] In fact, Hulst had been dogging him on this matter since February 1891.[67] By June of that year, Vos wrote: "In the long run I do not want to stay in my present position."[68] And the alternative route of escape from his dogged detractors? "More than once I have been approached . . . about accepting a chair in a seminary of the Presbyterian Church."[69] The seminary in question was most certainly his alma mater, Princeton—the home of his beloved former professor, William Henry Green.

The call to Princeton reveals a tortuous history of its own—much like Vos's sparring matches with his belligerent infralapsarian adversaries. As indicated above, Vos was approached by Princeton, perhaps

---

65. Hulst signed a protest, which he submitted to the Curatorium on September 3, 1891, "against the introduction of supralapsarianism . . . at our Theological School." Vos was specifically mentioned in this protest and was warned (by Hulst) to confine himself to the confessional standards of the church.

66. He called it "trouble and friction" (Vos to Warfield, July 7, 1891).

67. Compare his article on the supralapsarian/infralapsarian question on the front page of *De Wachter*, February 18, 1891. Henry Beets wrote, "In the controversy about 'Supra and Infra,' too, we deplore it exceedingly that he [Hulst] failed to see how both of the conceptions involved are imperfect attempts at solving a problem too deep and too high for the human mind to solve, and perhaps requiring a higher synthesis. We have a vague memory of unpleasant things occurring at ecclesiastical meetings, especially when candidates were examined during the early nineties. Apparently Dr. Vos' decision to leave our School was taken under the influence of Hulst's opposition," "Rev. L.J. Hulst, A Man of Note," *The Banner* 57 (August 31, 1922): 533.

68. Letter to Bavinck, June 30, 1891. The pattern that is emerging will become more and more consistent. Controversy sends Vos searching for an escape—for a refuge—a quiet place to compose his thoughts, concentrate his mental energies, and find himself drawn into mystical union with Christ. Roaring Branch, Pennsylvania, will not be a coincidence!

69. Ibid.

in the spring of 1891 (if not before). On February 23, 1892, a formal call was issued by the New Jersey seminary for Vos to assume a newly created chair of biblical theology.[70] Within weeks, Vos's former professor of Old Testament wrote three letters (two of which are extant) in a barrage of pleading for his former student to accept the call.

Princeton, N.J. Mar. 18, 1892

My dear Dr. Vos,

Permit me to add a few words by way of postscript to my letter of yesterday, which seems to me to describe the exact situation.

A serious break is threatened in the dykes of Holland or if you please in the banks of the Mississippi. All the available engineers are already at work on other points of danger and cannot be spared. One competent engineer remains, who is summoned to check the dangerous influx of the devastating waters. But he is already employed upon a work in the interior of local importance. The residents in the vicinity besiege him with their urgency and he declines to go. There is no one to stop the river. The waters pour destruction over the whole region, and even the hamlet where he is does not escape. Does he do right? Is a man at liberty to decline a public duty in a time of general peril, however willing he may be to remain in obscurity and whatever local value may attach to his less conspicuous labour? My dear Dr. Vos, this may be the turning point of your whole life, on which your entire future shall hinge, and the service you can render to the cause of Christ. Remember that the Master, under whose orders you serve, rules the whole field of battle, and not one corner of it merely. Is he not calling you to a point where you can do his work more effectively, and where there is a more pressing need than where you are now?

Yours truly,
Wm. H. Green

---

70. *New York Times*, February 24, 1892, p. 8. I owe this reference to Alice (Mrs. Martin) Hamstra.

Princeton, N.J. Mar. 19, 1892

My dear Dr. Vos,

Suffer me to add to what I have previously written a few words more. The heavy hand of divine Providence upon us during the past year has created serious breaks in our faculty. *Four vacant professorships* must be filled next spring. We must have capable men, fitted for the place, in harmony with the theological position of this Seminary. We are in great perplexity—such men are difficult to find. In the providence of God this Seminary occupies a very important place in this time of theological unrest. If we can fill these chairs with the right men the prospect is very fair that this Seminary can breast the rising tide of rationalism in theology and criticism. But if these chairs must remain unfilled or given to incompetent men this Seminary will be crippled, its influence broken and the results to sound conservative theology will be disastrous. I wish I could disclose to you the anxieties and forebodings which distress our minds. We feel that interests of the utmost consequence to religion and to the church are in jeopardy. If it were not for the present theological crisis and the position which Princeton holds before the church, the case would be very different. If it was the mere question of the temporary prosperity or abasement of the Seminary—and other seminaries more prosperous would do Princeton's work, the case would be different. But as matters stand, if Princeton goes down, the cause of orthodox theology and evangelical religion will receive a heavy blow. This is the reason that such grave issues hang upon your decision and that we cannot regard the possibility of your adhering to your declinature with any equanimity. If you could be brought to see the real situation of things and how much depends upon your acceptance, I think you could not hesitate for a moment. I must renew my earnest request that you will not decide adversely without coming to Princeton and allowing us to put the case before you in its proper light. Your expenses shall be borne in so doing. You will inflict, I fear an incalculable and irreparable injury on the cause which is dear to your heart, if you insist on declining.

Very truly yours,
Wm. H. Green[71]

It is clear that Green envisioned an appointment for the spring of 1893.[72] Vos's letter to B. B. Warfield (March 18, 1892) states his reasons for declining the call.[73]

But the theological controversy evidently did not abate—father and gold watch notwithstanding. On June 15, 1892, Vos appeared before the Curatorium to ask "if it would not be best that some other docent be allowed to teach dogmatics." The relentless Hulst and his allies were having an effect. A vote of confidence (a "unanimous vote . . . to have . . . Dr. G. Vos to remain as docent in dogmatics") on the part of the Curatorium (June 29, 1882) only delayed the inevitable.[74] Princeton never vacated its call to Vos, nor did they pursue any other candidate. And their patience, if not importunity, was rewarded. By the spring of 1893, Vos was determined to move east. The Princeton graduation day notice for May 9, 1893, which appeared in the *New York Times* (for May 10), announced Vos's intent to take up the chair of biblical theology—a chair "offered him a year ago."

71. Letters provided in 1969 to Dr. Richard B. Gaffin of Philadelphia, Pennsylvania, by the late Bernardus Vos, son of Geerhardus. On July 3, 1967, Bernardus wrote to Roger Nicole, "I have two letters written to my father by Dr. William Henry Green strongly urging him to accept this call." (I am indebted to John Muether of Reformed Theological Seminary, Orlando, Florida, for a copy of this letter.)

72. The Curatorium responded with a meeting on March 11, 1892, and determined "to make every effort to keep Dr. Vos" in Grand Rapids. Vos's daughter, Marianne (Mrs. William) Radius, has indicated that Vos's father advised his son to decline the call so that "the family [might] remain together." Filiopiety strikes again! Even the students at the Theologische School weighed in: they presented a gold watch to Dr. Vos in appreciation of his decision to remain in Grand Rapids (Marianne Radius to the author, July 30, 1994).

73. Hence, a note in the *New York Times*, March 26, 1892, on "Princeton University," indicating Vos's "acceptance" of the call, is in error.

74. A few days later, Vos became a citizen of the United States. On July 5, 1892, he renounced his allegiance to "the King of the Netherlands" before the Superior Court of Grand Rapids, Kent County, Michigan (document on file in the State Archives of Michigan, Michigan Historical Center, Lansing).

Vos had appeared before the Curatorium on April 11, 1893, and heard a heartfelt pledge by the curators "to remove everything that might cause Dr. Vos a problem." But how does one change incompetence and poor educational background (not to mention carping criticism)? Vos wrote to Bavinck, "The appeal of the work here would not have been enough to keep me here in the long run. The young people who study are so poorly educated that despite the diligence of instructors the results that they accomplish are so small that you have to lose heart. . . . The two other instructors are not doing much solid work."[75] On June 29, 1893, Vos informed the Curatorium that he felt "compelled" to accept the renewed call to Princeton. That word "compelled" appears in several contexts regarding Vos's change of mind. Filiopiety no longer compelled him; the academic backwater of Grand Rapids no longer compelled him. William Henry Green compelled him, as did the prospect of a large library, small class schedule, adequate time to study and write, and a genuinely academic environment. As in the parable, the Lord of the banquet went out to Grand Rapids and compelled Geerhardus Vos to come in (to Princeton). By mid-September 1893, he was in his new quarters at 209 Hodge Hall. The Curatorium granted him all necessary testimonials: a document explaining that his diploma of 1882/83 entitled him to preach the gospel, and a letter of commendation.[76] When the new school year at the Theologische School opened on September 7, 1893, Vos was invited by the Curatorium to address the seminary family in a farewell speech; he was unable to accept the invitation.[77] In his place, as temporary instructor in theology (1893–94), the Curatorium nominated his father.[78]

The larger context of the Vos appointment involved Charles Augustus Briggs. Here was the world of the sophisticate—the suave, elite, intellectual bent on leaving his indelible mark upon history and the

75. Vos to Bavinck, July 3, 1893.
76. Minutes, June 30, 1893.
77. Minutes, September 7, 1883.
78. J. W. Brink, "Personal Reminiscences of the Late Rev. J. H. Vos," *The Banner* 48 (March 6, 1913): 155. This is confirmed by J. G. Van Den Bosch, "Historical Sketch of Our Seminary and College," *The Banner* 43 (September 3, 1908): 558. Vos's uncle, Hendericus Beuker, assumed the chair from 1894 until his death in 1900.

church.[79] As early as the 1870s, Briggs began to deconstruct traditional orthodoxy with respect to revelation and history. Briggs averred that the doctrine of the infallibility of the Bible had been invented by Francis Turretin and swallowed by Archibald Alexander, Charles Hodge, and other benighted Princeton fellows.[80] To this myth manufactured by Briggs, he added the historical confusion—even contradiction—of the Biblical narratives: Briggs maintained that the Bible could only be authoritative for "faith and practice," *not* for history, geography, and other subjects. This view of "limited inspiration" arose from Briggs's enthrallment with biblical theology of a rationalistic variety. From the rise of the German Enlightenment, the Bible was regarded as a cultural relic yearning to be set free from hide-bound traditionalists—benighted pietists with confessional or dogmatic attachments to a book that never mingles with fallible, ordinary men and women. Scriptural infallibility and inspiration, he believed, was repressive and reactionary. A truly "modern" approach to the Bible jettisoned the dogmatic approaches of the precritical era and opened the Scriptures with truly scientific methods. Biblical supernaturalism was an outdated handicap.[81] Reliable Biblical history was an impossibility given the prejudices of all writers of history (Biblical writers included). Everyone had an agenda—even the writers of the books of the Bible. Biblical theology was Briggs's theology of liberation of the day and he himself was its greatest critical advocate.

79. Briggs wrote of himself, "The author has done his best to turn away from the Christ of the theologians and of the Creeds and of the Church, and to see the Messiah as He is set forth in the writings of the Apostles." To that Vos responded, "Such wholesale condemnation of historic Christianity we have long been accustomed to from certain quarters where the contempt of so-called tradition is equaled by the lack of historic information, but in the case of a scholar and student of history like Dr. Briggs it is inexcusable" (review of *The Messiah of the Gospels* and *The Messiah of the Apostles*, by Charles A. Briggs, *PRR* 7 [1896]: 719).

80. See Charles A. Briggs, *Whither? A Theological Question for the Times* (New York: Charles Scribner's Sons, 1889), 20–21; Briggs, *Theological Symbolics* (New York: Charles Scribner's Sons, 1914), 378; John J. McCook, compiler, *The Appeal in the Briggs Heresy Case* (New York: John C. Rankin Co., 1893), 309.

81. Perhaps the most penetrating and incisive review of this shift is provided by Hans W. Frei, *The Eclipse of Biblical Narrative: A Study in Eighteenth and Nineteenth Century Hermeneutics* (New Haven: Yale University Press, 1974).

Briggs was brought to trial for heresy by conservatives in the Presbytery of New York, PCUSA, in 1892. He was suspended from office by the General Assembly of the Presbyterian Church, USA, the following year. But the long-simmering infiltration of liberal fundamentalism (of which Briggs was the figurehead) could not be stopped—not even by the boy from the dykes of Holland. The academic progressives and the evangelical cultural accommodationists were more alike than different—both were reductionists, treating the Bible merely as a book of practical application. For the critical fundamentalists, that meant the triumph of ethics and social crusading. For the evangelical accommodationists, ethics was the heart of applied Christianity. If the "Redeemer Nation" was to advance to the millennial pinnacle, proper moral behavior was essential. If "salvation" was morals to theological liberals, it was the essential *a priori* to cultural evangelicals, who urged this prerequisite in order to provide the basis for the proper, moral preservation of civilization. William Henry Green, B. B. Warfield, and others on the Princeton faculty may have seen the threat from higher-critical fundamentalism, but they were eventually betrayed, blind-sided and dumped by their erstwhile evangelical allies. In less than forty years, Old Princeton fell to the cultural liberals (in the reorganization of 1929) with the help of progressive, accommodationist "conservative" evangelicals. Warfield's well-documented disenchantment with Princeton's "conservative" president J. Ross Stevenson (in truth, a progressive evangelical) ended in cynicism—he refused to attend faculty meetings after Stevenson became president.[82] And Vos— the man recruited to stem the influx of liberal-critical biblical theology? He lived to see the disintegration of the Princeton he loved. His failure to join the Westminster Theological Seminary faculty in 1929 was more

---

82. Warfield indicated that Stevenson "was not the man for the place" ("Transcript of the Hearing of the Faculty of Princeton Theological Seminary by the General Assembly's Special Committee to Visit the Seminary," November 23–24, 1926, p. 158.) Cf. Ned B. Stonehouse, *J. Gresham Machen: A Biographical Memoir* (Grand Rapids: William B. Eerdmans Publishing Co., 1954), 219. For more on the reorganization of 1929, see David Calhoun, *Princeton Seminary* (Edinburgh: Banner of Truth Trust, 1996), 2:365–93; Bradley J. Longfield, *The Presbyterian Controversy: Fundamentalists, Modernists, and Moderates* (New York: Oxford University Press, 1991), 162–79. For the characterization of Stevenson, see Edwin H. Rian, *The Presbyterian Conflict* (Philadelphia: Committee for the Historian of the Orthodox Presbyterian Church, 1992), 40–43.

a testimony to the futility of the enterprise than to his advancing years, poor health, or isolation in the classroom.[83]

I have digressed to the dénouement of our story. In 1893, all this was in front of Vos. He could not see the dismal future of 1914, 1929, 1932, and beyond. He could only see a fresh opportunity in the halcyon corridors of Reformed orthodoxy. The wet-behind-the-ears young man from Grand Rapids would sit down at faculty meetings with Warfield, Green, Hodge, Patton, Armstrong, and other hoary heads of orthodoxy.[84] He was the junior faculty member, and he must have been thrilled. Kuyper said that the move from Grand Rapids to Princeton rescued Vos from "academic murder."[85] Kuyper was surely right!

Professor of Biblical Theology at Princeton

Vos taught from September 1893 to May 1894 before his famous inaugural address defined his biblical-theological methodology.[86] But

---

83. It is important to note that after Vos published *The Pauline Eschatology* in 1930—a work which he initially published himself, as no publishing company would print it—he laid his theological pen down and *never* took it up again. Vos may have replaced Charles Augustus Briggs on the tongues of Old Princeton in 1893, but in 1932 Briggs displaced Vos at his alma mater. Princeton belonged to the heirs of the Union Seminary "heretic," not to orthodox Geerhardus Vos. Vos walked away from Mercer Street in the summer of 1932 into obscurity. Not even Westminster Seminary fathomed the measure of the man. "In spite of Machen's admiration for Vos, I doubt that he came . . . fully under the impact of his thought and approach" (Ned Stonehouse to Louis Berkhof, December 17, 1954). To Machen, Murray, MacRae, Allis, and perhaps Van Til, Vos was like them: another fundamentalist fighting merely for the conservative turf and constituency they once controlled.

Ned Stonehouse wrote: "It is significant that the professors Drs. Vos, Armstrong and Hodge do not join in these protestations as to the soundness of Princeton. They seem to be much more sympathetic with Westminster than with President Stevenson's policy. Everyone here feels that the position of these men is therefore wholly inconsistent and misleading. They should really come out for their conviction, but whether they really will is something that only time will tell" (letter to F. W. Grosheide, cited in George Harinck, "Valentijn Hepp in America: Attempts at International Exchange in the 1890s," in *Sharing the Reformed Tradition: The Dutch-North American Exchange, 1846–1996*, ed. George Harinck and Hans Krabbendam (Amsterdam: VU Uitgeverij, 1996), 138, n. 62.

84. "Initially the change pleases me. It is much better here for my health, and also the intellectual atmosphere, in which people live, is preferable to the one in my former surroundings" (Vos to Bavinck, October 20, 1893).

85. Cited in Gaffin, introduction to *RHBI*, xi, n. 6. For the original, see Kuyper to Bavinck, January 24, 1894, in R. H. Bremmer, *Herman Bavinck en zijn tijdgenoten* (Kampen: J. H. Kok, 1966), 81, 291.

86. "The Idea of Biblical Theology as a Science and as a Theological Discipline," in *RHBI*, 3–24. The address was delivered on May 8, 1894. Cf. James T. Dennison Jr., "What Is Biblical

as early as July 1893, in a letter to Bavinck, he had broached his approach to the new course—the new Charles T. Haley Chair—the new mandate assigned to him by the God he loved. The key word in the letter is "revelation."[87] Vos believed in objective, concrete, divine revelation in history.[88] *Revelation* was not a weasel word for Vos[89]—he had experienced enough of that in the philosophical prostitution of revelation to prevailing nineteenth-century ideology. Nor was *revelation* a dialectical term for Vos—a chimerical paradox, seemingly granting "revelation" on the one hand, but whisking it away with the other in a "crisis" of contradictions. Revelation for Vos was essentially an eschatological concept. Out of his transcendentally eschatological arena, God initiated word and deed revelation, intruding them into history—the warp and woof of the creation that he spoke into existence. One must never forget the bookends of Vos's biblical-theological paradigm: Creation—Consummation. The linear aspect connecting these two vectors

---

Theology? Reflections on the Inaugural Address of Geerhardus Vos," *Kerux: A Journal of Biblical-Theological Preaching* 2/1 (May 1987): 33–41 (online at kerux.com).

87. "It was not my intention to take the covenant idea as a guiding principle in Biblical Theology to the exclusion of *Revelation*. I also give the latter priority. Biblical Theology is for me History of Revelation. But beneath that I place the covenant concept, because God has revealed himself in the covenant" (Vos to Bavinck, November 21, 1893).

88. Observe Vos's expression of this concept in a review of E. H. van Leeuwen's book *Prolegomena van bijbelsche godgeleerdheid*: "The objective character of revelation is maintained in a very positive manner. The temptation to weaken this may become especially strong in Biblical Theology. It would seem as if the idea of a progressive, living revelation, that gradually unfolds the perfect doctrines from their perfect germs, no longer suffices to satisfy the prevailing demand for so-called historical, or, more accurately speaking, evolutionary treatment of sacred things. Hence many, in an altogether subjective manner, make the *religion* of Israel the object of Old Testament Theology" (*PRR* 4 [1893]: 143). Again, in a review of *De letterkunde des Ouden Verbonds naar de tijdsorde van haar ontstaan*, by G. Wildeboer, he stated, "Evolutionary criticism . . . strikes at the very roots of supernatural revelation, not to say of theism" (*PRR* 5 [1894]: 699).

89. "The idea of revelation . . . is actually coextensive with the whole course of sacred history, if only revelation be taken not in the abstract theological sense of a communication of truth, but in the practical sense of a self-manifestation of God for the purpose of establishing and cultivating the true religion" (review of *The Theology of the Old Testament*, by A. B. Davidson, *PTR* 4 [1906]: 116). Vos here makes practical the genuine connection between revelation and relation, i.e., God drawing sinners into relation with himself *in history*, not in abstraction. Genuine practical theology requires biblical theology or it becomes abstract, ahistorical, and unconnected with real life. Is it only liberals, or are allegedly "orthodox" conservatives guilty of "the old delusion of rationalism that the world can be saved by teaching" (review of *The Prophet of Nazareth,* by Nathaniel Schmidt, *PTR* 5 [1907]: 496)? Substitute "application" for "teaching" and you get the point.

was joined by the supernatural person who originated and perfected them: God himself came out of his eschatological arena, in the act of creation, and God will again come out of his eschatological arena in the final act of consummation. For Vos, revelation is God-centered. This would not satisfy the nineteenth-century advocates of biblical theology, for whom "God" was merely a symbol in the philosophy of religion.[90] Thus, the religion of Israel (Old Testament) and the religion of Christians (New Testament) were the object of reconstruction on proper, scientific, and philosophical premises.[91] For Vos, the religion of the Bible was not subject to the changing whims of philosophy. Revelation was as absolute as God himself.

The second element of his biblical-theological program that Vos articulated to Bavinck was "historical development." Biblical theology was an historical discipline; it required attention to the ongoing historical continuum. God revealed himself concretely in history in an ongoing or progressive display of his person and work.[92] The capstone of that redemptive-historical revelation was the advent of God himself in the incarnation of his Son, the glorious and eternal second person of the Godhead. For Vos, the term *progressive* was not evolutionary or dialectical (in an Hegelian or post-Hegelian sense). That would redefine God by the creation, the Creator by the creature. *Progressive* for Vos meant "going on through history," i.e., revelation unfolding or progressing to its fulfillment in the person and work of

---

90. "The modern tendency to transform biblical theology into an out-and-out historical science ... proposes to make our science a purely naturalistic and secular branch of study, a mere subdivision of the history of religions" (review of *The Theology of the New Testament*, by George B. Stevens, *PRR* 11 [1900]: 702).

91. In reviewing Hermann Schultz's *Old Testament Theology*, Vos wrote: "The development of Israel's religion is throughout discussed with the utmost freedom, as something human and subjective; and on reading the discussion, we would not ascribe to the author any other than the naturalistic view. But all at once, and apparently unconnected with these premises, the idea of revelation is introduced. It is obvious that revelation, so conceived, must be a process forever inaccessible to inference or proof. The apparent conservatism of Schultz's work, therefore, is something accessory, not being due to what he obtains from a careful review of the facts in accordance with his own critical canons, but largely to certain philosophical ideas imported from without" (*PRR* 5 [1894]: 132).

92. *Progressive* for the critical-liberal fundamentalist meant contradiction and evolution. I.e., truth comes with man's progress in self-enlightenment, by which he liberates himself from the errors of the past. (Cf. Immanuel Kant's clarion call: *Sapere aude!*—"Dare to know!")

Christ. As the story unfolded, revelation unfolded; and as revelation progressed through history, more and more of that rich eventuation and fullness drew near. In other words, revelation was theocentric; redemptive history was Christocentric. And both were pneumatically and eschatologically oriented.

In Vos's mind, the concept of covenant integrated revelatory unity and redemptive-historical development. "I have come to the conclusion that the covenant idea fulfills the requirements best of all." But it was *Reformed* covenant theology in which Vos was grounded. This covenant theology was organically construed. That is, Vos explained that all revelatory covenants are organically connected. The covenant with Adam (Gen. 3:15) is organically connected with the covenants with Noah (Gen. 6:18), Abram (Gen. 12:1–3; 17:1–8), Moses (Ex. 19:5; 24:7), and David (2 Sam. 7:14). Furthermore, "in Scripture the new covenant every time occurs as a benefit in a former covenant." Vos is a purely Augustinian, Calvinistic Christian here—the new is in the "old concealed." The new covenant in Christ intrudes into every previous covenant.[93]

The euphoria of settling into the Princeton environment was a relief from the weekly grind of Grand Rapids. "For this year, I teach not more than four hours a week."[94] He was working in the Old Testament at the time, but anticipated assignments in the New Testament the following year. The catalogue of the seminary for 1893 lists his courses as

---

93. It should be observed that Vos preserves the gracious acts of God in redemption throughout the covenant program. "The main structure of history is that the covenant with Abraham, confirmed at Horeb, is renewed with David. This implies that the essence of the covenant is grace, not legalism" (review of *De theologie van kronieken*, by Jelte Swart, *PTR* 10 [1912]: 480). Postlapsarian salvation is ever and always by grace. And that grace penetrates into history through covenantal relation (i.e., "I will be your God, and you shall be my people"—an essentially gracious declaration), so that Old Testament saints, New Testament saints, all saints are saints by God's divine initiative and work, not, nor ever, by their own.

"It seems to me that when the covenant represents an *archetypical* covenant in eternity, the *absolute* and *unchangeable*, that then also the different covenant gifts as they historically follow each other can represent the *development* of revelation. Moreover the covenant idea is neither purely theoretical nor purely practical, so that it contains in itself word as well as deed revelation. Finally it presents this benefit, that each following covenant development revolves organically from the preceding one, while in Scripture the new covenant every time occurs as a benefit in a former covenant" (Vos to Bavinck, July 3, 1893).

94. Vos to Bavinck, October 20, 1893.

Syriac, Arabic, and Biblical Theology (undoubtedly the Old Testament portion of the discipline, as he had noted). With the light class load, "there is more opportunity here for conversation and scholarly contact than in Grand Rapids."[95] But his euphoria was tempered by a dim foreboding. "In the midst of the general defection, Princeton exerts a good influence. In the last years, they have become more firm here as matters unfold. In the church at large, things look miserable. Church discipline is fallen very much into disuse, and, what is more, the realization that it *must* be exerted dutifully has been lost. Even in an extreme case as that of Dr. Briggs, it was very difficult to move into action. They allow opinions to be expressed and spread unhindered—opinions which, without any doubt, assail not only the Reformed doctrine, but also the army of Christianity. And the worst is that through this, gradually the concept of discipline itself undergoes a change and falsification. It seems to be the curse of unsound practice, that at the same time it corrupts the theory and so perpetuates itself."[96] Vos prophesies the debacle of 1929 here. The Briggs heresy trial was the "last assize."[97] The conservatives had no more stomach for removing error from their midst—or even recognizing error in their midst. In order to get along, they went along. The crisis of modernism would produce the clash with fundamentalism—not historic Calvinism.[98] In 1929 and 1932, Vos's remarks in this letter became his own legacy—things were now worse than "miserable"; they were hopelessly and irretrievably lost.

By the spring of 1894, Vos was less euphoric and more realistic. "We continue to struggle here. I am not sure if we are making much progress. The German theology and criticism is imported with full zeal, and the worst is that the practice of doctrinal discipline in almost all American churches has gotten almost totally lost. Even in an extreme case as that of Briggs, it required the greatest effort to take action. Now that Briggs

---

95. Ibid.
96. Vos to Kuyper, February 26, 1894.
97. A. C. McGiffert, of Union Seminary in New York, was "charged" by the Presbytery of New York, PCUSA, but withdrew from the denomination in 1900 rather than face the music.
98. This is evident in Carl McIntire's rupture with the Presbyterian Church of America (later the Orthodox Presbyterian Church) in 1937. McIntire was never a Calvinist; he was a slick fundamentalist leveraging for power in conservative ecclesiastical politics.

is suspended, no one wants to do anything else and the accomplices of Briggs are left unhindered."[99] The conservatives gained only a Pyrrhic victory, losing the war for winning the skirmish. The liberal fundamentalists and progressive evangelicals would not permit the orthodox conservatives to best them again—indeed, ever again!

On April 24, 1894, Vos was finally ordained. His diploma, credentials, and record in the "Holland Christian Reformed Church" were recognized by the Presbytery of New Brunswick, PCUSA.[100] His ordination as an "evangelist" occurred at Second Presbyterian Church (PCUSA), Princeton, New Jersey. Two weeks later, he delivered his inaugural address to a full audience at First Presbyterian Church, Princeton, New Jersey. That summer, Vos left Princeton and returned to the home of his parents at 48 Spring Street, Grand Rapids. When he returned to Princeton in the fall, he had taken a wife.

Catherine

Catherine Frances Smith was born in Lima, Ohio, on August 11, 1865. Her mother, Mary Ann Smith, née Sherring, was born in Halstead, England. Her father, Henry Smith, was born in Vernon, Connecticut.[101] In 1880, Mary Ann Smith, by then a widow, arrived in Grand Rapids with her three daughters: Catherine (age 15), Emily (age 13), and Lidia O. (age 11).[102] On June 6, 1880, Catherine was received as a member of the South Congregational Church of Grand Rapids.[103] Strangely, it was not until 1886 that Catherine graduated from the

---

99. Vos to Bavinck, March 28, 1894.
100. See *The Presbyterian* 64 (February 7, 1894): 7.
101. See Death Certificate for Catherine Frances Vos, filed November 2, 1937, State of California #37-066338; Certificate of Marriage for Geerhardus Vos and Catherine F. Smith, September 7, 1894, Kent County, Michigan, book 11, p. 195. Bernardus Vos tells us that his maternal grandfather was a schoolteacher (letter to Roger Nicole, July 3, 1967). He also indicates that Henry, Mary Ann, and their daughter Emily died of tuberculosis. Catherine was afflicted with the disease in 1923 and spent several winters in Redlands, California, at an "orange ranch" to aid the full recovery of her lungs.
102. The 1884 Michigan State Census, from which this information is derived, lists her as a "Music Teacher."
103. Letter to the author from Joyce Maczka, Secretary, South Congregational United Church of Christ, July 12, 1999.

Grand Rapids public schools.[104] Perhaps this twenty-year-old high school graduate had been delayed on account of her family circumstances. In any event, it is clear that her late graduation was not due to academic problems! Immediately upon graduation, Catherine was hired as an elementary school teacher at the Madison Avenue School in Grand Rapids, where she taught from 1886 to 1892.[105] In 1892, she was hired as a librarian at the Grand Rapids Public Library.[106] When she resigned two years later, it was to marry Geerhardus. The couple was wed, with Vos's father officiating, on Friday, September 7, 1894, in Grand Rapids.[107]

How did Vos meet his best beloved? Over a book? His son, Bernardus, provides the answer: "My father met my mother in an unusual way. After his return to Grand Rapids from Strassburg in 1888 he became a member of the faculty of Calvin Theological Seminary. In the years that followed he frequently was found in the Grand Rapids Public Library. My mother was at the time doing volunteer work at the circulation desk of the Library, and this is how they met."[108] Geerhardus brought his bride to Princeton in September 1894, where they took up "two rooms and board in the family of a widow of a former professor."[109] The house in which they would reside for thirty-eight years (at 52 Mercer Street) would not be ready to accommodate them until April 1895.[110]

Geerhardus and Catherine were to be the parents of four children, all of whom were born in New Jersey and baptized at First Presbyterian Church, PCUSA, Princeton. Catherine had joined this con-

---

104. See Grand Rapids Board of Education Minutes, p. 100, "Graduating Class, 1886."
105. Her continuing interest in the education of children is reflected in her article "Can Education Be Both Secular and Christian?" *Sunday School Times* 60 (August 2, 1924): 461 (reprinted in *The Banner* 59 [August 8, 1924]: 508–9). Here she champions the "Hollander" commitment to establishing Christian schools in their communities. She was converted from her former public school ways by her husband, no doubt!
106. See Grand Rapids Public Library Board Minutes, May 31, 1892, to December 10, 1894, passim.
107. A printed announcement of the wedding by Mrs. Mary A. Smith is deposited in the Archives of Princeton Theological Seminary. See also the notice of issuance of the marriage license in the *Grand Rapids Herald*, September 8, 1884, p. 5.
108. Bernardus Vos to Roger Nicole, July 3, 1967.
109. Geerhardus Vos to Bavinck, December 22, 1894.
110. In fact, they were not to occupy it until May 1895; see Vos to Bavinck, July 6, 1895.

gregation by letter of transfer on October 3, 1896.[111] Their firstborn, Johannes Geerhardus, was born on February 4, 1903.[112] Bernardus Hendrik followed on April 19, 1905.[113] Marianne Catherine (later Mrs. William Radius) was the lone daughter, born on December 7, 1906.[114] Geerhardus Jr. was the last, born on March 7, 1911.[115]

Dutch Ties

In 1898, Vos became involved with the General Dutch Alliance established by Abraham Kuyper.[116] In fact, Vos became the first secretary of a branch that met in New York City.[117] As his letters to Kuyper demonstrate, Vos was an ardent fan of Kuyper's agenda, with some doctrinal caveats. While this may have resulted from his own Dutch roots and Kuyper's long friendship (though not necessarily endorsing Kuyper's neo-Calvinist goals), Vos nonetheless maintained cultural ties with the two worlds—Holland and America. In America, this Alliance

---

111. Catherine's literary talents are displayed in the justly famous *Child's Story Bible*. First published in 1935 and many times thereafter, this "children's Bible" retells familiar stories from the Old and New Testaments. It remains in print and is a favorite at family devotions still. Bernardus Vos indicates that she began writing the book in the 1920s while wintered at Redlands, California, for the health of her tubercular lungs (letter to Roger Nicole, July 3, 1967).

112. Baptism, May 30, 1903; profession of faith, February 3, 1917; death, June 8, 1983. The *New York Times* contains a humorous story about his birth. The senior class of the seminary presented a baby carriage to Dr. and Mrs. Vos the day after his birth. "Dr. Vos . . . expressed his thanks in a short speech, saying that the donation might have been postponed until to-morrow with great propriety, as the subject of his lecture then would be 'The Fatherhood and the Sonship'" (February 6, 1903, p. 8).

113. Baptism, October 25, 1905; profession of faith, December 6, 1919; death, July 14, 1998.

114. Baptism, March 31, 1907; profession of faith, December 6, 1919; death, November 9, 2000.

115. Baptism, October 1, 1911; profession of faith, April 5, 1924; death, July 14, 1988. The family's baptismal and profession of faith records are in the Archives at Speer Library, Princeton Theological Seminary, *sub* First Presbyterian Church, PCUSA, Princeton.

116. Cf. James D. Bratt, "Abraham Kuyper, American History, and the Tensions of Neo-Calvinism," in *Sharing the Reformed Tradition: The Dutch–North American Exchange, 1846–1996*, ed. George Harinck and Hans Krabbendam (Amsterdam: VU Uitgeverij, 1996), 97–114.

117. The organizational meeting occurred on June 10, 1899, in the office of Augustus Van Wyck, former justice of the State Supreme Court of New York. W. Elliot Griffis and William Melanchthon Jacobus (of Hartford Theological Seminary) were also present; see "General Dutch Alliance," *New York Times*, June 11, 1899, p. 14. Compare Vos to Griffis, December 15, 1898, and January 13, 1902.

produced little if any fruit. Kuyper himself was not always well received, even in Dutch circles in the States. The American cultural context was different. Looking back to the Old World, even to its great Calvinistic statesman, may have been honorable, but it was not, in the main, culturally transforming.[118]

Vos's continued contacts with Kuyper were devoted to cajoling him into delivering the famous Stone Lectures—eventuating in 1898 with *Lectures on Calvinism*. Vos then turned his "charm" on Bavinck with an invitation from the seminary faculty for him to visit Princeton in order to deliver the Stone Lectures too. Vos was rewarded when Bavinck obliged with the Stone Lectures for 1908 (published as *The Philosophy of Revelation*). Dr. and Mrs. Bavinck were guests in the Vos home during their visit to Princeton.[119]

The change in Vos's correspondence took place in 1894. After March 28, 1894, he no longer provided his own self-reflections on theological or ecclesiastical matters. He became a businesslike correspondent, and we no longer read the thoughts or feelings of the man's mind and heart. While it is true that he unceasingly devoted himself to writing (his greatest literary output spans the period 1894 to 1917), we nevertheless miss the elements of appraisal, criticism, and reflection. What happened? Was he soon disenchanted with Princeton? Not likely, since he remained in a satisfying academic post for more than thirty-nine years. Did he realize that his scholarly pursuits would have to suffice for his personal sense of accomplishment and satisfaction? His personal Christ-centered devotion never flagged—his sermons demonstrate this. But he was no longer open and self-expressive. The fact that this shift corresponds with his marriage may be coincidental; it may not. Perhaps he found in Catherine a sole sounding board for his inner feelings. Or perhaps he was beginning to see the fulfillment of what he had predicted following the Briggs trial.[120] Whatever

---

118. Bratt, "Abraham Kuyper, American History, and the Tensions of Neo-Calvinism," 103.
119. See Vos to Bavinck, January 7, 1909.
120. Is the following remark indicative of an emerging sense of futility? "They are . . . men of so-called evangelical color, though in our estimation not Calvinists" (Vos to Kuyper, April 30, 1896). While it is true that the men listed were to receive honorary degrees at Princeton Uni-

the reason, the shift immersed his creative processes deeper and deeper into the Scriptures. In that fathomless reservoir, Vos plunged and recovered and uncovered streams of refreshing—for his own soul as well as for the souls of those seeking to comprehend *mens Dei* ("the mind of God").

But Vos needed a place for this quiet, scholarly reflection. The library of Princeton and the campus atmosphere were stimulating, but distracting. He needed a place for extended, quiet, uninterrupted thought, composition, and penetration of God's mind and heart in his self-revelation. That is what Geerhardus Vos needed; that is what he found.

Roaring Branch

In a small mountain village in north-central Pennsylvania, Geerhardus Vos spent his summers reading, thinking, writing, and praying. Nestled in the Lycoming Valley, Roaring Branch contained two general stores, a post office, and a Methodist (or Methodist Episcopal) church alongside a state highway and a railroad line.[121] Isolated from the bustle of Princeton, it was a place of retreat—of escape—of another world. Catherine and Geerhardus first visited the rural village at the suggestion of his brother, Bert John.[122] On March 12, 1906, Vos purchased a home in Roaring Branch from Theodore H. and Amanda Lieb.[123] In 1908 and 1910, he subsequently purchased eight and five acres, respectively, north of the Ogdensburg Road, just west and north of the village.[124] He purchased this acreage in order to move his house

---

versity, the relation between the University and the Seminary had historically been symbiotic. A chilling of relations set in, which was to be exacerbated during the administration of Woodrow Wilson (who was president of Princeton University from 1902 to 1910). Wilson was a revisionist reformer and educator, a visionary idealist, a "progressive" who would eventually lead the shift away from the historic Calvinism of the College of New Jersey.

121. Roaring Branch is so named for the "roaring" Mill Creek that descends through a rocky gorge from the northwest to join Lycoming Creek (Union Township, Tioga County, Pennsylvania). See *History of Union Township* (Union Township Historical Society, 1986), 15.

122. Marianne Radius to the author, October 31, 1994.

123. Deeds of Tioga County, Pennsylvania, book 131, pp. 19–20.

124. Ibid., book 135, p. 258, and book 138, p. 467. Vos sold the summer house for one dollar to his four children on October 26, 1937. The transaction was no doubt prompted by the

out of town.[125] In 1910, Vos had the two-story house[126] that originally stood in town "almost" across from the I.O.O.F. Hall (Independent Order of Odd Fellows) blocked and moved on rollers with horse-drawn teams to a hillside north of the village. This hillside vista commanded a view of the town and the surrounding north-central Pennsylvania mountains. According to a notice in the *History of Union Township*, the house had about eight rooms. Needless to say, the whole town turned out to see a house jacked up and moved about one thousand feet to a site above the village.

Marianne Radius remembered that this summer home was the idyllic location of her childhood.[127] The family gathered on the porch in the afternoons for Dr. Vos to read the classics to his children. He would also walk to the post office in the morning and in the afternoon to pick up the mail.[128] Mornings and evenings were spent in his study, which is alleged to have been located in the "attic." On Sundays, the family walked into town to worship in the lone Methodist church. Family prayer was the custom each day. Catherine read the Scriptures and provided running commentary. Dr. Vos would then lead in prayer.[129]

---

burial of Catherine in Roaring Branch following her death in Santa Ana, California, on September 14, 1937.

125. Ibid., 18.

126. Actually, the house appears to have had a full attic as well, judging from an undated photo in the author's possession.

127. Is there a reflection on that idyllic family setting in the following remark? "When the Spirit of God moves the centre of our life, transferring it from self to God, there immediately awakes a longing to come in touch with God and possess him and enjoy him for his own sake. We can best illustrate this from the relation of a child to its parents. We do not blame the child because it often turns to its father or mother for the simple reason that it wants something which it can procure in no other way. But what would you think of a child which never sought its father's arms or climbed upon its mother's lap unless there were some external want to be supplied? The true child will spontaneously, instinctively turn to the presence and smile of its parents as a flower will seek the face of the sun. And in the same way the true child of God will have moments in which he turns to his Father in heaven unconscious of any other desire than the desire to be near unto God" ("Songs from the Soul" [sermon on Ps. 25:14], in *Grace and Glory* [Edinburgh: Banner of Truth Trust, 1994], 178).

128. There are several hints that Vos was an eager walker. His promenades were noted in Princeton, Roaring Branch, and Grand Rapids.

129. It is likely from this custom that Mrs. Vos's *Child's Story Bible* evolved. Cf. "Faculty Memorial Minutes: Gerhardus [sic] Vos," *Princeton Seminary Bulletin* 43/3 (Winter 1950): 45.

Sadly, the Vos summer home burned to the ground on August 17, 1937.[130] The Vos heirs suspected arson, but no investigation or proof was ever provided. Marianne Radius maintained that some of her father's books and papers (left in the attic) were destroyed in that blaze.[131] Why the papers were left in the home by Vos's children is an even greater mystery, if, in fact, papers *were* left there for the flames of 1973.

A short distance from the burned-out hole marking the site of the Vos summer home lies Griffin Cemetery. Here are interred the mortal remains of Catherine and Geerhardus Vos. On the eastern side of the cemetery's loop road is a simple flat stone marker: the words "Catherine F. Vos (1865–1937)" and "Geerhardus Vos (1862–1949)" are separated by a cross labeled "Blessed are the dead who die in the Lord."

Vos's summer world was the world beloved to him perhaps most of all. Else why choose this spot for burial? Why not Grand Rapids? Or Princeton? Or Santa Ana (for Catherine)? Why return to this tiny mountain hamlet, remote from the intellectual and ecclesiastical worlds in which he moved? The answer is as poignant and enigmatic as the poetry that Vos wrote.[132] Here was a place of quiet, peaceful reflection, a place for family and solace and meditation. Vos escaped to Roaring Branch for at least twenty-six consecutive summers (1906–1932).[133]

---

130. "Friday Fire Destroys Home; Articles Needed," *Canton* [Pennsylvania] *Sentinel*, August 23, 1973.

131. This observation should be weighed against Vos's disposal of most of his books following his retirement. Many of them went to professors at Westminster Theological Seminary. See Vos's correspondence with Machen and Woolley.

132. "Their [the Psalmists'] attachment to the house of God is at bottom an attachment to the person of God himself, just as the love which we cherish for our house would, when analysed, ultimately appear to be a love fed not so much from association with the material structure but from that intimate contact with the spirit of our family and friends of which the house is, as it were, the external embodiment" (*Grace and Glory*, 179). Cf. Vos's poem "My House," in *Spiegel der natuur en lyra Anglica*, 162. The only house that Vos ever owned was the one in Roaring Branch.

133. The year 1923 was probably an exception, on account of a sabbatical year (actually, spring and summer) spent in Southern California. Compare his poems with California motifs, including the mention of San Diego, Sierra Madre, (Mira) Mesa, and La Jolla. A notice in the *Princeton Seminary Bulletin* (17 [May 1923]: 19) indicates that Dr. and Mrs. Vos resided in La Jolla during this period. This California sojourn included visits to Christian schools in Los Angeles and Redlands, as Catherine attests in "Can Education Be Both Secular and Christian?" *Sunday School Times* 60 (August 2, 1924): 461.

Introduction

The isolation at Roaring Branch may have extended to the local residents, too. Charles Cole once owned the farm that bordered on the Vos hillside property.[134] He does not remember ever talking to Dr. and Mrs. Vos,[135] although he did have occasional conversations with Bernardus and Geerhardus Jr. Cole echoes some of the lines in the *History of Union Township*. The Vos family "was highly educated and remote." Even the relocation of the summer house from in-town to the hillside out-of-town was regarded as a "privacy" matter (p. 18). Cole states that the family did not "mix in."[136] The summer home appears to have been a place of total escape—from Princeton, from Grand Rapids, from Holland—and even from Roaring Branch!

There are tidbits indicating socialization in the Princeton world: a dinner for Valentin Hepp,[137] a guest room for Cornelis Van Felderen,[138] a dinner for newly appointed professor John Murray,[139] Mrs. Vos assisting at a reception for seminary graduates in the class of 1930.[140] And then there is the intriguing information from the U.S. Census form for 1910. The Vos address indicates a full house: Geerhardus and Catherine plus three of the four children (Jerry, as Geerhardus Jr. was nicknamed, was a year away). But two of Catherine's sisters were also staying at the house: Emily Smith (age 42) and Lidia O. Smith (age 40)—both listed as "single." One more name appears on the roll: Katherine Bolan, "nurse," age 34 and single, from England. The title "nurse" is probably equivalent to "nanny." In a letter to Mrs. Herman Bavinck (February 16, 1909), Catherine notes that her "nurse" has gone to Michigan and that an "Irish Protestant girl" has taken her place.[141] Ten years later, there were no aunts or nannies at 52 Mercer Street.[142]

134. Cole (then 82 years old) to the author, October 24, 1999.
135. He was only 15 years old in 1932, Vos's last summer in Roaring Branch.
136. Phone conversation, June 10, 1999.
137. *New York Times*, April 3, 1930, p. 38.
138. Vos to Van Felderen, September 5, 1921.
139. *New York Times*, March 9, 1930, p. 36.
140. Ibid., May 6, 1930, p. 35.
141. Letter in the H. Bavinck Archive, Free University of Amsterdam.
142. U.S. Census 1920, Princeton Township, Mercer County, New Jersey.

Vos was an inveterate walker. His daughter recalls him walking "arm in arm" with B. B. Warfield.[143] This last portrait—Vos and Warfield walking arm in arm about the Princeton quadrant—is a symbolic tribute to the harmony of the theological disciplines: the great Princeton systematic theologian and the great Princeton biblical theologian in perfect, brotherly harmony and affection. Such a portrait evades the polarizers and agenda-manufacturers of the present day. For Vos and Warfield, biblical theology and systematic theology were simpatico.[144]

And teaching? Vos's thirty-nine-year career at Princeton was a teaching career. In addition to the staple Old and New Testament Biblical Theology, he taught: Eschatology of the Old Testament, Pauline Eschatology, Theology of the Epistle to the Hebrews, Teaching of the Eighth Century (B.C.) Prophets, Peter's Speeches in Acts, Messianic Consciousness of Jesus, The Teaching of the Fourth Gospel, Teaching of Paul in Survey, Arabic, Syriac, Pauline Christology and Soteriology, The Petrine Teaching, The Mode of Prophetic Revelation—The Psalter, Prophetism or Teaching of the Prophets, Application of Redemption in Paul, The Self-Disclosure of Jesus.[145] Most of these courses will be recognized as the titles of books or major articles by Vos. Some are preserved only in brief course syllabi or student notebooks. Others are not extant in any known form.

The Biblical-Theological Legacy

Vos formulated a distinctively evangelical and Reformed approach to biblical theology.[146] Positioning himself over against every form of

---

143. Cf. also Calhoun, *Princeton Seminary*, 2:210. Calhoun's volume contains a photograph of the seminary campus with a key labeling the Vos home and others (plates between pp. 298 and 299 of volume 2). "[Dr. Warfield] and my father both liked to take walks along the stretch of Mercer Street in front of the Seminary campus" (Bernardus Vos to Roger Nicole, July 3, 1967).

144. Jerry and Bernardus Vos reported to friends and relatives that Warfield collapsed from a heart attack in the Vos's front yard at 52 Mercer Street on his way home from class on February 16, 1921. Warfield died that evening at his home. See *New York Times*, February 18, 1921, p. 11, for a brief obituary notice. J. Gresham Machen wrote his mother an account of Warfield's last day; see Stonehouse, *J. Gresham Machen*, 309–10.

145. This list is compiled from the catalogue of Princeton Theological Seminary from 1892 to 1932.

146. The following paragraphs are based upon the unedited version of the author's contri-

liberal reductionism, he affirmed the supernatural character and integrity of the Word of God.[147] But this antithetical stance was not merely the affirmation of a son of the historic orthodox church against Lessing's ugly ditch and Kant's epistemological divide.[148] Vos's adherence to the objectivity of supernatural revelation was anchored in the objectivity of God himself. The God who has spoken in history. That revelation is not mere witness (*Zeugnis*), not mere religious insight, not mere idealism or rationalism, not mere developmental comparison of Semitic and Hellenistic religions (*Religionsgeschichte*[149]). Rather, that revelation is the objective self-communication of the very words of God (*ipsissima verba Dei*) from his throne room, his arena, his heavenly domain, his very being. In other words, Vos eschatologizes revelation. His biblical theology is theocentric because it is the very word from the above to the below. That arena in which God himself dwells is the arena from which he speaks. And that speech is intended to reveal that eschatological arena to the listening creature.

Even before the Fall, even before Eve, Adam was invited by God to come "up a little higher"—to enter into the eschatological arena. The earth was never intended to be the locus of man's eschatological rest. It was an arena of probation, protologically oriented to the

---

bution on Vos in *Bible Interpreters of the Twentieth Century*, ed. Walter A. Elwell and J. D. Weaver (Grand Rapids: Baker Book House, 1999), 82–92.

147. Commenting on the critical principles of Abraham Kuenen (1828–1891), Vos wrote: "These principles to be sure are, as Kuenen himself does not conceal, from the outset, incompatible with any form of supernaturalism" (review of *Historisch-critisch onderzoek naar het ontstaan en de verzameling van de boeken des Ouden Verbonds: De profetische boeken des Ouden Verbonds*, by A. Kuenen, *PRR* 2 [1891]: 139).

148. "As long as our thinking regulates itself by the real and objective world, it cannot ignore the distinctions by which it is confronted on every side. But once the notion having gained prevalence that the "Ding an sich" is shut off from our knowledge, and that at least the forms of representation and thought are products of our own mind, this great objection is easily disposed of. Through Kant's subjective idealism this view became predominant in modern philosophy. Human thought naturally tends towards unity, and this tendency did the rest. The result was, that in the great Pantheistic systems following upon Kant, all difference between Creator and creature, between time and eternity, between good and evil, between the holy and the profane, is done away with" (review of *De verflauwing der grenzen*, by Abraham Kuyper, *PRR* 4 [1893]: 331).

149. Vos's familiarity with this method, which he labels "utterly unscientific," is detailed in his review of *Die Menschensohnfrage im letzen-Stadium*, by Eduard Hertlein (*PTR* 10 [1912]: 324–30).

eschatological heavens. In his magnum opus, *Biblical Theology: Old and New Testaments*, Vos teaches us that eschatology is prior to soteriology, even as heaven is prior to Adam's fall. The implication of this observation profoundly alters one's view of revelation in history. The earth is the temporal and temporary. This world will pass away. God's dwelling place is permanent, eternal (in the heavens), never to fade away.

If the protological Adam fails, the eschatological Adam will not. If the First Adam will dissolve to his dusty origins, the Second Adam will not see corruption, but is raised a life-giving Spirit. Vos taught his students (and continues to teach his readers) that to understand the Bible, one must begin with God. And to begin with God is to begin with the eschatological arena. Every word from God is a summons to that heavenly arena. In this fallen world, the only ladder to that arena is the Son of Man himself. Christ Jesus, the man from heaven, covenantally binds himself to bring heaven down to earth in order that the sons and daughters of the earth may be brought up to heaven.

The progress of the history of revelation (*historia revelationis*) is, for Vos, the outworking of this protological/eschatological pattern ("eschatology becomes the mother of theology and that first of all theology in the form of a philosophy of redemptive history"[150]). Using his favorite analogy, Vos traces the unfolding history of redemption from the Garden of Eden to the New Jerusalem in terms of a flower blooming from bud to blossom. Inherent in the earlier stages of the flower are the later. Indeed, retrospectively and prospectively the flower, at every stage of growth, is organically related to history past, history present, and history future. This linear or horizontal dimension in the development of the history of redemption has been called the typological. But for Vos, typology is not enough. The dynamic of a theocentric (and Christocentric) revelation must recognize the vertical dimension. In other words, Vos transforms traditional biblical study by introducing an intersecting-plane hermeneutic: the intrusion of the vertical into the horizontal, the

---

150. "Hebrews, the Epistle of the Diatheke," in *RHBI*, 193.

penetration of the temporal by the eternal, the intersection of the protological and the eschatological. His famous diagram of the two-age construction of the New Testament era testifies to the overarching and interpenetrating "age to come" (above) into this "present evil age" (below).

The church thus finds itself in a semi-eschatological tension—between the "now" and the "not yet." The reality of this experience comes to expression particularly in the Pauline indicative-imperative. The believer is now seated in the heavenly places in Christ Jesus (Eph. 2:6), while he yearns for the consummation and the resurrection of the body ("not yet"). However, his life, "hidden with Christ in God" (Col. 3:3), possesses even now the status of the sons and daughters of God as an indication of what is yet to come. And the moral imperative of the Christian life is the realization of the indicative—the living out of the heavenly arena even now in the present evil age.

Vos carefully delineated his biblical-theological method at the inauguration of his career at Princeton (in his 1894 address). This method was evident in the final manuscript to flow from his pen, *The Eschatology of the Old Testament*. In between, each essay, each sermon,

I. The Original Scheme

This age or world	The age or world to come

II. The Modified Scheme
The world to come,
realized in principle

| Resurrection of Christ | [in Heaven] [in earth] | Parousia | Future age and world fully realized in solid existence |

This age or world

each book, each review, and each article explored the intersection of the eschatological with the temporal. His address on the covenant enabled him to position the Reformed doctrine of the covenant as the subsidiary organizing principle of the history of redemption. Covenant becomes an archetypal pattern for the disclosure of God's words and deeds. Revelation is primary, but that revelation occurs in history. How are the transcendent unity and developmental diversity of that self-disclosure maintained together? The relationship that binds creature and Creator throughout time and space—the relationship that draws the creature into union with his Creator, the relationship that breathes the mutuality of being chosen and being grateful—is the covenant: the covenant of the Father and the Son, the covenant of works between the Creator and his protological creation, the covenant of grace between the Creator and his eschatological (un)creation.

When the covenant reaches its semi-eschatological climax at the inbreaking of the kingdom of heaven, the church becomes the heir to the fullness of the promises. She is nothing less than the new Israel in which the sojourners (the "Hebrews") of the end of the age live out their odyssey to the New Jerusalem, the heavenly Zion, the land of eschatological Sabbath rest. The Pauline eschatology is but a species of this sublime drama conceived in the encounter with the risen Christ on the Damascus road. The Pharisee is transformed by an encounter with the eschatological life from the dead. Now Saul, bond-slave of the law of Judaism, must be the servant of the Messiah for the Gentiles. Old is displaced by new: the law does not justify; the blood of Abraham does not save; the mysteries of the seers do not enlighten. Only Christ Jesus justifies, as he himself has been justified by resurrection from the dead (1 Tim. 3:16). Only faith in Christ saves, as he himself has been faithful to and through death. Only the mystery of Christ enlightens, as he himself is the effulgence and radiance of the Father.

The church that Paul plants is the church in which this eschatological lifestyle is dramatically rehearsed. In Christ, the church has died to the curse of the law, so that she may be raised to reflect the moral character of heaven itself. In Christ, the church walks by faith because she even now possesses the reality of the heavenly arena. In Christ, the church sees the light of glory and reflects that radiance to a dark and dreary world.

Vos penned four revolutionary volumes after his appointment to the faculty of Princeton Seminary. Each volume accents Vos's unique contribution—the priority of eschatology: eschatology and the kingdom, eschatology and the homiletic moment, eschatology and the messianic self-consciousness of Jesus, eschatology and the Pauline theology.

Vos's first book-length contribution to the biblical-theological discussion of his day was *The Kingdom of God and the Church* (1903). His exegesis of the kingdom of God proclaimed by Jesus is positioned so as to contrast with: (1) first-century Jewish kingdom expectations, (2) nineteenth-century liberal views of the kingdom of God, in which Jesus is not the bringer of the kingdom (God is!), but rather the one who prepares men for the appearance of the kingdom (which he mistakenly expected in his own lifetime), and (3) early twentieth-century explanations of Jesus' apocalyptic-eschatological expectations (i.e., Albert Schweitzer), in which Jesus attempts to extort the kingdom from God, only to die in dereliction when God abandons him.[151] The fundamental error of all three views is that they desupernaturalize the kingdom. For Vos, the coming of the kingdom which Jesus announced was the presence of supernatural events (visible in the miracles, hidden in the parables). This kingdom begins in regeneration (supernatural rebirth) and continues in the immanent gifts derived from the

---

151 "The kingdom is a gift of God (not a task, a goal, an ideal, an idea or a community); the attitude of man with reference to it is purely receptive, not productive; the kingdom is wrought by God; human activity comes into consideration only in so far as it conditions the reception or loss of the kingdom; the kingdom is a product specially of the creative activity of God, it is not evolved out of the world, but imported into it from heaven; the kingdom is hidden, celestial, future, in so far as it consists in the fullness of life, angels, light, power surrounding God in heaven, not in the sense of being a resting treasure preserved in heaven or merely ideally preexistent in the purpose of God; the world receives the kingdom in so far as the latter steps forward out of its hidden state and by drawing the world into its sphere becomes manifest; God brings the kingdom, though in Christ, and Christ through the power of God, these two being synonymous" (review of *Das Reich Gottes nach den synoptischen Evangelien*, by W. Lütgert, *PRR* 11 [1900]: 172).

spiritual person and work of Christ. Incorporation into this spiritual aspect of the kingdom is the ongoing function of the Spirit of Christ, who brought it with his very own advent. And yet, there is a "not yet."[152] The kingdom that Jesus announces has a future eschatological dimension. It will be consummated in a sudden crisis so cosmic and visible in scope that its outcome will be utterly and totally final. Supernatural incorporation into the kingdom now; supernatural consummation of the kingdom in the future. The "now" and "not yet" (or the two ages) of Jesus' kingdom proclamation surpass Judaism with its nationalistic, political, sensual kingdom hopes. The presence and future of the kingdom that Jesus brings contravenes classic liberalism that immanentizes the eschaton. And Vos's presentation of Christ's kingdom avoids the dereliction of Schweitzer's (non)historical Jesus,[153] because it presumes the credibility and historicity of the gospel records.

In 1922, Vos published six sermons that he had delivered in the Chapel of Princeton Theological Seminary. These sermons represent the craft of the biblical theologian applied to the homiletical moment. In each sermon, the priority of God's invitation to his creature to dwell with him is portrayed. It is as if Vos reverses the traditional preaching event by drawing his listeners into the living text of Scripture, rather than by extracting truths from the text in order to impose them upon the listeners. *Grace and Glory* presents a homiletical method in which God's people find their life hidden with Christ in God; their life is united to and identified with the life of Christ revealed in that partic-

---

152 "The kingdom is not merely future, it is also a present reality" (review of *Die Predigt Jesu vom Reiche Gottes*, by Johannes Weiss; *Jesu Predigt in ihrem Gegensatz zum Judenthum*, by W. Bousset; *Jesu Verkündigung und Lehre vom Reiche Gottes in ihrer geschichtlichen Bedeutung dargestellt*, by Georg Schnedermann, *PRR* 5 [1894]: 146). "The ordinary formula . . . harmonizes the present and the eschatological aspects of the kingdom by representing the former as the incipient, partial realization of the latter" (review of *Das Reich Gottes nach den synoptischen Evangelien*, by W. Lütgert, *PRR* 11 [1900]: 173).

153 A trenchant comment on the "quest for the historical Jesus" drew from Vos the following remark: "But precisely because of this utter dispassionateness of the discussion the reader will rise from its perusal with all the stronger conviction that the form of skepticism which it combats borders nigh upon the psychopathic" (review of *Der geschichtliche Jesus*, by Carl Clemen, *PTR* 10 [1912]: 489).

ular word of God. In other words, preaching for Vos is not primarily application, nor is it fundamentally introspection—it is supremely identification and incorporation. The eschatological perspective dominates even the sermons that Vos preaches![154]

Vos published *The Self-Disclosure of Jesus: The Modern Debate about the Messianic Consciousness* in 1926. In a scintillating survey of Christ's messianic self-consciousness, Vos examined the evolution of the modern critical discussion from Gustav Volkmar, James Martineau, and Nathaniel Schmidt (denial of messianic consciousness in Jesus), to Wilhelm Wrede's famous "messianic secret" (agnostic conclusion derived from Jesus' prohibition, especially in Mark's gospel, of the disciples' revealing his messiahship[155]), to David Friedrich Strauss, Ernest Renan, and Heinrich J. Holtzmann (Jesus grows from not being conscious of being the Messiah to "thinking" he is the Messiah). Always hovering in the background is the "eschatological" Jesus of Albert Schweitzer and Johannes Weiss.[156] At heart, each liberal reduction is an attempt to eliminate the eschatological element from the person of Jesus. In other words, desupernaturalize Jesus of Nazareth, and messiahship must be explained centrifugally, not centripetally (p. 37). What Vos

---

154. The compatibility of modern evangelical and Reformed preaching with classic nineteenth-century liberal preaching is not coincidental, since both agendas are moralistically and ethically reductionist: "The spirit of the age is not over friendly to eschatology, and on the other hand is inclined to ethicize in every direction" (review of *Die Reichsgotteshoffnung in den ältesten christlichen Dokumenten und bei Jesus*, by Paul Wernle, *PTR* 1 [1903]: 303). Whatever objective revelation (if any) these moralizers admit, each one "speaks as if the revelation value of the [biblical] record [lies] exclusively in the lesson which the history is made to teach, so that in the last analysis it would not make any essential difference whether the statements were history or legend or pure fiction" (review of *Joseph and Moses*, by Buchanan Blake, *PTR* 1 [1903]: 471). Application that is ahistorical has no connection to the supernatural. Application that is merely ethical or moral is fundamentally pagan, not Christian (or even biblical).

155. "Did not our Lord Himself find it necessary . . . to throw during the larger part of His public teaching nearly all the emphasis upon the idea of the kingdom of *God*, so as to hold the idea of His own Messianic kingship in reserve, until the time when, the conception of the kingdom having been fully set forth in its spiritual import and carefully guarded against all political misconceptions, the idea of the Messiahship could be safely brought forward and placed in the light of the regenerated kingdom-idea? Is it not possible to believe that this method was anticipated in the development of Old Testament prophecy?" (review of *Der alttestamentliche Unterbau des Reiches Gottes*, by Julius Boehmer, *PTR* 1 [1903]: 131).

156. Actually, it was a noneschatological Jesus. See Vos's review of Schweitzer's *The Quest for the Historical Jesus* in *PTR* 9 (1911): 132–41 (reprint, *RHBI*, 517–25).

brilliantly points out is that to reduce Jesus to the level of human religion, liberalism must make him part of the world, not distinct from the world. Supernatural and eschatological messiahship would set him apart from the world (while yet in the world) as wholly unique. All liberalism must re-create Jesus of Nazareth in its own immanentistic image.

Vos spends the bulk of the volume in an exegetical tour de force of the messianic titles: "the Christ," "the Lord," "the Son of God," "the Son of Man," "the Savior." He concludes with an exposition of the messianic death that, in itself, is not only exegetical of the prophetic projection (notably Isaiah 53), but also revelatory of the glory of the passion of Jesus.

Vos's legacy regarding the messianic consciousness of Jesus is the rehabilitation of the orthodox, supernatural view. Jesus of Nazareth is the Messiah because he is the supernatural Son of God anointed to be the Savior of his people. To patronize Jesus as a moral example, while rejecting his supernatural person, *is* pathological.

The final volume from the Princeton years was *The Pauline Eschatology*, self-published in 1930. Vos has his eye primarily on the critical reduction of eschatology and Paul, but he casts a glance at burgeoning premillennialism (chiliasm) and its competitor (postmillennialism). The lengthy first chapter on the structure of Pauline eschatology repeats a Vosian theme: "To unfold the Apostle's eschatology means to set forth his theology as a whole" (p. 11). It is the end (of history) that shapes the beginning of Paul's estimate of Christ. In particular, as Richard B. Gaffin Jr. has demonstrated, the resurrection of the dead is the central motif of Paul's system.[157] With the resurrection of Christ, the future eon has burst in upon the present (see the diagram above). The believing Christian is even now in possession of the eschatological arena because he too has been raised up together with Christ.[158] The Christian's life in this

---

157. Indeed, the whole Christian ethos is dominated by Christ's resurrection—"the turning point of the ages," as Vos writes in *Grace and Glory*, 75. Cf. Richard B. Gaffin, *Resurrection and Redemption: A Study in Paul's Soteriology* (Phillipsburg, NJ: Presbyterian and Reformed Pub. Co., 1987), originally titled *The Centrality of the Resurrection: A Study in Paul's Soteriology* (Grand Rapids: Baker, 1978).

158. "The whole saving work of Christ was, strictly speaking, an exemplification of the principle that life can come out of death" (review of *Die Erwählung Israels nach der Heilsverkündigung des Apostels Paulus*, by Johannes Dalmer, *PRR* 11 [1900]: 170).

world is dominated by the age to come—he walks as one who reflects the character of heaven's Lord.[159] The Pauline church is conscious of living in the "heavenlies" even now as she sojourns toward the consummation. In both soteriology and ethics, Vos demonstrates that for Paul and his churches, the ultimate is determinative of the present, not vice versa. For Vos, eschatology is prior to, and determinative of, ethics. All moralism, whether liberal or conservative, is unbiblical because it is, fundamentally, religiously conditioned anthropocentrism.

Vos's contribution to the centennial celebration of Princeton Seminary in 1912 ("The Eschatological Aspect of the Pauline Conception of the Spirit"[160]) should be integrated at this point (for it forms the backbone of chapter six of *The Pauline Eschatology*). The function of the Holy Spirit after the glorification of the risen Lord Jesus is to incorporate the believer now into the life of the age to come. The down payment (Greek, *arrabōn*) of the life of heaven is displayed in the life of the believer. This is so because the Holy Spirit unites the Christian to his ascended Lord and energizes his existence in the world (the so-called "indicative-imperative" relationship).

Vos's sermons, essays, books, and poems were a constant litany of the difference Christ makes. That difference is anticipated in the eschatological intrusion of the biblical theology of the Old Testament. That Christocentric difference is inaugurally (semi)realized in the eschatological intrusion of the biblical theology of the New Testament. That difference will be swallowed up in face-to-face consummation at the death of the believer and the second advent of the Son of glory.

---

159. How little the contemporary church understands the mind of Paul is illustrated in the following quotation. Tragically, few modern preachers think, act, or preach with this mind of Paul. "The first chapter well brings out the dominating place eschatology occupies in the apostle's view of salvation. We believe the matter could have been even more strongly put than the author puts it. The question is not so much whether the doctrines of justification and possession of the Spirit and union with Christ carry with themselves an outlook into the future, but rather whether those acts and states to which these doctrines refer are not from the outset eschatological acts and states, or, more strictly speaking, anticipations in this life of what had previously been regarded as reserved for the end. Only by realizing the extent to which this is true can we appreciate the profound eschatological interest that pervades all Paul's teaching" (review of *St. Paul's Conception of the Last Things*, by H. A. A. Kennedy, *PTR* 3 [1905]: 485). For Vos, Paul's doctrine without Paul's eschatology amounts to a denial of Paul's Christianity.

160. Reprinted in *RHBI*, 91–125.

The practice of biblical theology in Vos's sense draws the believer into union with the Christ of Scripture—as he is displayed from heaven from Genesis to Revelation. And life in Christ is the most practical form of Christianity for the New Testament church. Geerhardus Vos has provided us with the key for this preeminently biblical lifestyle.

Santa Ana

Vos retired to Southern California in 1932.[161] The decision was due, in part, to his health.[162] He had been hospitalized in the spring of 1932 and had not fully recovered when he left Princeton for the last time. Then it was off to the summer house to recuperate even further before the arduous trip across the United States. It was to be his last summer in the mountains of north-central Pennsylvania. A sabbatical trip to the Southwest in 1923 had convinced him that the land of "gold" bordering the vast Pacific, fragrant with orange blossoms and warm—bright, sunny, and warm—was akin to paradise. His son Jerry was already living in Santa Ana. Vos and his wife moved in with him at 1212 South Sycamore Street.[163]

But "paradise" became a tragic nightmare.[164] Within months of relo-

---

161. It was not his first visit to this "fair land," as his poems, thematically associated with the region, indicate (i.e., "California," "San Diego," and "The Mission Bell," in *Western Rhymes*). As previously noted, La Jolla appears to have been home for the sabbatical of 1923.

162. Albertus Eekhof says that Vos retired there "vooral ook om gezondheidsredenen" ("especially for health reasons"). See A. Eekhof, "Prof. Dr. Geerhardus Vos," *Neerlandia* 37 (January 1937): 9.

163. Bernardus Vos indicates that it was late in September when he drove his parents across country (letter to Roger Nicole, July 3, 1967). Cf. Geerhardus Vos to Paul Woolley, September 9, 1932, and Vos to Albertus Eekhof, October 28, 1932.

164. Vos referred to the theological climate in Southern California with the words of Eugene O'Neill's play *Ah Wilderness!* (Vos to Stonehouse, December 15, 1938). He had previously reflected upon the premillennial mania that predominated in fundamentalist circles (Vos to Machen, May 7, 1936). But it was not merely chiliasm that distressed the amillennial Vos; it was the tepid, indeed vacuous, preaching that distressed him more. The gospel was crowded out from the pulpit and Sunday school in the interest of cultural relevance and contemporary moralizing. Vos would be revolted at what passes for preaching in the modern Southern California pulpit. In his words, the soteric significance of revelation is "rarely" heard. "I am sure that there are churches in which a great many other things can be heard, yet where one could listen in vain for the plain preaching of the cross of Christ as the God-appointed means for the salvation of sinners" (*Grace and Glory*, 237).

Introduction

cation, Catherine began to fade with senile dementia.[165] The family worshiped in a Covenanter church (Reformed Presbyterian Church of North America [RPCNA]), no doubt because of its proximity and the fact that Johannes, their oldest son, had been ordained a missionary for the RPCNA to Manchuria (Manchuko). Catherine was received as a member of the Santa Ana RPCNA by letter of transfer on May 6, 1933.[166] But Geerhardus never altered his ministerial membership in the Presbytery of New Brunswick, PCUSA—he was still on the roll of that judicatory at his death in August 1949.

For nearly five years, Geerhardus and his son tended to Catherine. On September 14, 1937, she died of pneumonia at their home. The funeral was held at the house on Saturday, September 18, with her pastor, Rev. Sam Edgar, officiating.[167] Her body was transported to Roaring Branch, where she was buried in the hillside cemetery near the beloved summer house. Did Dr. Vos accompany the body? We do not know for sure. On October 26, 1937, he sold the summer house and property to his four children, but he was in Santa Ana when he completed the transaction.[168] Bernardus was living on the property at the time; hence, it is possible that Geerhardus remained in California when his wife's remains were interred at Roaring Branch. As early as 1886, he had acknowledged that travel was difficult for him.

Vos disposed of most, if not all, of his personal library by donating and selling portions to Westminster Theological Seminary.[169] The letters raise some doubt about the rumored existence of books and papers in the house when it burned in 1973. If Vos had taken steps to dispose

---

165. Her death certificate indicates the "date of onset" of the dementia as November 1932. The irony is that she had cared for her husband all through the years of their marriage. Now he had to care for her.
166. Session Minute Book, RPCNA, Santa Ana, California, meeting of May 6, 1933, p. 143 (deposited in the Library of Reformed Presbyterian Theological Seminary, Pittsburgh, Pennsylvania).
167. *Santa Ana Journal*, September 17, 1937, and *Santa Ana Register*, September 15, 1937.
168. Deed book 213, p. 490ff., Tioga County, Pennsylvania.
169. See Vos to Machen, April 28, 1932; Vos to Woolley, September 9, 1932; Vos to Woolley, January 27, 1936; Vos to Woolley, February 22, 1936.

of many of his books between 1932 and 1936, it is unlikely that any remained in the "attic" in 1973.[170]

Grand Rapids Again

Following the death of Catherine, Vos's health began to decline. In 1939, he was moved to the home of his daughter at 1319 Colorado Street, S.E., Grand Rapids, Michigan.[171] Here he passed the last ten years of his life. He continued his walking, ambling up the sidewalk in front of the house virtually every day. And he received visitors. It is reported that on several occasions in the summer, Cornelius Van Til and Ned Stonehouse visited their former professor in the Colorado Street house. Vos's attention to Stonehouse (and vice versa) is confirmed by his correspondence. It was Stonehouse who produced the acknowledgment that Vos was aware of Rudolf Bultmann and Karl Barth. The phrase "ilk of him" (referring to Barth) is telltale. The May 18, 1940, letter to Stonehouse suggests that Vos was also already acquainted with the views of Martin Dibelius—

---

170. Vos wrote to Rev. Edwards Elliott that his library had been "scattered" following his retirement in 1932 (letter of January 25, 1946). Bernardus Vos wrote to Roger Nicole: "During the summer of 1935, being unemployed and consequently with plenty of time to do it, I removed the books from the large wooden boxes in which they had been packed at Princeton when leaving there, and catalogued all of them. There were at that time some 2091 volumes in all, excluding some dozen or two that have turned up in various places in the Roaring Branch house which I did not know about at the time of cataloguing the books. Since 1936 quite a number of the books have been sold to various persons and organizations—to Dr. Van Til, to Westminster Seminary, to Dr. Rudolph of the Reformed Episcopal Seminary in Philadelphia, to Rev. John Meeter, who edited several of Dr. Warfield's books, etc. Very unfortunately only a very imperfect record was kept of which books were sold, so that at present the catalogue would hardly be an accurate record of what remains. Further, after 1935 some of the books were sent to my father at Santa Ana, and I have at present no idea what ever eventually was done with these." Bernardus goes on to note that in about 1947 he removed all books published before 1800 and brought them to his home in Harrisburg, Pennsylvania. However, he does write the following: "Last November [1966], while a well was being drilled at the Roaring Branch house, I had several hours to browse through old papers and family belongings. I came upon a pack of letters that my father, living then in Santa Ana, had written to me in Roaring Branch during the 1930's. I brought them back to Harrisburg and re-read all of them carefully" (letter of July 3, 1967).

171. An address card in the faculty file of Princeton Theological Seminary (#85a) indicates the following: "7/39 1341 Colorado Ave. S.E. Grand Rapids, Mich." Bernardus Vos indicates that it was Marianne who moved him (letter to Nicole, July 3, 1967); Marianne reported that Jerry brought him.

who, with Bultmann, was one of the principle founders of New Testament form criticism.

No More Sorrow

On Saturday, August 13, 1949, Geerhardus Vos entered the "city which hath foundations." He died at the Hessel Convalescent Home (218 Sheldon Avenue, Grand Rapids) after a bout with bronchial pneumonia. He had been moved to the Home a week earlier. His funeral was held on Monday, August 15, with H. Henry Meeter, President of Calvin College, officiating.[172] Forty-five people attended the funeral service, three of whom were his children: Marianne (Radius), Johannes, and Jerry. Bernardus appears to have remained in Roaring Branch to await transfer of the body and make arrangements there.[173]

The macabre black-and-white photo of the open casket at Roaring Branch contains two of the attendees at the burial: Rev. John DeWaard, pastor of Memorial Orthodox Presbyterian Church, Rochester, New York, and Dr. Cornelius Van Til, professor of apologetics at Westminster Theological Seminary, Philadelphia, Pennsylvania.[174] Dr. Van Til preached from 2 Corinthians 5:1.[175] Geerhardus Vos was laid to rest beside his wife in the summer retreat he loved so well. No one

172. Funeral record from Zaagman Memorial Chapel, Grand Rapids, Michigan.
173. In a previous article, I suggested that no one from Vos's family was present at the Roaring Branch interment. I appear to have been mistaken, and I am happy to correct the misapprehension. It has subsequently been reported that Bernardus was one of perhaps six people present at the rites on August 17, 1949.
174. The photo was probably snapped by DeWaard's wife, Hattie, who was also present. A man and a woman who sang a duet at the service were from the local Methodist church. Charles Cole has suggested to this writer that the woman likely was Odessa Evans Proctor, well known for singing and playing the organ at the church during that era.
175. On May 21, 1977, during a visit to Mrs. John (Hattie) DeWaard in Grand Rapids, Michigan, Van Til took her copy of Catherine Vos's *Child Story Bible* and wrote the following: "John de Waard offered the final prayer after I had given a short exposition about II Corinthians 5:1: 'For we know that if our earthly house of this tabernacle were dissolved, we have a building of God, an house not made with hands, eternal in the heavens.' Dr. and Mrs. Vos had gone to Roaring Branch, Pennsylvania for many summer vacations. Apparently they attended a church there; a man of about eighty and a woman of about sixty sang a duet: it was a melody of love to the Saviour, whom Geerhardus Vos and Katherine [sic] F. loved so deeply and served so well at Princeton Theological Seminary many years. I am writing this at Hattie's dining room table. May 21, 1977" (William D. Dennison to the author, September 18, 1985).

from Princeton was present; no one from the PCUSA paid any attention; only two from the community were there. He was obscure in life, and obscure in death.

Periodization

We now have a body of material sufficient for a more thorough biographical sketch of our subject than has previously been available. The volume in hand adds a dimension previously wanting, yet more discursive than the pieces heretofore assembled. We observe that the literary remains of Geerhardus Vos fall roughly into the "epochal" periods of his life. The book reviews date from 1889 to 1919—a thirty-year period in which he was at the top of his powers. The articles date from 1897 to 1929 and, although they extend ten years beyond the reviews, are major contributions only insofar as they contribute to *The Self-Disclosure of Jesus* and the magisterial *The Pauline Eschatology*. The sermons, with three exceptions,[176] are dated from 1902 to 1914.[177] The published books, with two exceptions,[178] appeared from 1922 to 1930—as if he was winding down his career with book output. The volumes of poetry are spread from 1922 to 1936; it is crucial to note that they extend beyond the conclusion of the specifically theological, homiletical, and biblical-theological output.

An outline of Vos's career would look like this:

---

176. One sermon (on Isaiah 57:15) is dated December 12, 1896, and another (on Ephesians 2:4–5, in Dutch) is undated. The latter certainly originated in the Grand Rapids period (1888–1893). There is also a "graduation sermon" on Ephesians 1:4, dated June 25, 1883, in Vos's hand (with his signature), deposited in the Heritage Hall Archive at Calvin College.

177. Vos's publication of the original six messages in the 1922 edition of *Grace and Glory* indicates that he had ceased preaching in the Princeton Chapel services. This is consistent with Vos's gradual withdrawal from writing reviews, articles, letters, etc. There is a decided shift in Vos's Princeton career following the end of World War I (1918) and the death of his closest friend on the faculty, B. B. Warfield (1921).

178. *The Mosaic Origin of the Pentateuchal Codes* (1886) and *The Kingdom of God and the Church* (1903), which are strangely omitted from the list of his publications that Vos drew up in 1932 (see *Neerlandia* 37 [January 1933]: 10). The original edition of *Grace and Glory* (1922) is also absent. Cf. James T. Dennison Jr., "Editor's Introduction," *Kerux: The Journal of Northwest Theological Seminary* 19/3 (December 2004): 3–5.

Early Transitions: 1862–1888
Spurt of Scholarly Activity: 1888–1902
Era of Greatest Scholarly Productivity: 1902–1919
Period of Waning Scholarly Output: 1919–1930
Era of Nonproductivity: 1930–1949

Enigmas

Let me attempt—for an attempt is all that can be made from the data available—to assess the incongruities of Geerhardus Vos. First, let us reflect on some raw data bespeaking the enigma of the man. In his only printed self-reflection, Vos makes very little reference to his career staple, biblical theology. Why? Having received an honorary D.D. degree from Lafayette College in 1893, he was never again the object of such recognition—not even by Calvin College and Seminary.[179] After 1919, he wrote no more theological or biblical book reviews. Why? And for the final ten years of the *Princeton Theological Review* (1919–1929), he virtually disappeared from its pages. Why? Following publication of *The Pauline Eschatology*, his scholarly output ceased.[180] After 1930, he wrote no more theological books or articles. Why? His last nineteen years of life were virtually silent, theologically speaking. Why? After promoting Abraham Kuyper and Herman Bavinck for their famous Stone Lectures, he ceased corresponding with them: with Abraham Kuyper in 1897 (though Kuyper lived until 1920) and with Bavinck in 1909 (though Bavinck lived twelve more years). Why? Having stayed abreast of developments in liberal-

---

179. This is remarkable, considering the fact that Vos was the *first* university-educated professor at Calvin, as well as the *first* to earn a Ph.D. and then teach within her walls.
180. The *Eschatology of the Old Testament* manuscript was being completed during the Princeton years, i.e., as a foundation or product of his class lectures under that name. Bernardus Vos wrote to Roger Nicole: "So far as I know, the only major work of my father which has never been published in any form is his Eschatology of the Old Testament, a manuscript of about 500 double-spaced typed pages. He was working on this at the time of his retirement in May 1932. Presumably the manuscript was sent to Santa Ana when he moved there in October 1932. Since then the manuscript has become lost" (letter of July 3, 1967). There is a story, reportedly told by Cornelius Van Til, that the full manuscript of this work, numbering perhaps 400 pages, was lost in the move from Santa Ana to Grand Rapids in 1939. Van Til said that Vos remarked, "It was like losing a child." Cf. *The Eschatology of the Old Testament*, ed. James T. Dennison Jr. (Phillipsburg, NJ: P&R Publishing Co., 2001).

critical fundamentalism from 1894 to 1924, thereafter he evidenced little interest in advancing non-orthodoxies. There is minimal awareness of the Bultmannian and Barthian dominance of theology after World War I (and that was stimulated, apparently, by Ned Stonehouse),[181] and no reflection on the emerging postwar biblical archaeology phenomenon. Why? He alleged sympathy with Westminster Seminary, but did not join her faculty. Why? He showed no support for the organization of the Presbyterian Church of America in 1936 (renamed the Orthodox Presbyterian Church in 1939), nor did he ever mention the denomination by name.[182] Why, particularly when his former students—Machen, Murray, Van Til, Stonehouse—were pillars of her formation? He never altered his ecclesiastical standing, even after departing from Princeton. Furthermore, after 1932, he apparently never worshiped in a PCUSA church again, attending an RPCNA church from 1932 to 1939 and then returning to the vicinity of the conservative CRC from 1939 to 1949. Why? Even more baffling, apart from one oblique reflection (in 1881), he never mentioned worship in a particular church, nor the life of a congregation, nor the impact of a pastor, although he undoubtedly attended church all his life. Why? His written materials show no emphasis upon distinctively Reformed truths after the Confessional Revision movement of 1889–1890 (and, again, 1900–1903), and this from a man who had written his own Reformed dogmatics. Why? He departed from Grand Rapids in part over "useless bickering," but stayed at Princeton in the face of the bickering unleashed by J. Ross Stevenson and his reorganization agenda. In fact, he was downright passive, submissive, and repentant for causing any unrest at the seminary. Why? When providing readers in the Netherlands with an autobiographical sketch (1932), he highlighted almost none of his biblical-theological work, choosing rather to place the emphasis on his interest in poetry. Why? The enigmas are staggering.

181. Emil Brunner visited Princeton Theological Seminary in 1928 and insisted on meeting J. Gresham Machen. Machen was suspicious of the neo-orthodox pioneer. Was Vos aware of the visitor? See Calhoun, *Princeton Seminary*, 2:387–89.
182. Not even in his letter of condolence to her founder's brother, Arthur Machen, on January 5, 1937.

Introduction

Vos's provocative and spirited correspondence was essentially over by 1894. The period of his greatest literary output was from 1889 to 1929. The letters ceased altogether from 1909 to 1921,[183] during his peak years of sermonic output and scholarly production. And after 1932? Nothing came from Vos's pen save poetry, a few letters, the *Neerlandia* items, and the preface (dated September 1, 1948) to his edited classroom lectures, *Biblical Theology: Old and New Testaments*. To explain the man, this apparent periodization must be kept in mind. His extant remains are meager (Vos's "privacy" is legendary), and much has no doubt been discarded or lost forever; nonetheless, there is a pattern here that intrigues the biographer and periodizes the life of the "father of Reformed biblical theology."

The incongruities of this apparently contradictory personality are baffling to this observer. Vos's worlds shifted routinely, but he remained constant—a personal enigma. After 1893, we have no display of the mind, the inner man, the heart or feelings, the angst, apart from the profusion of poetry. The poetry does indeed indicate a sensitive, reflective personality. But we discover precious little of the biographical commodity in his other writings after his wedding. We gather up bare facts and attempt to compose the persona of the man. He eludes us, mystifies us, leaves our world behind. Was he so attached to heaven that the earth and its trials became unimportant? Such a conclusion would make him a practitioner of the magnificent biblical theology set forth in his books. But we hesitate. He confessed to being an insomniac, his nights were nightmares, and his nerves were frayed. He retreated relentlessly from the spotlight; he was even virtually antisocial in the rural Pennsylvania town where he spent his summers for more than twenty years. How is it possible for a person and his wife and children to return summer after summer and not "mix" with a small rural community in some sense? The Methodist folk of Roaring Branch were not of his theological tradition, but they were professing Christians. Two of them, apparently, sang at his Roaring Branch

---

183. We cite two exceptions: the letters to Henry Beets dated March 16, 1912, and October 4, 1915.

funeral. Was this, too, part of the unassuming portrait of the man? Even in the summer at that Arminian church, simplicity and a shy expression of Christianity were all that he could offer in person. He could not give of himself outside the family circle.

Finally, what Vos did *not* write, especially after retirement in 1932, speaks volumes about what was uppermost in his mind. Mostly, he wrote poetry—a virtual return to his youth. Is this a veritable confirmation of the Freudian paradigm, i.e., infancy returns with geriatrics? Most all of what Vos wrote after 1932 was matter-of-fact, reflecting little interest in ecclesiastical politics or developments. In other words, Vos appears to have dropped out after 1932. I would suggest that this was the extension of his own conscious odyssey that began in 1906 with the retreat to Roaring Branch (and perhaps stemmed from his earlier disillusionment with the downgrade resulting from the Briggs heresy trial and the Confessional Revision movement). And I am suggesting that it was the extension of his Old World pietistic roots.

A second curious enigma to be explained is the neglect and dismissal of Vos's biblical-theological method and insights during his lifetime. While many lamented the neglect of Vos's writings and exegetical insights after his death, it seems clear that few assimilated and applied them while he was alive. If scholars manifested little or no interest in his writings,[184] this was all the more glaringly true of his students. With the possible exception of James Oscar Boyd and a few Dutch students (Henry Schultze, for example), Vos was largely forgotten as soon as his students completed his classes or earned their degrees. With the possible exception of John DeWaard, PCUSA and CRC graduates did not base their approach to Scripture, preaching, pastoral ministry, or the Christian life on the Vosian paradigm. And after the formation of the OPC, Vos was an enigma to her pastors—especially after the death of Machen on January 1, 1937. It was not until the early 1970s that students who read Vos began to rethink preaching and ministry on the

---

184. A mere handful of reviews constitute the interaction, both before and after his death. The majority of those were from Christian Reformed circles. See the Christian Reformed Periodical Index at the Hekman Library at Calvin College (available online).

basis of his exegesis of the semi-eschatological Pauline theology (or the eschatological perspective that he articulated so well in general). Vos was an assigned reading at many conservative, even Reformed, seminaries—but his system was not being "applied" to ministry. Academics used Vos to bolster their course bibliographies, but dismissed him as dense, impractical, and too hard.

Some will argue that Westminster Theological Seminary preserved and advanced Vos's biblical theology. While it is true that some of the figures associated with the early Westminster in Pennsylvania claimed to be Vosian in their approach to Scripture, more recently some have distanced themselves from him—even repudiating the very Christocentric hermeneutic he espoused and replacing it with "Reformed" anthropocentrism.

The interesting question is: Was this inevitable? That is, realizing that Vos was the "club key" for the early days of Reformed conservatism (i.e., the 1930s through the 1960s), numerous individuals eagerly attached their names to the sainted Princetonian. But having advanced to positions of prominence in the conservative Reformed movement, they increasingly ignored Vos or otherwise distanced themselves from him in thought and manner.

And thus Vos continues in death as in life: obscure, ignored, and insignificant. This would not have surprised Vos himself. And this opens up another avenue of consideration regarding the career of our subject. Vos demonstrated repeatedly his careful assessment and analysis of liberal-critical fundamentalism, but he was also familiar with biblical fundamentalism, especially its millenarian proclivities. Added to his conservative theological orientation and background were the emerging progressive evangelical and Reformed movements of his day. Vos was quite aware of the evangelical-fundamentalist mainstream. And he was aware that it was *not* Reformed. When the shift in theological emphasis reared its ugly head at Princeton in 1914 (when J. Ross Stevenson became president), it was the maturation of a long, gradual capitulation of progressive evangelicals on the faculty, on the board, in the student body, and in the denomination. Determined to make

Princeton look like the Presbyterian and American mainstream culture,[185] Stevenson and his cadre succeeded where the nineteenth-century New School failed—he completely gutted and neutered the Old School Princeton tradition. There is no one today who takes seriously Stevenson's claim that he was merely "adjusting" Princeton's Old School heritage to the church at large and the times as they were. Stevenson was an innovator (as Machen pointed out and Warfield perceived) and intended nothing less than the subversion of the tradition he secretly despised.[186] In 1929, he succeeded.

But J. Ross Stevenson brought to a head the long-simmering resentment of Old Princeton's orthodoxy and unique place in the American Presbyterian tradition. The drift away from the Westminster Confession after the Civil War was an acknowledgment that the mainline PCUSA had no real ties to seventeenth-century orthodoxy. The Confessional Revision movement proved this. At the same time, the Social Gospel drained the energies of Reformed conservatives, but in a hopeless cause. Social amelioration was the "messiah" of liberals—and still is.[187] And messianisms are not countered with theological tomes or seventeenth-century Reformed confessions. These anti-messiahs are "irrelevant." And finally there was burgeoning modernism—or the rabid liberalism of the Auburn Affirmationists, Pearl Buck, Shailer Matthews, and a host of others. Modernism ate away at the fabric of biblical Christianity like a corrosive acid. The modernist movement was the most demoralizing. Because the church at large was increasingly controlled by leaders with a modernist agenda, the seminary was placed on the defensive. And the withering onslaught of the media, which was sympathetic to modernism, compelled change, adaptation, and compromise inside Princeton. President Stevenson did not want Princeton left outside the cultural and ecclesiastical mainstream (as

---

185. "There is not much demand in this country" for encyclopedic works in theology, Vos wrote, "as people are apt to consider theology under an exclusively practical aspect" (Vos to Warfield, October 22, 1889).
186. In this writer's opinion, this is precisely why Stevenson destroyed his personal papers.
187. Cf. Vos's trenchant remarks on social "reconstruction" following the First World War in "The Eschatology of the Psalter," in *The Pauline Eschatology*, 357–65. This essay was originally published in *PTR* 18 (1920): 1–43.

his impassioned speech on the floor of the 1926 General Assembly indicated[188]). Vos was embroiled in the effects of creeping modernism in the church and in the seminary.

All these were bearing in, bearing down on Old Princeton in Vos's era. J. Ross Stevenson destroyed the tradition and theology for which Vos left Grand Rapids. By 1914, if not before, Vos surely knew that Stevenson was no friend of what he himself believed. The socio-ecclesiastical activism of the liberal practitioners seized the headlines as it seized the relevance-oriented minds of Princeton students (as in the student rebellion of 1909[189]). By 1909, Vos knew that most of the students sitting before him were merely required to be there. Most of them had *not* come to learn and apply what he delivered. For them, English Bible courses (which they demanded) were sufficient. "More practical theology!" was the cry of the student body, the church, and eventually President Stevenson and the Board. Vos was a pariah—a Neanderthal—even in 1909.

So far, all the pieces are consistent with the profile of Vos that we have presented. He was being marginalized as the institution was marginalized. But then, when we expect him to embrace the orthodox alternative—the Machen-led opposition to the Plan of Reorganization, the organization of Westminster Seminary, Machen's new Presbyterian denomination—when we expect him to move with the theological conservatives—he does not.[190] What he had done in 1893, he refused to do in 1929, 1932, and 1936. In fact, he did nothing, save send expressions of sympathy and the remnants of his library. We are

188. See Loetscher, *The Broadening Church*, 141.
189. See Stonehouse, *J. Gresham Machen*, 149–53.
190. His son Bernardus writes, "During the latter part of my father's tenure at Princeton Seminary the lengthy battle for the control of the Seminary was being fought. The President of the Seminary, J. Ross Stevenson, favored allowing the Seminary to fall into the hands of those liberal in their theological outlook and who favored operating the Seminary as an institution catering to all factions of the Presbyterian Church, liberal and otherwise. This policy was vigorously fought against by Drs. Machen, Allis, Robert Dick Wilson, Van Til, and others. With these my father agreed, although he himself took no active part in the controversy. He was also agreeable to the formation of Westminster Seminary when the control of Princeton Seminary by the liberal faction of the Church became an actuality, although again he took no active part in the formation of Westminster Seminary" (letter to Roger Nicole, July 3, 1967).

surprised. Machen, Stonehouse, and Westminster Seminary were surprised. What happened?

The usual excuse Vos receives is old age—he was near retirement in 1929, and his health was poor. Yet so was Robert Dick Wilson, 73, and that did not stop him.[191] So why did Vos hesitate; indeed, why did Vos refuse to "cross over"? What did he perceive or detect that kept him at Princeton and in the PCUSA?

His noncontroversial, nonmilitant personality may be urged as an explanation. Plausible support for this interpretation is found in his letters of 1928 to Sylvester Beach and Frank H. Stevenson on the matter of the reorganization of the seminary. The letters to these two men suggest an ambivalence.[192] His cautious expressions may veil a sense of injustice about the reorganization, but nevertheless he signed the "loyalty" documents *ex animo* with no "mental reservations":[193] "The Directors and my colleagues will, I can assure you, find me most peacefully inclined, forgivingly disposed, and ready to do what I can to render the present action successful."[194] Here is the language that makes J. Gresham Machen expendable—indeed, language that suggests Vos did *not* favor Machen's view of the reorganization.[195] Five months later,

---

191. Wilson (1856–1930) died on October 11, 1930. His demise may have been hastened by the hardship of the first year at Westminster Seminary.

192. The ambivalence is accentuated by the transcript of the discussions of the General Assembly's Special Committee with the faculty of the seminary. In those discussions, Vos indicates his adherence to the system of doctrine in the Westminster standards and suggests that that is the majority of the faculty's stance. In addition, he indicates that the resolution proffered by C. R. Erdman ("We the members of the Faculty of Princeton Seminary do hereby affirm that to the best of our knowledge, no member of this Faculty desires to alter the historic position of the Seminary in its absolute loyalty to the standards of our Church") was "not nearly as explicit as the pledge I subscribed to when I was inducted into my professorship" ("Transcript of the Hearings by the General Assembly's Special Committee to Visit Princeton Theological Seminary," January 5–6, 1927, pp. 251–52). But a year later, Vos appears to have mellowed or altered his position. Keep in mind that Erdman was the man against whom Vos signed a protest in the Presbytery of New Brunswick on April 25, 1925!

193. Ibid. Vos to Sylvester Beach, July 13, 1928. It should be noted that Beach had been the Vos family's pastor from 1906 to 1922. Is there a veiled reference to the style of ministry that Vos was exposed to at First Presbyterian Church, Princeton, in *Grace and Glory*, 237–39? Significantly, Vos never says a word about Sunday worship at Princeton anywhere in his extant remains. Again, the silence may speak volumes.

194. Vos to Beach, July 13, 1928.

195. In this letter of July 13, 1928, Vos returns his signature to a statement required by the Board of Directors under the date of June 20, 1928: "The undersigned members of the Faculty

Vos addressed Rev. Frank H. Stevenson with the assurance that he had agreed to "two of the formulas laid before the Faculty by the Committee of Six."[196] Machen noted that Caspar Wistar Hodge and Robert Dick Wilson were "disgusted."[197] Vos, apparently, was not. What Vos recognized and opposed in 1893—i.e., incompetence (CRC) and creeping liberalism (PCUSA)—he was resigned to tolerate in 1928. Stonehouse rightly detected the "inconsistency."[198] The "pacific," "non-militant," "retiring" Vos no longer had the stomach for controversy.

Vos certainly did not join with those who were railroading Machen. Was this due to his retiring, seceder, pietist upbringing? Or was it due to a realization that the catch-22 prevailed with Machen as much as with Princeton? In a letter to Machen (April 25, 1936), David Craighead indicated that he visited the Vos home in Santa Ana daily.[199] As he conversed with Vos, one of his goals was to "brace him up." Why? Writes Craighead, "I had felt for some time that his faith was growing wobbly." This telltale remark is consistent with the portrait of withdrawal and denial that characterizes Vos after 1932. Craighead even notes, perceptively, that part of Vos's discouragement was due to the absence of his old friends, i.e., B. B. Warfield and Robert Dick Wilson. Yet Vos refused to jump from the frying pan into the fire.

These multiple enigmas are capable of two interpretations: (1) he was a compromiser along with others who remained in the Modernist PCUSA, or (2) he recognized the deleterious and portentous influence of the fundamentalist element in the breakaway group. While his lack of militancy does support the first explanation, this writer is increasingly inclined to the latter. Vos may have perceived the "pox on *both*

---

hereby withdraw and express our regret for all statements which we have (may have) made which have seemed to fellow members of the Faculty to be unjust or unkind or untrue, and we assure the Directors of our purpose and determination to maintain peace and harmony and concord in our personal and official relations in the work of the seminary."

196. Vos to Stevenson, December 19, 1928.
197. Letter from Machen to his mother, May 31, 1928, cited in Stonehouse, *J. Gresham Machen*, 436.
198. Stonehouse to Grosheide, January 12, 1930, cited by Harinck, "Valentijn Hepp," p. 138, n. 62.
199. This letter is among the Machen Papers at Westminster Seminary.

houses," Princeton's drift into modernism *and* the personality-centered tendency of the conservative separatists.

Craighead makes a revealing declaration in his letter: "I have never had very much confidence in some of the men who came out so boldly and strikingly at the first, particularly so in connection with the Princeton upheaval. I am not surprised that they have turned back to their old places and associations." These remarks are a reflection of the daily conversations with Vos. Vos himself "never had much confidence in some of the men." So why would he join those in whom he had no confidence? Better to "passively submit" than to jump ship into even more turmoil.

Machen's letters to Vos are cordial and appreciative. But there is no reflection on distinctively Vosian motifs in Machen's letters, his books, or his articles. While he may have sat through New Testament Biblical Theology with appreciation (see Machen to Vos, April 28, 1936), he appears never to have imbibed Vos's penetrating insights.

Would this explain Vos's ambivalence? Did he commend Machen for defending basic Christian truths, but realize that Machen and his movement were able only to rally to the surface, not plumb the depths of the infinite mind of God in Christ? Machen's character was never in doubt to Vos. Machen was a champion of fundamental orthodoxy, but perhaps naïve to the influence mongers who sought to use him for their own purposes. Vos may have detected this and avoided sweeping clean his own house in realization of seven demons worse than the first entering in.

And yet there is another possible explanation. Vos had been shaped by the revelation of the Lord Jesus Christ in his humiliation and glorification. The trough of the incarnational parabola was making himself of "no reputation" (Phil. 2:7). It was this condescension to servanthood, which impressed Vos—a major motif in his *Grace and Glory* sermons, as even a cursory perusal will detect. The eschatological Ebed Yahweh incarnated the paradigm to humiliation on the cross, leaving behind the inconsistencies and injustices of this present evil world. Accordingly, Geerhardus Vos could not enlist in a crusade to promote himself or even to promote his principles; that would be a denial of his own servanthood. And those who did? He would admire them, even commend them—from afar—but he would not join them. His solitary path could trace out neither the footsteps of liberalism nor the pathway of fundamentalism. His path was the lonely path of an Old Reformed German pietist, born in Friesland, transported to America, summering in splendid isolation in Pennsylvania, dying in obscurity in Michigan.

Jeremiah—Epexegetical of Geerhardus Vos?

The pattern that emerges in Vos's old age is, in fact, consistent with the Vos of each age. The impress of the pietism of his childhood was never erased. Withdrawal from the limelight, as he himself confessed, was a dominant personality trait of the man. And what he eschewed had its antithesis—communion with God in Christ by the Holy Spirit. This too was a dominant motif of the personality of the man. Vos was always content (even in his apparently militant moments) with self-effacing humility (no lime light) and union with Christ. These characteristics are omnipresent in all he wrote. The privacy, the shyness, the reserve, and even the hesitancy were due to the intimacy of meeting his heavenly Father and his precious Son by the effusion of the Holy Spirit in secret, in the closet (Matt. 6:6).

It is possible to find these characteristics embedded in the article "Jeremiah's Plaint and Its Answer."[200] With the exception of the parts of *The Pauline Eschatology* that appeared in the *Review* for 1929,[201] this was the final article that Vos wrote for a theological journal. In essence, "Jeremiah's Plaint" was Geerhardus Vos's swan song. Did he plan it that way? Did he intend to make his final biblical-theological statement in this article? Remember the larger context—this was the year of his two letters regarding the reorganization of Princeton Seminary. The texture of this article is an eerie echo of his sermons. It does not breathe a specifically academic air; rather, it carries the tone of a

---

200. *PTR* 26 (1928): 481–95.

201. "The Pauline Doctrine of the Resurrection," *PTR* 27 (1929): 1–35, became chapter 6 ("The Resurrection") in *The Pauline Eschatology*; "The Structure of the Pauline Eschatology," *PTR* 27 (1929): 403–44, became chapter 1.

last will and testament, even in homiletic strains. It is as if Vos is preaching his farewell, indeed his "eschatological," sermon.

Considering, for a moment, "Jeremiah" as Vos's valedictory, what do we learn from its content? First, the element of anxiety and resolution is reposed in the prophetic corpus—a return to the canonical element that Vos first chose as the vehicle of his biblical-theological focus.[202] If there is a return to the prophets (as there was in the beginning of his career), we are at the antipodes—at the end of his career. Here we are confronted with the symmetry of the bookends of our subject's writing career. But even more pertinently, we are back to the themes of angst and resolve, which dominated Vos's writing from 1886. In 1928, the prophet Jeremiah became the foil for Geerhardus Vos. Vos saw himself in the prophet.

And what did he see? First, a person transported "into the final world-order, when the chaos and ruin, the sin and the sorrow shall have been overpast, nay changed into their opposites" (p. 481). Vos dissolved his own sorrowful world into that of Jeremiah's Jerusalem, and in the same breath laid hold of the prophet's eschatology. We do not learn something new from this Vosian identification (the biblical theologian identifies with the biblical prophet). This identification was present from the outset of the old pietist's career. Vos's final article projects us from this world of sinful sadness to the final eschatological world of no more tears—and that is where his writings always project us.

Second, the prophet Jeremiah exemplifies "a retiring, peace-loving disposition" (p. 482). Surely this is Vos speaking of himself through the personality of the prophet. At this critical date (1928), when Vos has chosen retirement from confrontation—indeed, has chosen peace (see his letters to Beach and Stevenson)—this article is a mirror of the author's soul, even as it is a mirror of the prophet's.

The conflict induced by the surroundings in Vos's outside world clashed with the inner feelings of the world of his own soul. "He sat

---

202. Compare his articles on the eighth-century B.C. prophets published between 1897 and 1899.

alone because of God's hand, filled with indignation" (p. 482). Vos, like Jeremiah, had been left alone—not even Machen could quell the solitary feeling. And indignation? Where was the indignation in Vos's life in 1928? It had been crucified, because "in God he discovered his wayfarer's lodge with its profound peace" (p. 483). Vos took his place within Jeremiah's person so as to resolve the tensions in his own.

After affixing his signature to the 1928 epistles, did Vos find himself "coming out of the waste of the wilderness into a land of paradise" (p. 484)? Was the preciousness ("sweetness and beauty") of Jehovah's pledge—"Yea, I have loved thee with an everlasting love, therefore I have drawn out long lovingkindness unto thee" (Jer. 31:3)—so powerful to the heart of Geerhardus Vos that he melted into contentment and rest, notwithstanding the jarring iniquities and incongruities around him? Was the vision of the parade of returning captives from Babylon to Jerusalem so ethereal and heavenly a hope that it set Vos free from any potential dereliction, alienation, or betrayal?

"Surely this prophet bore within himself a great poet" (p. 484). Here a resilient chord echoed out of the whole mind and heart of Geerhardus Vos. If the sublimation of the disjunction between sin and grace was reduced to the poetry of redemption, forgiveness, and eschatological anticipation, then Vos became exempt from the machinations, the politicizations, the tergiversations of both sides in the reorganization dispute. Poetry rescued Jeremiah; it would rescue Vos too!

But retreat to the poetic idiom left him outside the camp of Old Princeton. In fact, it isolated him from his colleagues on the faculty, not to mention the student body. The poet would be reduced to himself alone. The individual prophet-poet (Jeremiah) was the model of the individual professor-poet: "The normal goal of the entire religious movement must lie in the individual" (p. 486). Yet not the individual in solitary exclusion; rather the individual in face-to-face communion with God; "If the features of the face of God remained strange to us and we had no experience of the divine embrace and benedictions, it would profit us nothing" (p. 486). Geerhardus Vos, the individual, sought the embrace and benediction of the face of God, even as his counterpart, Jeremiah, did. And in that embrace, he was no longer an individual—no longer alone—in that embrace, he was possessed by the perfect fullness of him who is all in all.

The dissonance, the disjunction of the prophet's world drove him to the one refuge of solace: "The prophet rises out of the perplexing maze and the thick atmosphere of his field of labor towards the serenity of the presence of God" (p. 488). Serenity! That was what drew Vos like a magnet to "the possession of the heart of God" (p. 487). And the heart of God was the object of Vos's prayers. The thin line between Jeremiah's complaints and Jeremiah's supplications was drawn down into the experience of the Princetonian. Where did this "disconnect" lead the weary professor? To "relief and unburdening of the soul . . . [in] repeated prayer-episodes" (p. 488).

But these prayer encounters in which the soul of the suppliant—even plaintive suppliant—was drawn to the heart of God, could not leave aside the history of redemption. No indeed! If Jeremiah pulled back the veil of the eschatological hope so as to catch a glimmer of the throne room of the almighty, triune God, then his darkening eye beheld the Son of the Father in all his preincarnate glory. And if Vos entered that same chamber of eschatological fruition, he could do so only by focusing on great Jeremiah's greater Lord and Savior. The eschatological Jeremiah—the once-and-for-all weeper over the city of God—he was the object of Vos's vision, his heart, his blessed possession. Only Jesus Christ, as the fullness of Jeremiah's gaze, and Vos's faith could perfect and complete the resolution of Jeremiah's—of Vos's—complaints. The prophet-poet *must* drive us to Christ, or there is only complaint and chaos and brutality.

And at the intersection of these vectors—at the pinpoint of the intrusion of the eschatological arena into the existential arena—at that point there was redemption. The salvation of the prophet from his despairing, plaintive protests was swallowed up in the long lovingkindness of the Lord. How much more sweetly was this so for Vos in view of the life, death, and resurrection of his Lord (of Jeremiah's Lord) Jesus Christ. "There is no joy like the joy engendered by redemption"

(p. 491). Navel-gazing was useless to Jeremiah; introspection, with its morbid by-product of perennial failure and insufficiency, was useless to Jeremiah. Only the upward and outward gaze of the faith fixing upon the glory-object, the Christ of glory, the glory-Godhead—only such a gaze could resolve the turmoil of the weeping prophet's heart. And the weeping professor? He too found his supreme, eschatological rest in the glory-Christ.

There, in the Christ of glory, was the embodiment, the incarnation, of the love of God. Was he not the love-gift of God the Father by the indwelling of God the Holy Spirit? And was that not the craving, nay the hungering and thirsting, of the soul of both Jeremiah and Vos? Was not love itself between person and person the most sublime of the spiritual graces? To be loved by God, and to love God—such reciprocity was more sublime than the love of a man for a woman or a woman for a man. "Love is . . . the highest form of the spiritual embrace of person by person" (p. 492). Vos sought "the heart-to-heart union between the pious and Himself" (p. 493). And that sweet, ecstatic, sublime union was enough. In the face of deceit, betrayal, injustice, and sin, to be grasped by the Lord God in love and to grasp the Lord God reciprocally in love—that was "the one supremely desirable reality" (p. 463). Apart from this, "it were folly to seek aught in heaven or on earth" (p. 463). Christ! Christ! Christ! That was Vos's heart-object, heart-love, heart-joy, and heart-peace.

And Princeton in 1928? "Each one carries for himself through life the consciousness of what cannot be undone" (p. 494). Jerusalem in 586 B.C. could not be "undone"; Jerusalem in A.D. 30/33 could not be "undone." The reorganization of 1928 could not be undone. But Vos left his statement—his statement of the resolution of this bitter antithesis. It was his valedictory—as damning and shaming of those on both sides who positioned themselves outside the eschatological Jeremiah and his victory over complaints and cries and groans and tears and sighs.

"The best proof that He will never cease to love us lies in that He never began. What we are for Him and what He is for us belongs to the realm of eternal values. Without this we are nothing, in it we have all. Ours is the paean of Paul: 'For we know that to them that love God all things work together for good . . . for those whom he foreknew [that is, eternally loved] he also predestinated to be made like unto the image of his Son . . . for I am persuaded, that neither death nor life, nor angels nor principalities, nor things present nor things to come, nor powers, nor height nor depth, nor any other creature, shall be able to separate us from the love of God which is in Christ Jesus our Lord' (Rom. 8:28, 38, 39)" (p. 495).

And so Geerhardus Vos was content. In his quiet, solitary, isolated world, Geerhardus Vos was content with the face-to-face, person-to-person, inestimable riches of Christ Jesus, his Savior and his Lord.

Vos's valedictory contribution to the *Princeton Theological Review* was his commentary on thirty-five years at Princeton. It was especially epexegetical of the most recent three. His valedictory contribution would remain his final biblical-theological reflection. Beyond it, only poetry (?prophetic-poetry) would express the songs of his soul.

Déjà Vu?

But there was also something more. As Vos could never combine Christlikeness in humility and servanthood with militancy in activism (because it would not integrate into his persona), so Vos was alert to cant, hypocrisy, and the pretence of orthodoxy that lacked the power thereof. If Machen never grasped Vos,[203] and Vos reciprocated by not joining Machen's exodus, is it because Vos detected something in the "Reformed" fundamentalists that reminded him of L. J. Hulst, the middle-of-the-road evangelical advocates of confessional revision, the rebellious conservative reductionists (i.e., classes in English Bible), or the graspers for power and control (e.g., J. Ross Stevenson)? Was Vos's distance from Machen's struggle, Westminster Seminary, and the formation of the OPC an acknowledgment of the horns of a dilemma? Did he see already in 1928 what Machen would experience in November 1936? Would the betrayal by Carl McIntire and the rejection of Machen by the Independent Board for

---

203. See Ned Stonehouse to Louis Berkhof, December 17, 1954.

Introduction

Foreign Missions in November 1936[204] represent the unveiling to Machen of the vicious nature of tyrannical conservatism? Had Vos detected this in those who surrounded Machen, and did he know—as Machen learned, at last—that these people were not interested in orthodoxy, but rather were singularly bent on gaining power? They would increase even at the expense of "Valiant-for-Truth" Machen. In other words, Vos realized that Machen was a mere pawn in a larger game. And as soon as the arbiters of that game had sufficient leverage and money, Machen would be expendable—even as Old Princeton had become expendable for the forces seizing her prestige, her tradition, and her endowments. Vos knew that depravity does not bypass evangelical and Reformed hearts. Liberals alone have no corner on contrivance, deceit, brutal abuse of power, injustice, and subjugation of human beings. Vos had suffered from it in Grand Rapids. He had seen it seep into the fabric of Princeton Seminary from so-called broadly evangelical sources. Westminster Seminary could be no more than a temporary respite in the inevitable march of the "evil star" of progressivism, liberalism, and antisupernaturalism. Machen was surrounded by erstwhile conservatives whose dispositions were millennial—tyrannical (Carl McIntire, H. McAllister Griffiths).[205] Vos knew—did he detect it from the character of the men in his classrooms?—that the spirit of these men was triumphalist. And as he had drifted from

---

204. Machen was unseated and replaced as president in a bitter feud with McIntire and his lackeys, especially H. McAllister Griffiths. See George M. Marsden, "Perspective on the Division of 1937," in *Pressing toward the Mark: Essays Commemorating Fifty Years of the Orthodox Presbyterian Church*, ed. Charles G. Dennison and Richard C. Gamble (Philadelphia: Committee for the Historian of the Orthodox Presbyterian Church, 1986), 308–11; Dennison, *History for a Pilgrim People*, 103–8, especially p. 106; *Presbyterian Guardian* 3 (November 28, 1936): 91. Mark Noll comments, "[Machen's] ideal of Presbyterian confessionalism was also rejected by most of the fundamentalist allies who joined him in battling theological modernism" (*The Old Religion in a New World: The History of North American Christianity* [Grand Rapids: William B. Eerdmans Publishing Co., 2002], 25). Noll astutely observes that modernists and fundamentalists alike were opposed to confessional traditions. In essence, they were cultural accommodationists: for the left, social ethicists and activists; for the right, "Redeemer nation" appliers of American civil religion. Both agreed that the supreme biblical canon was its morality; only the specific application differed. Machen never saw it coming. November 1936 and his lamentable letters to his family afterwards are the proof.

205. The Machen family (brother, Arthur; sister-in-law, Helen; niece, Mary Gresham; Laura Woods, Helen's mother) filed affidavits in Baltimore, Maryland, on October 5 and 6, 1937, attesting that "the action of the Independent Board was the cause of his death" (Laura Hall Woods). See copies of the originals among the Machen Papers.

Kuyper's neo-Calvinist triumphalism, so he stood off from fundamentalist triumphalism. Vos was averse to the power brokers of both the left and the right.

Legacy

The legacy of Geerhardus Vos consists in what he wrote and preached. Few of his students[206] applied what he taught them to the pulpit, the pastoral ministry,[207] or the academy. The evidence of this is found in the vacuum in developing Vos's insights from 1932 until the 1960s. And even then, only one voice in Holland (Herman Ridderbos) and one in America (Richard B. Gaffin Jr.) drew more deeply from the well that Vos left.[208] But even here, the translation from book to pulpit, pastorate, pew, or denominational office was not followed. Academically, Vos has been a great footnote; practically, Vos has been left out of the pastorate, the pulpit, the life of the church, and the "application" of Scripture to life.[209] The irony, of course, is that those

---

206. More than four thousand students may have passed before him in his thirty-nine-year career. See the estimate in the retirement notice printed in *De Heraut*, August 21, 1932, p. 1.

207. John DeWaard may have been an exception: "I loved him when I studied there [Princeton Theological Seminary, 1922–25], I love him more now. . . . As we listened to the lectures we forgot about the man speaking, while our minds were fixed on the wonders of the Word. . . . Perhaps there is no one in our fellowship who can do what Dr. Vos succeeded so well in doing. But we can attempt to do the same thing in a small way" ("Higher Ground," *Presbyterian Guardian* 3 [December 12, 1936]: 97).

208. Marianne Radius tells of Herman Ridderbos's tour of the United States in 1975. When he visited Grand Rapids and was feted at a dinner on the campus of Calvin College and Seminary, he eagerly anticipated greeting Vos's daughter. She reported that he seized her hand warmly when introduced and confessed a great dependence upon her father in his own thinking. Virtually all that Richard Gaffin has written manifests the influence of Vos.

209. Jay Adams insists on this. "Preaching that wrongly uses the insights of biblical theology, bringing into the pulpit what belongs in the study . . . will grow old fast. . . . Biblical-theological study, then, like systematic-theological study, is primarily for the sake of the preacher" ("Proper Use of Biblical Theology in Preaching," *Journal of Pastoral Practice* 9/1 (1987): 49). Adams even writes that Vos's sermons have "no application in them" (*Truth Applied: Application in Preaching* [Grand Rapids: Ministry Resources Library, 1990], 20). Vos would have regarded Adams as myopic and fundamentalistic: "The gathering of exegetical data should be followed by the grouping of these under well-defined historical conceptions, not indeed to be indiscriminately derived from the sphere of Dogmatic Theology, but from the range of thought of the Biblical writers themselves. These various conceptions should be made to supplement, to interpret and to illumine one another, in order that thus we may reproduce within our own minds the perspective in which the writers saw the truth. If this be neglected we lose ourselves in exegetical details, the various lines

vociferously demanding the most in "applicatory" preaching and pastoral theology can be in fact the most belligerent and uncharitable.

Did Vos realize this tendency, even in his own day, in his own circles? Did the political pressure in Grand Rapids drive him to Princeton in an escape to quiet, even appreciated scholarship? But did he eventually realize, after the rise of the evangelical chameleons at Princeton (J. Ross Stevenson, C. R. Erdman, J. Ritchie Smith, Frederick W. Loetscher), that Christ-centered scholarship was merely a shibboleth? The real issue was money and control of the institution, in concert with the prevailing and controlling mood of the denomination. And did he come to understand that even the fundamentalist and allegedly "Old School" realignment of J. Gresham Machen and Westminster Theological Seminary was, in part, a posturing for ecclesiastical political power?[210]

And did Vos in retirement cease to write theologically, exegetically, and biblical-theologically because he was fed up—fed up with the deceit of his former students, who had chosen self-promotion and a "mess of pottage" for the riches of the glory-seated Jesus Christ?[211]

---

of thought remain unconnected, we obtain a catalogue of what was in the author's mind instead of seeing a living vision through his eyes, and, however rich the information imparted, the final effect produced must needs be confusing" (*PRR* 7 [1896]: 719–20). In an unsigned review, a reviewer says that Vos's sermons "are not superficial.... They dig deep into the Word, and leave one weightily conscious of the greatness of the grace and glory of the Gospel.... Not difficult of reading, yet these sermons give to the reader that delightful sense of the mastery gained in the effort of thinking through and appreciating the fullness of new light from the Word" (review of *Grace and Glory*, *Sunday School Times* 65 [February 24, 1923]: 116).

210. Did Machen himself finally realize this after the betrayal of Allen MacRae, Carl McIntire, H. McAllister Griffiths, Mark Matthews, and even Clarence E. Macartney? When he lay dying under a crucifix in a Roman Catholic North Dakota hospital, was Machen forced to focus on the heart of the Pauline soteriology as well as the center of the Pauline eschatology, i.e., on a person who identified with *him* in death and resurrection?

211. Is the following remark from a 1902 sermon prescient? "Now I do not mean to affirm that in all cases there need be the preaching of false doctrine which involves an open and direct denial of the evangelical truth. It is quite possible that both to the intention and the actual performance of the preacher any departure from the historical faith of the church may be entirely foreign. And yet there may be such a failure in the intelligent presentation of the gospel with the proper emphasis upon that which is primary and fundamental as to bring about a result almost equally deplorable as where the principles of the gospel are openly contradicted or denied. There can be a betrayal of the gospel of grace by silence. There can be disloyalty to Christ by omission as well as by positive offence against the message that he has entrusted to our keeping. It is possible, Sabbath after Sabbath and year after year, to preach things of which none can say that they are untrue and none can deny that in their proper place and time they may be important, and yet to forego telling people plainly and to forego giving them the dis-

The tone of disappointment and frustration in his letters after 1932 is more than the advance of enfeeblement from the frailty of old age. The world he had inhabited from 1881 to 1932 had been attenuated and acculturated by a "gospel" that Christ and Paul and the New Testament world would not comprehend—the gospel of the self-consciousness of modern man: man, only man, nothing but man! Posturing, preening, manipulating, dominating, moneymaking, power brokering: these are the mantras that drive the influence peddlers of contemporary Protestant orthodoxy. Such worldliness was incomprehensible to Vos; hence, he has remained incomprehensible to them. And perhaps Geerhardus Vos came to realize that what was stamped on the hearts, souls, and behavior of these gurus was but another variety of that age-old depravity—tyranny. Conservative Christianity is provincial—pedantic, morose, dull—even soporific; it is Christian conservatism with very little brain, let alone heart. And perhaps that is why the brighter adolescents of that tradition grow up to become liberals. Liberalism is, at least, engaging.

Did Vos recognize this? Is that why he reviewed so little "conservative" literature, interacted with so little "evangelical" scholarship? Is that why he penetrated Schweitzer, Bousset, Gunkel, Gressmann, and other avant garde critical liberals? Did Vos perceive the political hypocrisy of the allegedly orthodox Calvinists of his generation and react[212]—react by withdrawing from them, isolating himself against them, retreating to a refuge where they could not affect him?

If Vos did not engage much theological conservatism, he certainly took on the liberal fundamentalists. Fundamentalism is a mind-set; it is found on the theological right and on the theological left. Right-wing fundamentalism is biblicist; it is enamored of American civil religion, in which the Bible and conservative American politics are

---

tinct impression that they need forgiveness and salvation from sin through the cross of Christ" (*Grace and Glory*, 237–38).

212. His remark to Bavinck was revealing and prophetic: "If the revision movement goes on as it began, then the symbols of Westminster will be changed in an Arminian tone and I fear the right wing will put up with it" (letter, February 1, 1890). No less than H. G. Wells once quipped that "the Americans' 'right-wing' and 'left-wing' are just different species of liberalism," as cited in Mark Noll, *The Old Religion in a New World* (Grand Rapids: Eerdmans, 2002), 24.

melded. Left-wing fundamentalism is narcissistic—it sees its own reflection everywhere, especially in the Bible, and continually criticizes the Scriptures according to its own prevailing cultural and philosophical presuppositions. Critical-liberal fundamentalism is also politically enamored—it loathes America and the Western political ethos. Vos did not live to see the full-fledged blossoming of the left-wing political aspect of liberal fundamentalism (although he was aware of the Social Gospel movement of his era), but he was aware of critical-liberal theological fundamentalism, especially the insidious reductionism of liberal criticism applied to the Bible.[213] Virtually everything Vos wrote was a response to the erosion of supernatural, God-given orthodoxy (as revealed in the Scriptures and articulated in the Reformed confessional tradition) by liberal criticism. Examine the written corpus and one discovers that Vos was alive with penetrating (indeed eschatological) analysis and orthodox critique of contemporary liberalism. Read between the lines and Vos is just as deadly against a broad conservatism that was itself liberalism in sheep's clothing.

From Mimesis to *Visio Dei*

Geerhardus Vos, was a sojourner and a pilgrim living between two worlds.[214] He came from the Old World; he flourished in the New World. But this tension, this life between the old and the new, was a mimesis[215] (an imitation), a mirror of his sojourn between the present evil age and the age to come—his pilgrimage between the now and the not yet. Did he find himself mirrored in Abraham, that Hebrew sojourner, who went out looking for a better country, an eschatological city? Did Geerhardus Vos see himself reflected in Israel

---

213. Cf. James T. Dennison Jr., "What Is the 'Critical' Reading of the Bible?" *Kerux: The Journal of Northwest Theological Seminary* 17/1 (May 2002): 3–24.
214. Cf. James T. Dennison Jr., "Geerhardus Vos: Life between Two Worlds," *Kerux: A Journal of Biblical-Theological Preaching* 14/2 (September 1999): 18–31 (available online at kerux.com).
215. Cf. Erich Auerbach, *Mimesis: The Representation of Reality in Western Literature* (Princeton: Princeton University Press, 1968).

in the wilderness—pilgrims sojourning between the old and the new? Or did he see himself in the Eschatological Pilgrim—Jesus Christ— sojourning upon the earth between heaven and heaven? Yes, Jesus Christ, the Eschatological Pilgrim, the seed of Abraham, recapitulator of Israel's history: out of Egypt, through the waters, into the wilderness, to the mountain, over Jordan, to death and resurrection. Geerhardus Vos's pilgrim identity was reinforced by his God-gifted existential experience. He became a pilgrim in this world; he mirrored the sojourn of the pilgrims of the world to come. He belonged to the last Pilgrim—that Pioneer and Perfector. Geerhardus Vos belonged to the Lord Jesus Christ—his life was hidden with Christ in God.

In closing, I reprise the final journey. The body of Geerhardus Vos was transported from Grand Rapids, Michigan, to Roaring Branch, Pennsylvania, between Monday, August 15, 1949, and Wednesday, August 17, 1949. And there in that mountain cemetery just below the house he loved so well, the body of the great biblical theologian was laid to rest beside that of his wife Catherine. A small, plain stone marker tells the tale. Dr. Cornelius Van Til officiated at the interment of the mortal remains of his beloved friend and teacher. Van Til was there— not Princeton. Van Til was there—not Grand Rapids. But in the end it did not matter. Geerhardus Vos, pilgrim, had finished his journey and reached the one world of heaven, his sweet Lord Jesus, the love of God the Father, the communion of the Holy Spirit, the fellowship of the saints in glory. Geerhardus Vos had come home at last, never to sojourn any more.

THE WRITINGS OF GEERHARDUS VOS
A BIBLIOGRAPHY

Key to Abbreviations[1]

Bib. Rev. = *Biblical Review*
Bib. St. = *Bible Student*
DAC = *Dictionary of the Apostolic Church*, edited by James Hastings
ISBE = *International Standard Bible Encyclopedia*, edited by James Orr
PR = *Presbyterian Review*
PRR = *Presbyterian and Reformed Review*
PTR = *Princeton Theological Review*
RHBI = *Redemptive History and Biblical Interpretation: The Shorter Writings of Geerhardus Vos*, edited by Richard B. Gaffin Jr.

1886

The Mosaic Origin of the Pentateuchal Codes. With an introduction by William Henry Green. New York: A. C. Armstrong & Son; London: Hodder and Stoughton.

1888

Die Kämpfe und Streitigkeiten zwischen den Banū 'Umajja und den Banū Hāšim. Von Takijj ad-dīn Al-Makrīzjji. Herausgegeben und zur Erlangung der Doctorwürde bei der Philosophischen Facultät der Kaiser-Wilhelm-Universität zu Strassburg im Elsass, eingereicht von Geerhardus Vos. Leiden: E. J. Brill.

---

1. This bibliography originally appeared in the *Westminster Theological Journal* 38 (Spring 1976): 350–67. It was reprinted with slight revision in *RHBI*, 547–59. This version is further expanded and revised. Cf. Peter de Klerk, ed., *A Bibliography of the Writings of the Professors of Calvin Theological Seminary* (Grand Rapids: Calvin Theological Seminary, 1980), 40.0–40.18.

"The Prospects of American Theology." Translated by Ed M. van der Maas. *Kerux: The Journal of Northwest Theological Seminary* 20/1 (May 2005): 14–52.

1889

Review of *Die Psalmen und die Sprüche Salomos*, by F. W. Schultz and Hermann Strack, in Kurzgefasster Kommentar zu den Heiligen Schriften, Alten und Neuen Testaments, sowie zu den Apocryphen, edited by Hermann Strack and Otto Zöckler. *PR* 10:301–3.

1890

"Gereformeerde dogmatiek." 5 vols. Grand Rapids.
"Onlangslazen wij in . . ." *De Wachter*, April 30, p. 2.
"Das 22sten en . . ." *De Wachter*, May 7, p. 2.
"Rev. Riemersma verklart . . ." *De Wachter*, May 28, p. 2.
Review of *Leesboek over de Gereformeerde geloofsleer*, by H. E. Gravemeijer. *PRR* 1:146–49.

1891

De verbondsleer in de Gereformeerde theologie. Grand Rapids: "Democrat" Drukpers. (Also an edition by J. B. Hulst, 1891. Reprint, Rotterdam: Mazijk's Uitgeversbureau, 1939. Translation by S. Voorwinde and W. Van Gemeren: *The Covenant in Reformed Theology*. Philadelphia: published privately by K. M. Campbell, 1971. New revised translation by Richard B. Gaffin Jr.: "The Doctrine of the Covenant in Reformed Theology." In *RBHI*, 234–67.)
"Nog geen twee . . ." *De Wachter*, February 18, p. 1.
Translation of "Calvinism and Confessional Revision," by Abraham Kuyper. *PRR* 2:369–99.
Review of *Historisch-critisch onderzoek naar het ontstaan en de verzameling van de boeken des Ouden Verbonds: De profetische boeken des Ouden Verbonds*, by A. Kuenen. *PRR* 2:139–40.

1892

Translation of "Recent Dogmatic Thought in the Netherlands," by Herman Bavinck. *PRR* 3:209–28.

1893

Review of *Prolegomena van bijbelsche godgeleerdheid*, by E. H. van Leeuwen. *PRR* 4:143–45.

Review of *De verflauwing der grenzen*, by Abraham Kuyper. *PRR* 4:330–32. (Dutch version in *De Wachter*, January 11, p. 1; January 18, p. 1.)

1894

The Idea of Biblical Theology as a Science and as a Theological Discipline. New York: Anson D. F. Randolph & Co. (Reprint, *RHBI*, 3–24. Dutch version: "De bijbelsche theologie beschouwd als wetenschap en theologisch studievak." *De Wachter* 27: October 10, p. 2; October 17, pp. 2–3; October 24, pp. 2–3; October 31, p. 2; November 7, pp. 2–3; November 14, p. 2; November 21, p. 2.)

Notes from . . . Lectures on Biblical Theology, for Students' Use Only. Trenton, NJ: Naar, Day & Naar, Printers.

Translation of "The Future of Calvinism," by Herman Bavinck. *PRR* 5:1–24.

Review of *Old Testament Theology*, by Herman Schultz. *PRR* 5:132–33.

Review of *The Doctrine of the Prophets*, by A. F. Kirkpatrick. *PRR* 5:138–39.

Review of *Die Predigt Jesu vom Reiche Gottes*, by Johannes Weiss; *Jesu Predigt in ihrem Gegensatz zum Judenthum*, by W. Bousset; *Jesu Verkündigung und Lehre vom Reiche Gottes in ihrer geschichtlichen Bedeutung dargestellt*, by Georg Schnedermann. *PRR* 5:144–47.

Review of *Alexander Comrie*, by A. G. Honig. *PRR* 5:331–34.

Review of *De letterkunde des Ouden Verbonds naar de tijdsorde van haar ontstaan*, by G. Wildeboer. *PRR* 5:696–99.
Review of *Gisbertus Voetius*, by A. C. Duker. *PRR* 5:714–15.

1895

"Systematische theologie, compendium." Grand Rapids. (Other copies dated 1896, 1909, 1916.)
"Syllabus of Lectures on Biblical Theology." Princeton.
Review of *Theology of the Old Testament*, by Ch. Piepenbring. *PRR* 6:149–52.
Review of *New Testament Theology*, by Willibald Beyschlag. *PRR* 6:756–61.
Review of *St. Paul's Conception of Christianity*, by Alexander B. Bruce. *PRR* 6:761–66.

1896

"Dogmatiek, theologie, deel I." Grand Rapids.
"Dogmatiek, anthropologie, deel II." Grand Rapids.
"Dogmatiek, Christologie, deel III." Grand Rapids.
"Dogmatiek, soteriologie, deel IV," bound with "Dogmatiek, ecclesiologie, media gratiae, eschatologie, deel V." Grand Rapids. (Another version in 3 vols., Grand Rapids, 1910.)
Review of *Gereformeerde dogmatiek*, vol. 1, by Herman Bavinck. *PRR* 7:356–63. (Reprint, *RHBI*, 475–84. Dutch version in *De Wachter*, September 2, p. 2; September 9, p. 2; September 16, p. 2.)
Review of *The Messiah of the Gospels* and *The Messiah of the Apostles*, by Charles Augustus Briggs. *PRR* 7:718–24. (Dutch version in *De Wachter*, November 25, pp. 2–3; December 2, p. 2.)

1897

"Some Doctrinal Features of the Early Prophecies of Isaiah." *PRR* 8:444–63. (Reprint, *RHBI*, 271–87. Dutch translation by J. Keizer: "Het dogmatisch karakter van Jesaja's eerste profetie-en." *Gereformeerde Amerikaan* 1 [1897]: 254–61, 287–96, 334–38.)

Review of *De Mozaische oorsprong van de wetten in de boeken Exodus, Leviticus en Numeri*, by Ph. J. Hoedemaker. *PRR* 8:106–9.

1898

"The Modern Hypothesis and Recent Criticism of the Early Prophets." *PRR* 9:214–38 (on Amos and Hosea), 411–37 (on Isaiah), 610–36 (on Isaiah).

1899

"The Modern Hypothesis and Recent Criticism of the Early Prophets." *PRR* 10:70–97 (on Isaiah), 285–317 (on Micah).
"Fool." In *A Dictionary of the Bible*, edited by James Hastings. New York: Charles Scribner's Sons. 2:43–44.
Review of *Gereformeerde dogmatiek*, vol. 2, by Herman Bavinck. *PRR* 10:694–700. (Reprint, *RHBI*, 485–93.)

1900

"The Biblical Importance of the Doctrine of Preterition." *The Presbyterian* 70 (September 5): 9–10. (Reprint, *RHBI*, 412–14; reprint, *Outlook* 28 [January 1978]: 10–12.)
"The Ministry of John the Baptist." *Bib. St.* 1:26–32. (Reprint, *RHBI*, 299–303.)
"The Kingdom of God." *Bib. St.* 1:282–89, 328–35. (Reprint, *RHBI*, 304–16. Dutch translation by J. Keizer: "Het koninkrijk Gods." *Gereformeerde Amerikaan* 4 [1900]: 337–44, 392–98.)
Review of *Die Erwählung Israels nach der Heilsverkündigung des Apostels Paulus*, by Johannes Dalmer. *PRR* 11:168–71. (Reprint, *RHBI*, 494–98.)
Review of *Das Reich Gottes nach den synoptischen Evangelien*, by W. Lütgert. *PRR* 11:171–74.
Review of *Die Bedeutung des lebendigen Christus für die Rechtfertigung nach Paulus*, by E. Schäder. *PRR* 11:355–58. (Reprint, *RHBI*, 499–502.)
Review of *Gottes Volk und sein Gesetz*, by R. F. Grau. *PRR* 11:529–31.

Review of *The Theology of the New Testament*, by George B. Stevens. *PRR* 11:701–6. (Reprint, *RHBI*, 503–8.)

1901

"Our Lord's Doctrine of the Resurrection." *Bib. St.* 3:189–97. (Reprint, *RHBI*, 317–23.)

"The Pauline Conception of Reconciliation." *Bib. St.* 4:40–45. (Reprint, *RHBI*, 361–65.)

Review of *Die Jesajaerzählungen Jesaja 36–39*, by J. Meinhold. *PRR* 12:479–80.

Review of *Entwicklungsgeschichte des Reiches Gottes*, by H. J. Bestmann. *PRR* 12:480–81.

Review of *Grieksch-theologisch woordenboek, hoofdzakelijk van de oud-Christelijke letterkunde*, by J. M. S. Baljon. *American Journal of Theology* 5:564–67.

1902

"The Nature and Aims of Biblical Theology." *Union Seminary Magazine* 13/1 (February-March): 194–99. (Reprint, *Kerux: A Journal of Biblical-Theological Preaching* 14/1 [May 1999]: 3–8.)

"The Pauline Conception of Redemption." *Bib. St.* 5:51–58. (Reprint, *RHBI*, 366–71.)

"The Sacrificial Idea in Paul's Doctrine of the Atonement." *Bib. St.* 6:97–103, 151–58. (Reprint, *RHBI*, 372–82.)

"The Scriptural Doctrine of the Love of God." *PRR* 13:1–37. (Reprint, *RHBI*, 425–57.)

Review of *The Relation of the Apostolic Teaching to the Teaching of Christ*, by Robert J. Drummond. *PRR* 13:473–78.

1903

The Teaching of Jesus Concerning the Kingdom of God and the Church. New York: American Tract Society. (Reprint, Grand Rapids: Wm. B. Eerdmans Publishing Co., 1951 and 1958;

reprinted with a Scripture Index, Nutley, NJ: Presbyterian and Reformed Publishing Co., 1972.)
"The Theology of Paul." *Bib. St.* 7:332–40. (Reprint, *RHBI*, 355–60.)
"The Alleged Legalism in Paul's Doctrine of Justification." *PTR* 1:161–79. (Reprint, *RHBI*, 383–99.)
Review of *Der alttestamentliche Unterbau des Reiches Gottes*, by Julius Boehmer. *PTR* 1:126–31.
Review of *Die Reichsgotteshoffnung in den ältesten christlichen Dokumenten und bei Jesus*, by Paul Wernle. *PTR* 1:298–303.
Review of *Joseph and Moses*, by Buchanan Blake. *PTR* 1:470–72.
Review of *Die Gedankeneinheit des ersten Briefes Petri*, by Julius Kögel. *PTR* 1:472–76.
Review of *The Theology of Christ's Teaching*, by John M. King. *PTR* 1:653–54.
Review of *Theologischer Jahresbericht, 1901. PTR* 1:655.

1904

Review of *Die Religion des Judentums im neutestamentlichen Zeitalter*, by Wilhelm Bousset. *PTR* 2:159–66.
Review of *The Teaching of Jesus concerning the Kingdom of God and the Church*, by Geerhardus Vos. *PTR* 2:335–36.
Review of *Geschichte der jüdischen Apologetik als Vorgeschichte des Christenthums*, by M. Friedländer. *PTR* 2:528–31.

1905

Reviews of *Die Entstehung der paulinischen Christologie*, by Martin Brückner. *PTR* 3:144–47.
Review of *Die Begriffe Geist und Leben bei Paulus in ihren Beziehungen zu einander*, by Emil Sokolowski. *PTR* 3:317–21.
Review of *Die Offenbarung des Johannes*, by Johannes Weiss. *PTR* 3:321–25.
Review of *Biblische Zeitschrift in Verbindung mit der Redaktion der Biblischen Studien*, by Joh. Göttsberger and Jos. Eickenberger. *PTR* 3:482.

Review of *St. Paul's Conception of the Last Things*, by H. A. A. Kennedy. *PTR* 3:483–87.
Review of *Der Sohn und die Söhne*, by Julius Kögel. *PTR* 3:487–89.
Review of *The Spirit of God in Biblical Literature*, by Irving F. Wood. *PTR* 3:680–85.

1906

"Christian Faith and the Truthfulness of Bible History." *PTR* 4:289–305. (Reprint, *RHBI*, 458–71.)
"Covenant." In *A Dictionary of Christ and the Gospels*, edited by James Hastings, 1:373–80. New York: Charles Scribner's Sons.
"Salvation." In *A Dictionary of Christ and the Gospels*, edited by James Hastings, 2:552–57. New York: Charles Scribner's Sons.
"Saviour." In *A Dictionary of Christ and the Gospels*, edited by James Hastings, 2:571–73. New York: Charles Scribner's Sons.
Review of *The Theology of the Old Testament*, by A. B. Davidson. *PTR* 4:115–20.
Review of *The Eschatology of Jesus; or, The Kingdom Come and Coming*, by Lewis A. Muirhead. *PTR* 4:124–27.
Review of *The Messianic Hope in the New Testament*, by Shailer Mathews. *PTR* 4:260–65.
Review of *Der Sabbat im Alten Testament und im altjüdischen religiösen Aberglauben*, by Friedrich Bohn. *PTR* 4:406.
Review of *Christianity in Talmud and Midrash*, by R. Travers Herford. *PTR* 4:412–14.
Review of *Biblische Zeitschrift*, edited by Joh. Göttsberger and Jos. Sickenberger. *PTR* 4:414–15.

1907

"The Priesthood of Christ in the Epistle to the Hebrews." *PTR* 5:423–47, 579–604. (Reprint, *RHBI*, 126–60.)
Review of *Beiträge zur Förderung christlicher Theologie*, edited by A. Schlatter and W. Lütgert. *PTR* 5:115–19.

Review of *The Testimony of St. Paul to Christ Viewed in Some of Its Aspects*, by R. J. Knowling. *PTR* 5:324–28.
Review of *The Prophet of Nazareth*, by Nathaniel Schmidt. *PTR* 5:490–96.
Review of *Jesus und Paulus*, by Julius Kaftan. *PTR* 5:496–502.
Review of *Biblische Zeitschrift*, 1906. *PTR* 5:668.
Review of *Verzeichnis der von Adolf Hilgenfeld verfassten Schriften*. ... *PTR* 5:675–76.

1908

Review of *The Apostolic Age in the Light of Modern Criticism*, by James H. Ropes. *PTR* 6:310–14.
Review of *The Fourth Gospel: Its Purpose and Theology*, by Ernest J. [sic] Scott. *PTR* 6:314–20.
Review of *A Dictionary of Christ and the Gospels*, edited by James Hastings. *PTR* 6:655–62.

1909

Translation of "Calvin and Common Grace," by Herman Bavinck. In *Calvin and the Reformation*, edited by William P. Armstrong, 99–130. New York: Fleming H. Revell Co. (Also *PTR* 7 [1909]: 437–65.)
Review of *The Religion of the Post-Exilic Prophets*, by W. H. Bennett. *PTR* 7:123–26.
Review of *Der Zweifel and der Messianität Jesu*, by A. Schlatter. *PTR* 7:343–48.
Review of *Jesus und die Heidenmission*, by Max Meinertz. *PTR* 7:493–97.
Review of *The Religion and Worship of the Synagogue*, by W. O. E. Oesterley and G. H. Box. *PTR* 7:498–500.
Review of *Die religiösen und sittlichen Anschauungen der alttestamentlichen Apokryphon und Pseudepigraphen*, by Ludwig Couard. *PTR* 7:667–69.

1910

Review of *The Religion of the Old Testament*, by Karl Marti. *PTR* 8:295–96.

Review of *Echtheit, Hauptbegriff und Gedankengang der messianischen Weissagung Is. 9, 1–6*, by Wilhelm Caspari, and *Gottes Angesicht*, by J. Boehmer. *PTR* 8:296–98.

Review of *Jesus and the Gospel*, by James Denney. *PTR* 8:301–9. (Reprint, *RHBI*, 509–16.)

Review of *Spirit in the New Testament*, by Edward W. Winstanley. *PTR* 8:317–20.

Review of *The Background of the Gospels: or, Judaism in the Period Between the Old and New Testaments*, by William Fairweather. *PTR* 8:320–21.

Review of *Ahasver "der ewige Jude"* . . . , by Eduard König. *PTR* 8:345–46.

Review of *The Holy Spirit in the New Testament: A Study of Primitive Christian Teaching*, by Henry D. Swete. *PTR* 8:670–72.

1911

"The Pauline Eschatology and Chiliasm." *PTR* 9:26–60.

Review of *The Quest of the Historical Jesus*, by Albert Schweitzer. *PTR* 9:132–41. (Reprint, *RHBI*, 517–25.)

Review of *Israel's Ideal or Studies in Old Testament Theology*, by John Adams. *PTR* 9:482–83.

Review of *Biblische Zeitschrift*, 1909. *PTR* 9:660–61.

Review of *The Eschatological Question in the Gospels and Other Studies in Recent New Testament Criticism*, by Cyril W. Emmet. *PTR* 9:662–66.

Review of *New Testament Theology*, by Henry C. Sheldon. *PTR* 9:666–67.

1912

"The Eschatological Aspect of the Pauline Conception of the Spirit." In *Biblical and Theological Studies*, by members of the faculty of Princeton Theological Seminary, 211–59. New York: Charles Scribner's Sons. (Reprint, *RHBI*, 91–125.)

Review of *Die Menschensohnfrage im letzen Stadium*, by Eduard Hertlein. *PTR* 10:324–30.

Review of *Die Handauflegung im Urchristentum nach Verwendung, Herkunft und Bedeutung in religionsgeschichtlichen Zusammenhang untersucht*, by Johannes Behm. *PTR* 10:330–34.

Review of *De theologie van Kronieken*, by Jelte Swart. *PTR* 10:480–81.

Review of *Der geschichtliche Jesus*, by Carl Clemen. *PTR* 10:489–90.

Review of *Das Aposteldekret (Act 15, 28. 29): Seine Entstehung und Geltung in den ersten vier Jahrhunderten*, by K. Six. *PTR* 10:669–72.

1913

"The Range of the Logos-Title in the Prologue to the Fourth Gospel." *PTR* 11:365–419, 557–602. (Reprint, *RHBI*, 59–90.)

Review of *La Théologie de Saint Paul*, by F. Prat. *PTR* 11:126–29.

Review of *The Religious Experience of Saint Paul*, by Percy Gardner. *PTR* 11:316–20.

Review of *Der Begriff Διαθήκη im Neuen Testament*, by Johannes Behm. *PTR* 11:513–18.

Review of *Auferstehungshoffnung und Pneumagedanke bei Paulus*, by Kurt Diessner. *PTR* 11:664–68.

Review of *Der Begriff der Wahrheit in dem Evangelium und den Briefen des Johannes*, by F. Büchsel. *PTR* 11:668–72.

1914

"'Covenant' or 'Testament'?" *Bible Magazine* 2:205–25. (Reprint, *RHBI*, 400–11.)

Review of *Paul and His Interpreters*, by Albert Schweitzer. *PTR* 12:142–49. (Reprint, *RHBI*, 526–33.)
Review of *A Critical History of the Doctrine of the Future Life . . . and Immortality*, by R. H. Charles. *PTR* 12:297–305.
Review of *Primitive Christianity and Its Non-Jewish Sources*, by Carl Clemen. *PTR* 12:305–10.
Review of *Reden und Aufsätze*, by Hermann Gunkel. *PTR* 12:633–36.
Review of *Kyrios Christos*, by Wilhelm Bousset. *PTR* 12:636–45. (Reprint, *RHBI*, 534–43.)
Review of *The Christology of St. Paul*, by G. Nowell Rostron. *PTR* 12:645–47.

1915

"The Continuity of the Kyrios Title in the New Testament." *PTR* 13:161–89.
"Hebrews, the Epistle of the Diatheke." *PTR* 13:587–632. (Reprint, *RHBI*, 161–233.)
"Brotherly Love." In *DAC*, 1:160–62.
"Goodness." In *DAC*, 1:470–71.
"Joy." In *DAC*, 1:654–55.
"Kindness." In *DAC*, 1:673–74.
"Longsuffering." In *DAC*, 1:704–5.
"Love." In *DAC*, 1:713–17.
"Peace." In *DAC*, 2:159–60.
"Pity." In *DAC*, 2:240–41.
"Wicked." In *DAC*, 2:675–76.
"Eschatology of the New Testament." In *ISBE*, 2:979–93. (Reprint, *RHBI*, 25–58.)
"Gehenna." In *ISBE*, 2:1183.
"Hades." In *ISBE*, 2:1314–15.
"Heavens, New (and Earth, New)." In *ISBE*, 2:1353–54.
"Jerusalem, New." In *ISBE*, 3:1621–22.
"Lake of Fire." In *ISBE*, 3:1822.
"Last Time, Times." In *ISBE*, 3:1840.

"Omnipotence." In *ISBE*, 4:2188–90.
"Omnipresence." In *ISBE*, 4:2190–91.
"Omniscience." In *ISBE*, 4:2191–92.
"Perdition." In *ISBE*, 4:2320.
"Reprobate." In *ISBE*, 4:2560.
Review of *The Religious Ideas of the Old Testament*, by H. Wheeler Robinson. *PTR* 13:109–11.
Review of *The Theology of the Gospels*, by James Moffatt. *PTR* 13:111–14.
Review of *Buddhistische und neutestamentliche Erzählungen*, by Georg Faber. *PTR* 13:115–19.
Review of *Sporen van animisme in het Oude Testament?* by G. Ch. Aalders. *PTR* 13:288–89.
Review of *The Christology of the Epistle to the Hebrews: Including Its Relation to the Developing Christology of the Primitive Church*, by Harris L. MacNeill. *PTR* 13:490–91.
Review of *Die Entstehung der Weisheit Salomos*, by Friedrich Focke. *PTR* 13:677–81.
Review of *Zur Geschichte der alttestamentlichen Religion in ihrer universalen Bedeutung*, by W. W. G. Baudissin. *PTR* 13:681–83.
Review of *Das antisemitische Hauptdogma*, by Eduard König. *PTR* 13:683–84.

1916

"Hebrews, the Epistle of the Diatheke (concluded)," *PTR* 14:1–61. (Reprint, *RHBI*, 161–233.)
"Modern Dislike of the Messianic Consciousness in Jesus." *Bib. Rev.* 1:170–85. (Reprint, *RHBI*, 324–32.)
"The Ubiquity of the Messiahship in the Gospels." *Bib. Rev.* 1:490–506. (Reprint, *RHBI*, 333–42.)
"The Second Coming of Our Lord and the Millennium," *The Presbyterian* 86 (December 7): 6–7, 27–28. (Reprint, *The Banner* 51 [December 14]: 788–90. Reprint, *RHBI*, 415–22.)

Review of *The Books of the Apocrypha*, by W. O. E. Oesterley. *PTR* 14:135–38.

Review of *Paul's Doctrine of Redemption*, by Henry B. Carré. *PTR* 14:138–39.

Review of *Recht und Schuld in der Geschichte*, by A. Schlatter. *PTR* 14:361–62.

Review of *Het Evangelie van Markus*, by A. van Veldhuizen, and *Het Evangelie van Mattheus*, by J. A. C. van Leeuwen. *PTR* 14:494–95.

Review of *Israel en de Baäls afval of ontwikkeling*, by J. Ridderbos. *PTR* 14:495–98.

Review of *Der Märtyrer in den Anfängen der Kirche*, by A. Schlatter. *PTR* 14:656–58.

1917

"Kyrios Christos Controversy." *PTR* 15:21–89.

Review of *Paulus en zijn brief aan de Romeinen*, by A. van Veldhuizen. *PTR* 15:180–81.

1919

Review of *Het Evangelie van Lucas*, by J. de Zwaan. *PTR* 17:142–43.

Review of *Het eeuwige leven bij Paulus*, by Johan T. Ubbink. *PTR* 17:143–51.

1920

"The Messiahship: Formal or Essential to the Mind of Jesus?" *Bib. Rev.* 5:196–208.

"Eschatology of the Psalter." *PTR* 18:1–43. (Reprinted as an appendix to *The Pauline Eschatology*. Grand Rapids: Wm. B. Eerdmans Publishing Co., 1952.)

1922

Grace and Glory: Sermons Preached in the Chapel of Princeton Theological Seminary. Grand Rapids: Reformed Press.
Spiegel der genade. Grand Rapids: Eerdmans-Sevensma Co.
"The Name 'Lord' As Used of Jesus in the Gospels." *Bib. Rev.* 7:515–36.

1926

The Self-Disclosure of Jesus: The Modern Debate about the Messianic Consciousness. New York: George H. Doran Co. (Rewritten and corrected by Johannes G. Vos, Grand Rapids: Wm. B. Eerdmans Publishing Co., 1954. Another edition, Nutley, NJ: Presbyterian and Reformed Publishing Co., 1976, 2002.)

1927

Spiegel der natuur en lyra Anglica. Printed by the author.
" 'True' and 'Truth' in the Johannine Writings." *Bib. Rev.* 12:507–20. (Reprint, *RHBI*, 343–51.)

1928

"Jeremiah's Plaint and Its Answer." *PTR* 26:481–95. (Reprint, *RHBI*, 288–98.)

1929

"The Pauline Doctrine of the Resurrection." *PTR* 27:1–35.
"Alleged Development in Paul's Teaching on the Resurrection." *PTR* 27:193–226.
"The Structure of the Pauline Eschatology." *PTR* 27:403–44.

1930

The Pauline Eschatology. Princeton: Princeton University. (Reprint, with an appendix entitled "The Eschatology of the Psalter," Grand Rapids: Wm. B. Eerdmans, 1952; Grand Rapids: Baker, 1979.

Reprint, with Scripture Index, Phillipsburg, NJ: P&R Publishing Company, 1991.)
"The Eschatology of the Old Testament" (classroom syllabus).

1931

Charis, English Verses. Princeton: Princeton University Press.

1932

Spiegel des doods. Grand Rapids: Wm. B. Eerdmans Publishing Co. (Another edition, 1936.)

1933

Western Rhymes. Santa Ana, CA: by the author.
"Autobiographische aanteekeningen." *Neerlandia* 37 (January 1933): 9–10. (Translation by Ed M. van der Maas: "Autobiographical Notes." *Kerux: The Journal of Northwest Theological Seminary* 19/3 [December 2004]: 6–10.)
"Taal-afsterving." *Neerlandia* 37 (February 1933): 15–16. (Translation by Ed M. van der Maas: "Dutch: The Withering of a Language." *Kerux: The Journal of Northwest Theological Seminary* 19/2 [September 2004]: 6–10.)

1934

Zeis en garve. Santa Ana, CA: by the author.
Old and New Testament Biblical Theology. Philadelphia: Theological Seminary of the Reformed Episcopal Church. (Also 1942.)

1944

The Teaching of the Epistle to the Hebrews. Philadelphia: Theological Seminary of the Reformed Episcopal Church.
"Pinksteren (gedicht)." *Heiden Wereld: Missionary Monthly* 49:181.
"Kerstfeest bede (gedicht)." *Heiden Wereld: Missionary Monthly* 49:375.

1945

"Het kerst-evangelie (gedicht)." *Heiden Wereld: Missionary Monthly* 50:375.

1947

Old and New Testament Biblical Theology. Toronto: Toronto Baptist Seminary.
"Kerstfeest-treuren (gedicht)." *Heiden Wereld: Missionary Monthly* 52:347.

1948

"Preface." In *Biblical Theology: Old and New Testaments*, edited by Johannes G. Vos. Grand Rapids: Wm. B. Eerdmans Publishing Co. (Reprint, Edinburgh: Banner of Truth Trust, 1975.)
Biblical Theology: Old and New Testaments. Edited by Johannes G. Vos. Grand Rapids: Wm. B. Eerdmans Publishing Co. (Reprint, Edinburgh: Banner of Truth Trust, 1975.)

1949

"Kerstfeest-gebed." *Heiden Wereld: Missionary Monthly* 54:343.

1952

"Notes on Systematic Theology." Translated by Marten Woudstra. *Reformed Review* (Philadelphia) 1:18, 19, 37, 38, 58, 59, 76, 77, 93, 94, 98, 113–16, 133–36, 144–46, 155.
The Teaching of the Epistle to the Hebrews. Edited and rewritten by Johannes G. Vos. Grand Rapids: Wm. B. Eerdmans Publishing Co. (Reprint, 1956; reprint, Nutley, NJ: Presbyterian and Reformed Publishing Co., 1974 and 1977.)

1980

"Easter." *The Banner* 115 (April 4): 14. (Abridged from *Charis* [1931], pp. 3–5.)

1986

"A Sermon on Hebrews 12:1–3." *Kerux: A Journal of Biblical-Theological Preaching* 1/1 (May): 4–15.

"A Sermon on 1 Peter 1:3–5." *Kerux: A Journal of Biblical-Theological Preaching* 1/2 (September): 4–17.

1987

"A Sermon on 1 Corinthians 15:14." *Kerux: A Journal of Biblical-Theological Preaching* 2/2 (September): 3–13.

1988

"A Sermon on Psalm 25:14." *Kerux: A Journal of Biblical-Theological Preaching* 3/1 (May): 3–12.

"A Sermon on Isaiah 57:15." *Kerux: A Journal of Biblical-Theological Preaching* 3/2 (September): 3–19.

"A Sermon on Matthew 16:24, 25." *Kerux: A Journal of Biblical-Theological Preaching* 3/3 (December): 3–14.

1989

"A Sermon on Hebrews 13:8." *Kerux: A Journal of Biblical-Theological Preaching* 4/2 (September): 2–11.

1990

"The Spiritual Resurrection of Believers: A Sermon on Ephesians 2:4, 5." Translated by Richard B. Gaffin Jr. *Kerux: A Journal of Biblical-Theological Preaching* 5/1 (May): 3–21.

"A Sermon on 1 Corinthians 5:7." *Kerux: A Journal of Biblical-Theological Preaching* 5/3 (December): 1–8.

1991

"A Sermon on Mark 10:45." *Kerux: A Journal of Biblical-Theological Preaching* 6/1 (May): 3–15.

"The Wonderful Tree." *Kerux: A Journal of Biblical-Theological Preaching* 6/2 (September): 3–22.

"Hungering and Thirsting after Righteousness." *Kerux: A Journal of Biblical-Theological Preaching* 6/3 (December): 3–18.

1992

"Seeking and Saving the Lost." *Kerux: A Journal of Biblical-Theological Preaching* 7/1 (May): 1–19.

"Rabboni." *Kerux: A Journal of Biblical-Theological Preaching* 7/2 (September): 3–14.

1993

"The More Excellent Ministry." *Kerux: A Journal of Biblical-Theological Preaching* 8/1 (May): 3–19.

1994

Grace and Glory. Edinburgh: Banner of Truth Trust. (Contains all the sermons from the 1922 edition and several more.)

2001

The Eschatology of the Old Testament. Edited by James T. Dennison Jr. Phillipsburg, NJ: P&R Publishing Co.

2004

"Dutch: The Withering of a Language." Translated by Ed M. van der Maas. *Kerux: The Journal of Northwest Theological Seminary* 19/2 (September 2004): 6–10. (Original, "Taal–afsterving." *Neerlandia* 37 [February 1933]: 15–16.)

"Autobiographical Notes." Translated by Ed M. van Maas. *Kerux: The Journal of Northwest Theological Seminary* 19/3 (December 2004): 6–10. (Original, "Autobiographische aanteekeningen." *Neerlandia* 37 [January 1933]: 9–10.)

2005

The Letters of Geerhardus Vos. Compiled and edited by James T. Dennison Jr. Phillipsburg, NJ: P&R Publishing.

N.D.

Rhymes Old and New (by Desiderius—nom de plume for Vos).

Miscellaneous Manuscripts[2]

I. Dated Materials
   A. Graduation sermon on Ephesians 1:4 (1883).
   B. "Natuurlijke godgeleerdheid" (1885).
   C. "Geschiedenis der idololatrie" (1892 and 1895).
   D. Sermon on Isaiah 57:15 (the first page of 29 is missing; December 12, 1896).
   E. Personal sermon notebook used at Princeton Theological Seminary. Contains messages on the following texts:[3]
      1. Hebrews 12:1–3 (April 4, 1902).
      2. 1 Corinthians 5:7 (October 1, 1902).
      3. Psalm 25:14 (October 15, 1902).
      4. Hebrews 13:8 (January 7, 1903).
      5. Matthew 16:24–25 (November 19, 1903).
      6. 1 Peter 1:3–5 (October 31, 1904).
      7. 1 Corinthians 15:14 (April 21, 1905).
      8. Mark 10:45 (October 9, 1913).
      9. 2 Corinthians 3:18 (October 10, 1914). This manuscript is an earlier version of "The More Excellent Ministry" in *Grace and Glory* (1922), pp. 107–30.

---

2. Unless otherwise noted, these materials are deposited in the Heritage Hall Archive at the Calvin College and Seminary Library, Grand Rapids, Michigan.

3. These sermons are printed in *Kerux: A Journal of Biblical-Theological Preaching*, 1986–1993. The entire collection was published in the 1994 edition of *Grace and Glory*.

II. Undated Manuscripts
   A. "De geesteliike opstanding der geloovigen. Leerrede over Ephese II:4, 5." Grand Rapids: Melis. ("The Spiritual Resurrection of Believers: A Sermon on Ephesians 2:4, 5." Translated by Richard B. Gaffin Jr. *Kerux: A Journal of Biblical-Theological Preaching* 5/1 [May 1990]: 3–21.)
   B. "New Testament Biblical Theology." Princeton: Princeton Theological Seminary.
   C. Outline of notes on New Testament Biblical Theology. (Deposited in the Alumni Alcove of the Princeton Theological Seminary Library.)
   D. "The Teaching of the Epistle to the Hebrews."
   E. "Gereformeerde dogmatiek," 5 vols.
   F. "Hellenistic Greek Grammar." (Attributed to Vos by R. Stob in *Semi-Centennial Volume: Theological School and Calvin College, 1876–1926*, p. 296.)
   G. Outline of Old Testament Eschatology.
   H. "Old Testament Eschatology." (Two drafts of this work are extant and both are incomplete. The shorter is handwritten; the longer is a typescript.)
   I. "The Idea of 'Fulfillment' of Prophecy in the Gospels." (Printed in *RHBI*, 352–54.)
   J. Notebook entitled "Exegesis N. Testament." (This material is in Vos's hand and contains verse-by-verse exegetical notes on Isaiah 53:5–59:3 in Dutch, as well as verse-by-verse notes on Galatians 4:21–6:18 in English.)

Class Lecture Notebooks Belonging to Students of Professor Vos[4]

I. Among the Papers of Henry Beets
   A. Compendium systematische theologie.

---

4. The notes taken by Beets and Hoekstra are from classes at Grand Rapids, where Professor Vos taught from 1888 to 1893. The remainder are from lectures delivered at Princeton Theological Seminary. All notebooks are in the Heritage Hall Archive at Calvin College.

II. Among the Papers of William De Groot
   A. The Pauline Teaching in Survey, 1916–1917.
III. Among the Papers of J. B. Hoekstra
   A. Stellingen over den doop.
   B. Rede.
   C. Synopsis purioris theologiae: Theologie.
   D. Evangelien harmonie.
IV. Among the Papers of Dr. H. H. Meeter
   A. Pauline eschatology.
   B. The Fourth Gospel.
   C. Eighth century prophets.
   D. New Testament theology.
   E. Hebrews.
   F. Pauline soteriology, book II.
V. Among the Papers of Henry Schultze
   A. Biblical theology of the Old Testament.
   B. The eschatology of the Old Testament.

Select Vos Sources

Adams, Oscar Fay. *A Dictionary of American Authors*, 399. Boston: Houghton Mifflin Co., 1904.

Beets, Henry. *Christelijke encyclopaedie voor het Nederlandsche volk*, 6:429. Kampen: J. H. Kok, 1925?–1931?

Bouma, Clarence. "Geerhardus Vos and Biblical Theology." *Calvin Forum* 9/12 (August-September 1943): 5–6.

Brinks, Herbert. "Voices from Our Immigrant Past, the Christian Reformed Church: Phase II." *The Banner*, June 23, 1978, pp. 18–19.

De Jong, Peter. "The Vos Legacy." *Torch and Trumpet*, December 1979, pp. 13–14.

Dennison, James T., Jr. "Geerhardus Vos." In *Bible Interpreters of the Twentieth Century*, edited by Walter A. Elwell and J. D. Weaver, 82–92. Grand Rapids: Baker Books, 1999.

———. "Geerhardus Vos: Life in Two Worlds." *Kerux: A Journal of Biblical-Theological Preaching* 14/2 (September 1999): 18–31.

———. "What Is Biblical Theology? Reflections on the Inaugural Address of Geerhardus Vos." *Kerux: A Journal of Biblical-Theological Preaching* 2/1 (May 1987): 33–41.

"Ex-Calvin Professor Dies at 87." *Grand Rapids Herald*, August 14, 1949.

"Ex-Professor Here Passes." *Grand Rapids Press*, August 13, 1949, p. 1.

Gaffin, Richard B., Jr. "Geerhardus Vos and the Interpretation of Paul." In *Jerusalem and Athens*, edited by E. R. Geehan, 229–43. Phillipsburg, NJ: Presbyterian and Reformed Publishing Company, 1971.

———. Introduction to *Redemptive History and Biblical Interpretation*, edited by Richard B. Gaffin Jr. Phillipsburg, NJ: Presbyterian and Reformed Publishing Company, 1980.

"Geerhardus Vos." *Biographical Catalogue of Princeton Theological Seminary, 1815–1954*, p. 121. Princeton: Trustees of the Theological Seminary, 1955.

"Geerhardus Vos." *Princeton Seminary Bulletin* 43/3 (1950): 41–42 (Trustee Memorial Minute).

"Geerhardus Vos." *Princeton Seminary Bulletin* 43/3 (1950): 44–46 (Faculty Memorial Minute).

"Geerhardus Vos, Theologian, Dies." *New York Times*, August 14, 1949, 68.

Harms, Richard H. "Flashback: Geerhardus Vos, Calvin's First Ph.D." *Calvin Spark* 49/3 (Fall 2003): 13.

Harnick, George. "Geerhardus Vos as Introducer of Kuyper in America." In *The Dutch-American Experience: Essays in Honor of Robert P. Swierenga*, edited by Hans Krabbendam and Larry Wagenaar, 243–61. Amsterdam: VU Uitgeverij, 2000.

Herringshaw, T. W. *Herringshaw's National Library of American Biography*. Chicago: American Publishers' Association, 1909–1914, p. 559.

Jansen, John F. "The Biblical Theology of Geerhardus Vos." *Princeton Seminary Bulletin* 66/2 (Summer 1974): 23–34.
Meeter, H. Henry. "Professor Geerhardus Vos." *The Banner* 84 (September 2, 1949): 1046–47.
"The Rev. Geerhardus Vos, Ph.D., D.D." *Princeton Seminary Bulletin* 26/1 (June 1932): 15–16.
Vanden Bosch, Jacob G. "Geerhardus Vos." *Reformed Journal* 4 (November 1954): 11–14.
———. "Geerhardus Vos." In *Christian Reformed Worthies*, compiled by John H. Bratt, 82–87. N.p., n.d.
Vos, Geerhardus. "Autobiographical Notes." Translated by Ed M. van der Maas. *Kerux: The Journal of Northwest Theological Seminary* 19/3 (December 2004): 6–10. (Original, "Autobiographische aanteekeningen," *Neerlandia* 37 [January 1933]: 9–10.)
Webster, Ransom L. "Geerhardus Vos (1862–1949): A Biographical Sketch." *Westminster Theological Journal* 40 (1977–78): 304–17.
Woudstra, M. H. "Geerhardus Vos." *Kerux* [Calvin College], December 20, 1977, p. 4.

THE LETTERS OF GEERHARDUS VOS

To W. H. Roberts

August 17, 1883
Grand Rapids, Michigan
48 Spring Street
Rev. W. H. Roberts, D.D.[1]

Dear Sir,

You ask whether I intend to pursue a full course and advise me to do so. There are several reasons however, which make it very difficult for me to follow your advice, at least without further information.

1. As you will have seen from my testimonials, I studied theology two years.[2] Three additional ones would make five, a time rather too long. Besides, the matter might be too expensive for my parents. If possible my studies must be finished in two years.[3]

2. I studied in nearly all the branches appointed for the first year of a regular course. Also in Hebrew I passed an examination of which the diploma was not sent you, because it could not be of any influence on my admission. I will bring it with me however on my arrival.

This taken into consideration, it would suit me best to enter the middle class. As the Catalogue does not give evidence on this point, I must trouble you once more and ask:

1. Will I be admitted to the middle class?
2. Is it possible by studying successively or simultaneously all the branches to take a full course in two years?
3. To what kind of diploma or certificate will I be entitled when entering the middle class and leaving the Senior after a study of two years?

Expecting your information on these points and hoping to be present at your opening September 20th, I remain,

Most respectfully yours,
G. Vos

P.S. We received a Catalogue of Laurenceville School[4] and thank you very much for procuring it. My brother[5] will probably remain here to be prepared for entering college next year.

---

1. William Henry Roberts (1844–1920) was librarian and registrar at Princeton Theological Seminary from 1877 to 1886. He did not actually receive the D.D. degree until 1884 from Western University of Pennsylvania, Pittsburgh (now the University of Pittsburgh).
2. At the Theologische School (now Calvin Theological Seminary), Grand Rapids, Michigan; Vos was a student there from 1881 to 1883.
3. Vos completed his work at Princeton in 1885.
4. Now spelled Lawrenceville (New Jersey), the town is located about five miles northeast of Trenton. The Laurenceville School for Boys was established in 1810.
5. Bert John Vos (1867–1945).

To Abraham Kuyper

May 28, 1886
Friedrich Str. 205 III
Berlin bei Frau Oberstabarzt Bluhm

Valued and Very Learned Sir:

Please forgive me for not having answered you sooner. Your letter posed unexpected questions which I myself had never considered seriously, and upon which I also now, after further consideration, am only able to answer in part.

It is not because of lack of sympathy with your endeavors and with the institution which owes you her existence,[1] that makes me hesitate to meet you halfway. Directly and indirectly your book has exerted a formative influence on me.[2] Because of that, I willingly and thankfully grasp the opportunity to personally make your acquaintance, which you so kindly offer to me.

What makes it so difficult to agree with your proposal is mainly the following. Last autumn I came to Europe with no other plan than to sojourn there for some time for the continuation of my study. The possibility of a lasting stay on this side of the ocean was far out of my thoughts. Naturally I considered the country where my parents live as the assigned circle where God wanted me to labor to the measure of my capacities and opportunities.

Then you placed another prospect next to this one, that, if it were realized, would replant me into the old native soil and on the other hand pull me away from my newly won circle of friends and separate me from that which is dear to me.

I trust you will approve that I am not making a decision about the major issue of your correspondence for the reasons listed above. If you would demand this, more mature consideration with others and myself should precede.

Under this restriction I will be pleased to facilitate the closer acquaintance as much as I am able. I do not know however if the Pentecost recess offers the best opportunity to that end. It is almost too short to make such a long trip without urgent necessity; I was recently in the Netherlands. Allow me to make a counterproposal, and I shall be pleased to await your opinion about its acceptability. The summer semester semi-officially closes mid-August. At the end of that month, I hope to return to the Netherlands. Would we not be able without difficulty to find time and occasion at that point which would allow us to make the desired acquaintance?

If such a plan would present difficulties from your side, nothing else would remain for me to try to fulfil your kind invitation. The only time during this semester which I cannot attend classes for a few days without a proper excuse is during the Pentecost recess. Still, not yet thinking of the financial burdens, I do dread the trip a little, and would prefer to postpone it until the latter part of the summer.

Be so kind as to inform me with a few words what you think of my counterproposal.

Thanking you for your brotherly confidence, I remain after greeting and good wishes,

Yours in Christ,
Geerhardus Vos

---

* This letter has been translated from the original Dutch.
1. Vos refers to the Free University of Amsterdam, founded by Kuyper in 1880. The doors opened on October 20, 1880.
2. Vos probably refers to Kuyper's *Tractaat van de reformatie der kerken, aan de zonen der reformatie hier te lande op Luthers vierde eeuwfeest* (Amsterdam: Höveker, 1884). For a complete list of Kuyper's writings, see J. C. Rullmann, *Kuyper-Bibliografie* ('s-Gravenhage: J. Bootsma, 1923–40).

To Abraham Kuyper

June 7, 1886
Berlin

Valued and Very Learned Sir:

Please do not have a low opinion of me; I have to cancel a visit at Pentecost. Allow me to inform you briefly of the reason for that.

I cannot reconcile myself with the thought of taking even this temporary step without my parents' knowledge. It is true that the circumstances make preceding deliberations with them impossible. Still I would rather avoid the appearance that in such an important case I dared to act with an independence that showed a lack of piety.

A second objection is of a more personal nature. It seems to me that during my visit I may actually say more than I can account for at this moment, and would assume a position at the same time for others and myself, which gives me a nauseating feeling. I could have perhaps gotten myself over this last objection, if this was the only opportunity to meet you. But this is not the case, is it? Finally, my health also presents difficulties. I cannot make long journeys without harmful consequences to my system. I hope you will find these reasons sufficient to excuse me this time.

If all goes well and I come back to the Netherlands for the autumn vacation (mid-August to mid-October) I will willingly answer your request for a meeting, when and where that is possible, if you still desire to do so. I hope by then my first and third objections will be completely removed. Also the second one should be lessened as well.

Not considering all the other issues, I fervently wish nothing more than an opportunity to hear your thoughts concerning American church affairs. In the meantime, I remain after your greeting and good wishes

Yours in Christ,
Geerhardus Vos

* This letter has been translated from the original Dutch.

To J. W. Felix

September 4, 1886
Leiden

Dear Sir,
I shall accept with pleasure the kind invitation of Rev. Felix and call at his house at the time you mentioned.[1] Although I am not very familiar with Utrecht, I nevertheless hope to be able to find the way there

with little difficulty. With gratitude for your letters I remain, with regards and prayers for your well-being,

> Your willing servant,
> Geerhardus Vos

---

* This letter has been translated from the original Dutch. It is addressed to the curators of the Free University of Amsterdam through the chairman, Rev. J. W. Felix.
1. Rev. J. W. Felix was chairman from 1879 to 1888. The curators usually met at his home in Utrecht.

To Abraham Kuyper

October 7, 1886
Leiden

Valued and Very Learned Sir:

Receive my kindest thanks for your interesting letter. It has confirmed in me the strong conviction that your view is correct. Yet I felt obligated to act against that conviction.

The correspondence with my parents made it necessary for me to make a choice which had became doubly difficult after acquaintance with the Free University. Had not such tender motives as the relation between parents and child mixed up in our consideration and made that choice totally inevitable, that would not have been done. The impulse of undivided sympathy with the glorious principle that your institution represents and seeks to propagate drove me, as it were, within her walls. It would have been an honor and a delight to me to be permitted to serve the Free University with my frail energies.

The circumstances, as they have formed themselves under God's rule, apparently do not allow that. My parents cannot view the case in the same light in which I learned to look at it as of late. In case I, against their advice and wishes, dared to follow the inclination of my heart, I would bring grief to them, from which I have to save them at any cost. Taking this into consideration, I see no other way than to choose the field of activity assigned to me in America.[1]

With much sorrow I part with the cherished hope at one time to be allowed to live and work in the shadow of many highly esteemed men,[2] who have become, not without your influence, personally dear to me. Still I have the quiet prayer that God will use us in America, as from a distance, to join you in the fight. The Free University will always have in me a warm friend and a firm advocate.

May the Lord be with you and her cause.

>Your servant and brother in our Savior,
>Geerhardus Vos

---

* This letter has been translated from the original Dutch.

1. In the summer of 1886, the Synod of the Christian Reformed Church of North America had appointed Vos professor of theology at the Theologische School (now Calvin Theological Seminary).

2. In addition to Kuyper, the original faculty of the Free University at its opening in 1880 consisted of: Friedrich Wilhelm Jakob Dilloo, Faculty of Letters, who served until 1885; Damme Paulus Dirk Fabius (1851–1931), Faculty of Law, who served until 1921; Philippus Jacobus Hoedemaker (1839–1910), Faculty of Theology, who served until 1888; and Frederick Lodewijk Rutgers (1836–1917), Faculty of Theology, who served until 1910. Jan Woltjer (1849–1917), Faculty of Letters, was appointed in 1881 and served until his death. Arnold Hendrik de Hartog (1837–1895), curator, began his service in 1882 and served until his death. Jonkheer Alexander Frederik de Savornin Lohman (1837–1924), Faculty of Law, served from 1883 to 1896.

To Herman Bavinck

June 16, 1887
Schifflentgasse 29
Strassburg

Dear Brother:

It is high time that I answer your letters, especially since they contain direct questions to me. Let me begin by giving you as much as possible of the desired information.

I have in my possession a little book by the title: *Grundsatz und Bedingungen der Erteilung der Doktorwürde* ... [Principles and Terms of Entrance to the Doctorate ...]. I'll be pleased to send it to you for your perusal. You can then read it and judge for yourself.

There is no facility which administers an entrance examination to the university. Especially not if one possesses a gymnasium diploma, even if it is from a different country. I do not know if a literary degree from Kampen[1] would be considered sufficient. Such matters are not taken as seriously here as in the Netherlands. Both the rules and practice are much more liberal. I was admitted without hesitation to Berlin with my diploma from Amsterdam and Americans were admitted who only had a passport, regardless of their further documents. This will still be so. Of course here one has to reckon with local customs. Still I do not believe your brother[2] and his friends would have difficulties with matriculation. In any event, when they arrive here I would advise them to get themselves a passport.

The little book tells you when and how one can graduate. Also you will find the necessary information concerning the study time which one must spend at a university. I think for foreigners an exception can be made by taking their previous study into account and proportionally shorten the number of required German semesters.

Your other question, more difficult to answer, is which would be the shortest and least difficult study and where it would be most suitable. As you see, most of the theological faculties only give the licentiate degree. Theology is not held in high esteem here and I cannot say she earns it. To judge after all I have heard and seen, Theology is really for Professors, still it is for students "bread-winner study" (in the real sense of the word). All that Schopenhauer[3] says of the *Philosophen zunft* [profession of philosopher] is applicable to theology. Most of the students who are now enrolled in the theological faculty certainly would choose other professions, if scholarships were as numerous for the more humane professions, and an appointment in the future was as certain. It is so bad here that just by looking I can distinguish the theologians from the other students. Personally I would not attach much value therefore to a theological degree earned in Germany. Undoubtedly you have a much better and more ripe judgment than I have about these things.

For somebody who has already studied theology it would undoubtedly be the easiest way to graduate in that faculty. And as far as I know of the situations here that is a devil of a job. At any rate, one will not make as much progress as in the Netherlands. I doubt very much however whether the fruit of such a study would be materially great. From an encyclopedic point of view, Philosophy is a study which gives more satisfaction than German theology. I even believe that a not too superficial acquaintanceship with her further fundamental judgment of different theological trends shall appear of greater benefit than the concentration in one or another nuance of the newer theology itself. The theological faculty is after all too fragmented, the encyclopedic is too neglected, the method is often too historical, too little Philosophical, and even the higher criticism of Scripture is conveyed to the students in such a mechanical manner and *autoritätsmässig* [authority-wise] that the students are not able to internalize the principles on which this work of art is woven. It seems to me that under Kuenen[4] in Leiden students get more of the latter. On the other hand, philosophy automatically throws such a clear light on the radical difference in principle that one must think and stand. That makes the wine clear. I cannot express myself more precisely than by saying that the theology here in my opinion, is too little reflective and self-confident. It is better therefore that one looks at it from a distant point of view. That promotes clarity because the unconscious dulls and obscures.

I apologize for this deviation. It contains my personal judgment, nothing more, and therefore is of a very relative value.

At any rate, I would prefer a small university. One is better in touch there with the professors and does not have so many distractions. Also the notion of insignificance that one feels in Berlin and Liepzig is not without danger for the independence of the study. Finally at a smaller university one can make use of the library more easily.

I'm very pleased with Strassburg. The institutes are excellent and most of the chairs ably occupied. Moreover one has the advantage here when getting a degree in the Philosophy department to be able to take one theological subject. I chose for instance Semitic languages (Arabic, Egyptian, Hebrew) as my major and Philosophy and Church History as minors.[5]

One should not waste time too much, because writing a dissertation alone takes more than one semester. And one must be here for several months before one is sufficiently informed so as to make a good choice. I don't believe it can be done in less than two years.

I would advise everyone to stay at one particular university. It would have been desirable for me if I had chosen Strassburg right away and had not visited Berlin.

Living is more expensive here than in many cities in North Germany. I cannot live on less than 120 marks monthly. The tuition amounts to 50 marks per semester, and if you study medicine, it is more.

You probably know better than I do what the Theological Faculty is like. For Philosophy, they have Windelband[6] whom you know as Neo-Kantian.[7] You can learn much from him. I'm very sorry that Laas has passed away.[8] I wish I could have learned about his Positivism from the man himself.[9]

Without realizing it, I have detoured from answering your questions and instead have moved to personal matters. My health still leaves very much to be desired. Once again, in the midst of the work, my nerves have forced me to a standstill. My dissertation (the publication of a historical work of Makrizi[10] accompanied by a translation of a Leyden manuscript) is more than half finished. However on doctor's orders I have had to reduce my work-hours by half. More and more I realize that my health has definitely broken. Still I would like to attain my goal. It is here that the useless tie that binds me to Grand Rapids hurts me the most. I have to be there September 10. Most likely they will no longer grant an extension of time, partially perhaps in the hope that I will then decline. As far as I'm concerned, I would do that without hesitation. However my parents disapprove of that. Incidentally my position will be a false one. I have been appointed to teach English and to promote the importance of the English language; yet under the present circumstances there is nothing that I consider more harmful for our little church there than to introduce English ideas. No doubt the ideas follow the language closely.

Therefore my prospects are not very hopeful. I am going to America with the feeling that my place is not there. And I leave the Netherlands with the knowledge that even if my work be insignificant, I could do it there with joy and sympathy. More than once I have regretted that last year when they made me a proposal in Amsterdam, I did not make a decision. And I still sometimes doubt if I may or even should return, especially if it is wise to go there without having accomplished my goals here. It is very difficult for me to throw away two full years of study.

Right now I am less able to judge the prospects of unification between those from the Doleantie[11] and our church since I have not been informed for a while. Last autumn I agreed with what you wrote. But since that time much has changed. That is what they say, at least. If my hope is realized that the American Curators give me an extension, then in all probability I will spend some weeks in Amsterdam during the vacation and perhaps will meet you there. Or are you already travelling in August? If so, will you travel through Strassburg? And could you stay here for one night?

With special fondness, I am keeping busy now with Philosophy—and indeed most of the time with the theory of knowledge [*Erkenntnistheorie*]. Windelband teaches logic. I cannot attend that lecture because the hours conflict with the hours of Nöldeke.[12] In his class, he deals with Kant's *Kritik der Urteilskraft* [*Critique of Judgment*].[13] Then he lectures one hour a week about "Freedom of the Will." He drove freedom to its grave and with that I enjoyed a great deal of logical satisfaction. Now he braces himself up to save responsibility, and I'm afraid that my logical feeling will now have to pay dearly for the enjoyed pleasure. Without doubt we get a recommendation of Kant's "intelligent character".[14]

My health allows me to work only a very little. I can only use the morning hours for study. Originally it was my plan to be promoted mid-July. Now it cannot take place this Summer: provided I remain here, it will take place in December. However I am much afraid that they will summon me to America. I would then go forced to the land of the free!

Perhaps I feel more for the pessimistic side of Schopenhauer's Philosophy than you could reasonably have. Sometimes I can envy you for your beautiful and quiet sphere of work. From this you see that I'm not essentially pessimistic. And that is relatively true for every Christian.

Do you know a subject about which I can write an article for *De Vrije Kerk*?[15] Preferably something philosophical. Write me back before I leave here D. V.[16] within four weeks. The sooner the better.

With kindest regards
G. Vos

Would you please, after using it yourself, send the enclosed book to Uncle Beuker in Leiden?[17] Did you read or page through the work of du Marchie van Voorthuizen about Kant's *Critique of Pure Reason*?[18] Recently I saw a very favorable book review in the *Phil. Vierteljahrsschrift*.[19]

* This letter has been translated from the original Dutch.
1. Kampen Theologische Universiteit, founded in 1854.
2. Bavinck had two brothers: Coenraad Bernardus (1865–1941) and Bereneinus J. F. It is the former to whom Vos refers here. He had matriculated in 1885 and received his diploma in 1890.
3. Arthur Schopenhauer (1788–1860), German philosopher.
4. Abraham Kuenen (1828–1891), an Old Testament critical scholar, taught at Leiden from 1851 until his death; from 1855 onward, he was professor of Old Testament theology.
5. During the winter semester of 1885/86 at the University of Berlin, Vos took *Einleitung in das Alte Testament* (Christian Friedrich August Dillmann, 1823–1894), *Alttestamentliche Textgeschichte* (Dillmann), *Assyrische Schrift und Sprache* (Eberhard Schrader, 1836–1908), *Allgemeine Geschichte der Philosophie* (Eduard Gottlob Zeller, 1814–1908), *Galaterbrief* (Bernhardus Weiss, 1827–1918), *Arabische Grammatik* (Jacob Barth, 1851–1914), *Einleitung in die Philosophie* (Friedrich Paulsen, 1846–1908), *Ethik* (Paulsen), and *Buch der Sprüche* (Hermann Strack, 1848–1922). In the summer semester of 1886, he took *Kleinere exilische Stüche des Buches Jesaja* (Dillmann), *Alttestamentliches Seminar* (Dillmann), *Arabische Syntax* (Barth), and *Tier und Mensch* (Friedrich Heinrich Dieterici, 1821–1903). No detailed transcript of Vos's courses at Strassburg is extant. His thesis advisor was Theodor Nöldeke.
6. Wilhelm Windelband (1848–1915) was professor of philosophy at Strassburg from 1882 to 1903. A neo-Kantian, his standard work (*History of Philosophy*) was published in 1892 (English translation, 1893).
7. Post-Kantians regarded the *Ding an sich* (the noumenal realm) as a construct of the mind; only the phenomenal realm of ideas is real.
8. Ernst Laas (1837–1885) became professor of philosophy at Strassburg in 1872. He was more a neo-empiricist than a Comtian positivist.
9. Positivism regards the highest form of knowledge as that which is descriptive of sensory phenomena; there is no noumenal or metaphysical realm.
10. Taqi ad-Din Ahmad al-Maqrizi (1364–1442). The dissertation, entitled *Die Kämpfe und Streitigkeiten zwischen den Banū 'Umajja und den Banū Hāšim. Von Takijj ad-dīn Al-Makrīzijj*, was published in 1888 by E. J. Brill of Leiden.
11. Literally, "complaining." The movement was spearheaded by Abraham Kuyper in 1886. Kuyper's allies complained about the liberalism of the state church and, after suspension by that body, joined the churches of the 1834 Afscheiding to form the Gereformeerde Kerken Nederlands (1892).
12. Theodor Nöldeke (1836–1930) was professor of Oriental languages at Strassburg from 1872 to 1906.
13. Published 1790.
14. Cf. Immanuel Kant, *Critique of Pure Reason*, trans. Norman Kemp Smith (London: Macmillan, 1933), 468.
15. *De Vrije Kerk* was edited in 1887 by J. van Andel and H. Beuker (Vos's uncle).
16. *Deo volente* ("God willing").
17. Hendericus Beuker (1834–1900) was the brother of Vos's mother, Aaltje Beuker Vos.
18. Henri du Marchie van Voorthuizen, *De theorie der kennis van Immanuel Kant* (Arnheim: np, 1886).
19. The review is by E. Adickes in *Vierteljahrsschrift für wissenschaftliche Philosophie* 11 (1887): 117–22. This quarterly was published from 1876/77 to 1901.

To B. B. Warfield

February 2, 1889
Grand Rapids

Prof. B. B. Warfield
Princeton, N.J.

Dear Sir,

Enclosed you find the desired review.[1] I was not successful in trying to limit it to exactly 1,000 words (there are about 1,180), but perhaps you will find it necessary to omit something. You are at full liberty to do with what I have written, as you think best, and I can only hope that you will be able to use it at all. Accept my sincere thanks for your good wishes with reference to our Seminary, and allow me to send the same in return for Princeton.

>Yours very truly,
>G. Vos

---

1. Judging by the word count, this is the review of *Die Psalmen und die Sprüche Salomos*, by F. W. Schultz and Hermann Strack, in *Presbyterian Review* 10 (1889): 301–3.

To B. B. Warfield

October 22, 1889
Grand Rapids, Michigan

Prof. Benjamin B. Warfield
Princeton, N.J.

Dear Sir,

Some days ago I received a letter from Dr. Kuyper's publisher at Amsterdam, Netherlands. Dr. Kuyper is writing an *Encyclopaedia of Theology* not in the lexicographical sense of the term, but after the manner of Hagenbach's[1] and other more modern works. While the latter have all written from a German standpoint and hold views about theology that are irreconcilable with the Scriptural basis, Dr. Kuyper's work, if he is allowed to complete it, will no doubt present the material in an altogether different light. So far as I know the question was therefore put to me, whether I could make a rough guess at the size of the edition, which a work of this kind could have in America. I am asked for information as to a reliable firm which might be inclined to publish the book here. Finally there is a question as to whether, if the book were to be published in English, I would undertake to furnish the translation.

With reference to the first two questions, I do not very well know which reply to make. This is the reason why I have taken the liberty of addressing you in the hope that you would be kind enough to give me your opinion and advice. My own impression is that there is not much demand in this country for discussions of this sort, as people are apt to consider theology under an exclusively practical aspect, so that perhaps an *Encyclopaedia of Theological Science* would be received with a certain indifference which it would be hard to overcome. This may be a mistaken notion of mine however, and even if it should be correct, it would perhaps show all the more that theological opinion ought to undergo a change in this respect, and such a change might perhaps be brought about by this very publication. You know far better than I (a comparative stranger) the theological currents of the present day in this country, and could tell perhaps in a general way what chances of success a book as the one referred to would have. I should think myself that it might prove helpful in dispelling many half-German ideas, which are afloat and of which those, who adopt and defend them do not realise the dangerous tendency simply because they have no clear and firm convictions on the fundamental questions of Christian truth and theology. I need only refer to the looser views on Inspiration, Biblical Theology and Criticism.

My impression is that *Encyclopaedia* is not taught in our theological Seminaries as a regular branch of study. I remember very well however, during my Seminary days at Princeton, to have heard Prof. Patton[2] speak with great enthusiasm of the difficulties and attractions alike of such a work as Dr. Kuyper has undertaken.

I may say perhaps that the request was to mention a solid "congenial" firm. To an American ear this would sound somewhat strange, but religious and business-matters are much more mixed up over this than in our larger world here.

I hope that I do not exact too much from your kindness when asking for your opinion in these matters. On your judgment, the answer which I shall give, also in regard to translation of the book, will largely depend.

Permit me to thank you for your kindness in nominating me as a member of the American Society of Church History.[3]

          Yours very truly,
          G. Vos

---

1. Karl Rudolf Hagenbach, *Encyklopädie und Methodologie der theologischen Wissenschaften* (Leipzig: Weidmann'sche Buchhandlung, 1833); English translation (adapted) by George R. Crooks and John F. Hurst, *Theological Encyclopaedia and Methodology* (New York: Phillips & Hunt, 1884).

2. Frances Landy Patton (1843–1932) was Vos's professor of apologetics and ethics at Princeton Seminary. He held the chair of apologetics from 1881 onward; in 1888 he was chosen president of Princeton College and served until 1902. In that year he was elected the first president of Princeton Theological Seminary, a position he held until 1913.

3. Vos was a member of the Society from 1889 to 1892.

To Herman Bavinck

February 1, 1890
48 Spring Street
Grand Rapids, Michigan

Dear and Esteemed Brother:

Since I returned from Europe, it has been my continual intention to write you according to my promise. However my work keeps me so busy that I don't have the energy to begin a somewhat regular correspondence and yet I still have to fulfill my promise to you. Even now I would not have written if a particular occasion, which I will briefly share with you, had not furnished the motive.

As you might have noticed, last fall the *Presbyterian Review* ceased to exist.[1] Among the editors, who differed considerably in theological persuasion, a difference of opinion had manifested itself concerning the spirit in which the journal ought to be edited. The discord was connected with the present Revision Movement in the Presbyterian Church,[2] though I cannot say how closely. It was then decided by the more conservative group to publish a new review, which has just published its first issue under the title *Presbyterian and Reformed Review*.[3]

I was asked by the editor to furnish an annual or biannual account of what the Netherlands has produced in the field of theology. I would be pleased to honor that request. It cannot hurt for people here to become more familiar with the situation where you are. It is however very difficult for me to survey the field of Dutch theological literature from such a distance. Until now I have not read anything except the

Theologisch Tijdschrift[4] which keeps me insufficiently informed. Before anything else, I need someone who notes regularly what the different theological schools in the Netherlands produce and who can judge what would be worthwhile for the American theological public for discussion. I cannot think of anybody who could better supply this information than you can. Therefore I come to you with a friendly request. The request is this: could you by means of a bookstore, send me a copy of books (as soon as possible after publication) which you judge important enough to be reviewed in the *Review*? I will be content to depend totally on your discretion. Of course the color or leaning of the books need not present a problem. I will leave the decision to you to judge if they have scientific quality. The bookstore that you choose to order through, can of course send me the bill and will receive annual or biannual payments as he chooses.

Since the editors of the *Review* want an article for the April or July issue, I would like to receive books of importance that have appeared in the last year or six months—or any information which you perhaps could give me would be very welcome. However I feel that I have already asked too much of your kindness. I am reluctant to trouble someone particularly when it is not my own doing to have to count on someone else's service. Still, when the opportunity is there, I am willing and prepared to reciprocate.

Are you receiving the new *Review*? If not, I'll see that it will be sent to you starting in April. I can also send you the first issue which was recently printed. It contains some interesting articles of Shedd,[5] Patton[6] and others. I read with much interest what you wrote in the *Bazuin*[7] concerning the *Dogmatics*[8] of the first one (Shedd). He is still one of the most Reformed ones. From this, you can conclude what the identity of the left wing is, no doubt have already concluded from the *Presbyterian Review*. If the revision movement goes on as it began, then the symbols of Westminster will be changed in an Arminian tone and I fear that the right wing will put up with it. The Presbyterian church finds itself in a very critical period.

I hope to write you soon in more detail. For this time I greet you and yours, also for my parents, and may God be with you.

From your brother,
G. Vos

---

* This letter has been translated from the original Dutch.
1. The *Presbyterian Review* ceased publication in 1889. Launched in 1880, the managing editors were Charles Augustus Briggs (Union Theological Seminary, New York) and A. A. Hodge (Princeton Theological Seminary, New Jersey). B. B. Warfield was appointed coeditor in May 1888, at that point becoming coeditor with Briggs. Warfield resigned in October 1889. The Union Seminary faculty recommended that the *Review* cease publication.
2. The revision of the Westminster Confession of Faith was proposed at the General Assembly of the Presbyterian Church in the U.S.A. in 1889. The proposal was defeated, only to resurface in 1903.
3. The *Presbyterian and Reformed Review* was published from 1890 to 1902. B. B. Warfield was joined by W. G. T. Shedd in 1890 as part of a ten-member editorial board. William Greenough Thayer Shedd (1820–1894)was professor of systematic theology at Union Theological Seminary in New York from 1874 until his retirement in 1891.
4. Published at Amsterdam and Leiden from 1867 to 1919.
5. "The Meaning and Value of the Doctrine of Decrees," *Presbyterian and Reformed Review* 1 (January 1890): 1–25.
6. Francis L. Patton, "On Preaching," *Presbyterian and Reformed Review* 1 (January 1890): 26–41.
7. *De Bazuin* (1888–).
8. W. G. T. Shedd, *Dogmatic Theology* (New York: C. Scribner's Sons, 1888–94).

To Abraham Kuyper

February 1, 1890
8 Spring Street
Grand Rapids, Michigan

Highly Esteemed Sir and Brother:

After the receipt of your letter, I have given serious thought about the case of the translation of your *Encyclopedia*. Though there are not a few difficulties connected as a result of my heavy work load and my only partial familiarity with the English idiom, nevertheless I'll try to meet your wish. I hope to dedicate all my spare time, after carrying out my usual work, to the translation. However, because you will already be considerably ahead with the writing and I will not be able to furnish more than eight or nine pages each week, it is possible that through the slow progress of my translation the publication would be delayed for over two years. If you wish and can have patience with me, I'll do what is in my power. During the summer vacation the amount I translate per week can surely be doubled. If you can approve one or the other, I'll be pleased to leave further arrangement of the case to you. Naturally I should eventually wish to receive a part of the manuscript as soon as possible.

Allow me in return to present you with a request. Perhaps you are acquainted with the *Presbyterian Review*. Last autumn the publication ceased to exist because among the publishers a fundamental difference of opinion had arisen concerning the manner in which the journal ought to be edited. The differences related—just how closely I don't know—to the present revision movement in the Presbyterian Church. At present a new review association has been started by the conservative school, still mostly Reformed. This association publishes a quarterly journal under the title *Presbyterian and Reformed Review*. The January issue came out last week. The editor-in-chief of this new journal, Professor Benjamin B. Warfield from Princeton, N.J., wrote me some time ago that he would like to receive an article written by you about one of these two topics: "Recent Theological Thought in Holland" or "Recent Dogmatic Works in Holland." He asked me to inform you of this wish and to support his request to you. The topic should run to about 10,000 or 15,000 words. The honorarium is $2.00 a printed page.

Therefore I bring this request to you. I would be very glad if you could comply with it. Perhaps it would be useful to make your name known here in wider circles, and consequently prepare for the English edition of your *Encyclopedia*. Only a few know the circumstances in the Netherlands, and yet, in my opinion, the development of things there seem to have meaning for America. The Reformed church in this country is in a crucial stage. The issue is whether she will officially remove the Calvinistic doctrine of election from the symbols of Westminster and replace them with Arminian formulas. It is true, there is a side which puts up resistance against that, but I am afraid that side is in the minority and only time will tell how deeply it is rooted in the Reformed faith.

At any rate, it is a good sign that an organ has been found to stand up for these principles.

If it is at all possible, esteemed brother, write an article. It will be a pleasure for me to translate it for you into English. Would it be possible to publish it in the July issue? The publisher and I also would be pleased with a quick and affirmative answer.

I was moved by what you wrote about your wish to see me yet one day labor beside you. I would consider it an honor, but it seems as if I will have to labor here. Fortunately there are people here who live in the Reformed truth and who have brought love for the Reformed truth from the old country. Your name, too, is held in great esteem here.

May the Lord preserve you for his church.

                Your brother in Christ,
                Geerhardus Vos

---
* This letter has been translated from the original Dutch.

To Herman Bavinck

March 4, 1890
48 Spring Street
Grand Rapids, Michigan

Dear and Respected Brother,

It is with pleasure to see from your letter, that you will honor my request for a friendly service. I hasten to share with you the further information which you desire, which will have to do for the present with the promise to write more in detail in connection with what you have touched on as soon as time allows.

Don't worry that by exercising discretion in this matter you would lose my confidence. Still, if you prefer, I'll mention a certain amount, above which I would not want to go at the moment. Let us say, a yearly amount of 75 guilders.

From afar it will be very difficult for me to keep track of the theological alliances and shiftings. My intention therefore was not to give you an overview of the historical development, but only to discuss the most important works being published as such. I feel it is impossible to separate both points of view, but will try to limit myself to the latter. What is of ephemeral nature, brochures, etc. is less helpful to me. For the rest, you can certainly judge if such a writing, besides its usefulness for review in the *Review*, would be of value for me. If any money is left from the above mentioned amount minus the price of the more durable literature, you are given free rein in how to spend it.

I read all three, *De Heraut*,[1] *Bazuin*, and *Vrije Kerk*, as well as the *Theologisch Tijdschrift*. Would you advise me to read the *Theologische Studien*[2] in addition to or in the place of the *Theologisch Tijdschrift*?

I have both parts of the first volume (Hextaeuch and the rest of the Historical Books of the Old Testament) of the new edition of Kuenen's H. K. O.[3] I don't have the second volume yet and so your bookseller could start by sending it to me. Also I was happy to receive the book of Gooszen[4] about the Heidelberg Catechism.

At this time, I have not yet heard if the liberal school in the Presbyterian churches has published a new *Review*. Briggs[5] and Schaff[6] have been announced as contributors for the *Andover Review*.[7] I'll send you the 1890 issue of the latter. You can judge yourself what its usefulness is to you. I'm glad to render you this service in return for your trouble.

The Nation[8] is less important for you at the present because this publication spends so much time on politics that the literary-scientific part is in the background.

As I wrote you before, your bookseller can remit his bill to me annually, or if so inclined every six months. It will be necessary that he send the books with a wrapper, and preferably in not too large packages, since the little ones have a greater chance to reach me free of import tax.

Thanking you for the time being for your friendly trouble and with kindest regards also from my parents, to you and yours.

Yours truly,
Your friend and brother in Christ,
G. Vos

---

* This letter has been translated from the original Dutch.
1. *De Heraut* (The Herald), Dutch weekly newspaper (1877–1945).
2. Published at Utrecht from 1883 to 1917.
3. *Historisch-critisch onderzoek naar het ontstaan en de verzameling van de boeken des Ouden Verbonds* (Leiden: P. Engels, 1887–93).
4. Maurits Albrecht Gooszen (1887–1916), *De Heidelbergsche catechismus. Textus receptus met toelichtende teksten* (Leiden: Brill, 1890).

5. Charles Augustus Briggs (1841–1913) was professor of biblical theology at Union Theological Seminary, New York, where he began teaching in 1874. He was suspended from the ministry of the Presbyterian Church, U.S.A. in 1893 for (in part) his denial of the doctrine of biblical inerrancy, especially the verbal inspiration of the Bible.

6. Philip Schaff (1819–1893) was professor of church history at the German Reformed Seminary in Mercersburg, Pennsylvania, from 1844 to 1865. From 1870 to 1893, he was professor of church history at Union Theological Seminary, New York. There is no indication that Schaff actually contributed any material to the *Review*.

7. The *Andover Review: A Religious and Theological Monthly* was published from 1884 to 1893 in Boston and New York.

8. Launched in New York in 1865, the magazine is still published.

To B. B. Warfield

April 9, 1890
Grand Rapids

Dear Brother,

I have received Kuenen's *Historisch-critisch Onderzoek*, Vol. II on the Prophets,[1] and a book of Prof. Gooszen (University of Leiden) containing the textus receptus of the Heidelberg Catechism with extensive introductions. Shall I send the latter to Professor Steffens[2] to write a notice on for the *Review* of July and keep the former myself for the same purpose? To my great surprise I have not heard from Dr. Kuyper up to this hour. I do not know what prevents him from making a reply.

Yours truly,
G. Vos

---

1. Vos's review appeared in *Presbyterian and Reformed Review* 2 (1891): 139–40.

2. Nicholas M. Steffens (1839–1912) was a professor at Western Theological Seminary, Holland, Michigan, 1884–1895 and 1903–1912. He also served as professor at the German Theological Seminary, Dubuque, Iowa (now Dubuque Theological Seminary), 1895–1898 and 1900–1903. Steffens's review appeared in *Presbyterian and Reformed Review* 3 (April 1892): 350–52.

To B. B. Warfield

June 13, 1890
Grand Rapids, Michigan

Dear Professor,

I have just received a reply from Dr. Kuyper.[1] He expresses his readiness to furnish an article for the *Review* but thinks the subjects suggested less suitable in as much as he would either have to pass by in silence two orthodox movements or speak largely about himself. He therefore would prefer a different topic. I cannot but feel the force of his objection.

I insisted that you desire the series of articles complete. If you should be looking for somebody to take over Kuyper's place, allow me to suggest the name of Dr. Herman Bavinck, Professor in the Theological Seminary of the Free Church of Holland at Kampen.[2]

Will it be possible to comply with Dr. Kuyper's wish in assigning to him a different subject?

You will receive my review on Kuenen about the beginning of July according to agreement.[3]

Very truly yours,
G. Vos

---

1. The reference is to Kuyper's article (translated by Vos), "Calvinism and Confessional Revision," *Presbyterian and Reformed Review* 2 (1891): 369–99.
2. Bavinck took the chair of systematic theology and ethics at Kampen in 1882.
3. Vos's review was not published until 1891.

To B. B. Warfield

July 2, 1890
Grand Rapids

Dear Professor,
To my great regret I was not able to send the notice of Kuenen's book on Saturday last, as had been my intention.[1] I hope that my tardiness will not cause any serious inconvenience.
Your letters to Drs. Kuyper and Bavinck have been forwarded.

Truly Yours,
Geerhardus Vos

---

1. Vos refers to his book review of Abraham Kuenen's *Historisch-critisch onderzoek naar het ontstaan en de verzameling van de boeken des Ouden Verbonds: De profetische boeken des Ouden Verbonds*, which appeared in *Presbyterian and Reformed Review* 2 (1891): 139–40.

To Abraham Kuyper

July 12, 1890
48 Spring Street
Grand Rapids, Michigan

Highly Esteemed Sir and Brother,
Professor Warfield has asked me, after examination of what you had written in your last letter, to forward you the enclosed. As you see, he gave you complete liberty in the choice of your topic. I hope we will soon have the pleasure of reading something from your hand in an American journal.

I have nothing against the agreement concerning the *Encyclopedia*, nevertheless I would like to ask if it is your intention to let the work be published in Dutch also or only in English. If the first is the case, perhaps one should consider whether it would not be easier to translate from the Dutch edition than from the written copy. In the beginning it will be difficult perhaps for me to read your writing quickly. On the other hand, the English edition would be delayed considerably if I have to wait with the translation for the publication of the Dutch one. Most probably, however, I'll have more free time within the year to devote to the translation, since I have still more work to do on my courses. So it certainly will not make very much difference in time. Do you have an exclusive English edition in mind, or do you think it would be better to start immediately? Would you be so kind as to send me a part of the copy?

It gladdens me that you sometimes mention the happenings and situations here in the *De Heraut*. As you might have read, the General Assembly of the Presbyterian Church set up a committee in her recently held session in Saratoga to draft a plan of modification that might meet as much as possible the objections which are raised against the Confession.[1] With that, the revision movement has gone through its first stage. Now they will revise, and the question is only: how far and in what spirit? The General Assembly confined the freedom of her committee by the regulation that the Calvinistic character of the confession has to stay intact. In my opinion, however, that does not matter much. It is not easy to say how strict or how broad the term "Calvinistic System" has to be taken. Some are (though themselves orthodox) broadminded enough to include Amyraldianism in it. Also the terms "spirit of the Confession" and "system of doctrine" are used so often in all kinds of ways in the last years, even at the signing of the creed, and they are interpreted and practiced so freely, that such a phrase, added as a restriction with the revision assignment, cannot inspire much confidence. In 1871, when after a separation of thirty-four years the reunion between Old School and New School occurred,[2] the following three points were removed: (1) universal or individual redemption; (2) direct or indirect imputation of Adam's guilt; (3) moral or natural impotence of fallen man. At that time they permitted a non-Reformed way of thinking to exist within the church, and what they have justified in principle they will not be able to stop in its consequences.

After all, the evil is not limited to the Presbyterian church. It has spread in almost all Reformed churches. It is present also in the Reformed Church, to which a large part of our Dutch people belong.[3] It is in the air here and before one knows it, one is affected with it. It would be very desirable if all the Dutch people of Reformed principles, were one, and could form a separate denomination. It seems to me that isolation is the only thing that can protect us against washing away with the current. Most, however, have no eye for the dangers which threaten. One does not reckon with the invisible powers that make a total reversal of the creed of the church possible before there is an official threat to the Confession. The seriousness of the situation is not realized. One thinks that there is still enough time to stem the tide, until concrete facts shed light on how the tide is starting to carry us away. Dr. Steffens, who still sees the situation in the Reformed Church the clearest, is rather isolated and has heard much opposition already. *De Roeper* is mistaken when it thinks that Freemasonry is the only point of difference between us and the Reformed Church.[4] The question at issue is much deeper. Our simple people have felt by a sort of instinct the seriousness of the trend in which the large American churches move. That it in its simplicity has referred to something tangible as Freemasonry is no wonder. I myself view this only as an index of what lies deeper, but consider it then as an extremely sad sign.

The Reformed brethren in the Presbyterian Church have good courage and face the future with confidence. May the Lord justify their faith and may he put to shame our less favorable expectations!

Receive my greetings and may God be with you.

Your brother in Christ,
Geerhardus Vos

P.S. I want to add that Dr. Bavinck has been asked to write an article for the *Review* about the course of theological development in the Netherlands. I hope he will accept.

---

* This letter has been translated from the original Dutch.
1. The General Assembly of the Presbyterian Church in the U.S.A. met at First Presbyterian Church, Saratoga Springs, New York, from May 15 to May 27, 1890. The report on revision of the Confession is found on pages 122–25 of the Minutes. The names of the members appointed to the Committee are listed on page 127.
2. The division of the Old School and the New School occurred in 1837; the reunion vote was taken at the respective general assemblies in 1869 and came into effect in 1870.
3. The Reformed Church of America was known as the Dutch Reformed Church until 1867.
4. *De Roeper*, a Dutch secessionist periodical published from 1886 to 1889, was edited by Professor Lucas Lindeboom.

To B. B. Warfield

August 5, 1890
Grand Rapids, Michigan

Dear Professor,

Dr. Bavinck has agreed to write the desired article.[1] He promised to let me have it about January 1, 1891. I shall send it to you as soon as I can have the translation ready. From Dr. Kuyper there is no reply as yet.

Yours truly,
G. Vos

---

1. Vos's translation appeared under the title "Recent Dogmatic Thought in the Netherlands," *Presbyterian and Reformed Review* 3 (1892): 209–28.

To Abraham Kuyper

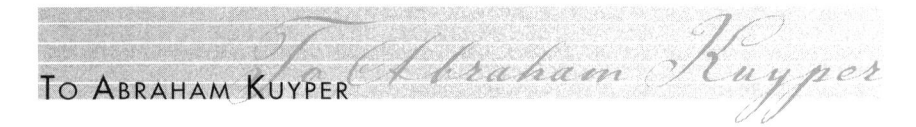

October 27, 1890
48 Spring Street
Grand Rapids, Michigan, U.S.

Highly Esteemed Sir and Brother,

Immediately after I received your article, I wrote to Professor Warfield. I was afraid that the size would present difficulty. As you will remember they had counted on about 10,000 words. However the article numbers at least 15,000. Still I hoped that the publishers of the *Review* would be able to insert it in full. I am disappointed in this expectation.

Professor Warfield writes in answer to my inquiry: "I am sorry to say it will be totally impossible for us to print so long a paper. We have to make our rules very stringent that 10,000 words (20 pages) is the maximum. Now and then this is unavoidably overstepped, but as seldom as possible. Do you think Dr. Kuyper would permit you to condense in translating it? If he would himself designate sections to be omitted; or would allow you to judge as to the portions most easily omitted without substantial loss, the paper might perhaps be reduced to the limit we can allow."

You will understand that I do not like to take the responsibility on myself to omit something, even though you would be willing to put such a great faith in me. It seems more desirable to me that you yourself indicate those parts which could be condensed or done without. If I may say something in this regard, I would like to remark that the answer on the fourth question ought to stay[1] and also that I would frown upon a change in the more theoretical and abstract part in the whole article. That which is concrete or relates indirectly to the Revision conflict here can rather be done without. Where the principles are being presented so clearly and sharply as you do here one cannot help to practice what one preaches.

I hope wholeheartedly that God may allow you to still be of service in this respect for the Reformed Church of America. The delay caused about this matter is surely somewhat of a pity. If it is possible for you to make the abridgment as needed, all may yet be well. If I have the article back by the first of December, the translation can be done by New Years. It could probably be published then in the April issue of the *Review*. I will comply with your request to send you the issue of the *Review* immediately after the publication.

Looking forward to an early reply, I remain

> Your brother and servant in Christ,
> Geerhardus Vos

---

1. Vos refers to the discussion on pages 391ff.—to what condition is the revision of the symbols, in the case of a progressive development of Calvinism, to be bound? "Calvinism and Confessional Revision," *Presbyterian and Reformed Review* 2 (July 1891): 369–99.

To B. B. Warfield

January 31, 1891
48 Spring Street
Grand Rapids, Michigan

Dear Professor,

I had communicated to Dr. Kuyper your proposal to condense his paper. He wrote back that it was absolutely impossible to condense without subtracting the entire argument. While requesting me to thank the *Review* for its offered hospitality, he further expressed his wish that I should publish the translation as best I could. Now this was a very difficult matter for me. If I translated before having secured a publisher, my labor might be lost, in the case I was not able to find one. On the other hand, I could not hope to find a publisher when not ready to show the translation. Nothing remained but to risk my time, and so I have done. I come to you now, and ask your candid advice as to how I shall act further. Of course I could perhaps have the paper printed here in pamphlet form, but then it will be buried. A great number of our Western ministers will procure a copy, and there it will stop. In order to reach the persons it was destined to at his disposal by the author, the paper ought to have an Eastern publisher, who has ample means of advertising—by Funk and Wagnalls for instance. But even then it could not reach all those it will reach when printed in the *Review*. Is it altogether impossible to have it appear in the *Review*? Do you think that the publication of it in two successive numbers would be a way out of the difficulty? I should be very much obliged to you for the sake of Dr. Kuyper if you still could so arrange it in some manner or other.

If it should be altogether impossible, could you make an effort for me to find a publisher in the East? Or would there be some other periodical perhaps that would take it? I think that Dr. Kuyper will not object to do without all honorarium, and I myself shall gladly contribute the trouble of translating his work without receiving the usual fee.

Enclosed I send the translation. Hoping you will receive it in good order, and favor me with a reply at your earliest convenience, I remain

Yours in Christ,
G. Vos

I have not yet received Dr. Bavinck's paper, but think it will come soon.[1]

---

1. "Recent Dogmatic Thought in the Netherlands," *Presbyterian and Reformed Review* 3 (1892): 209–28.

To B. B. Warfield

February 12, 1891
48 Spring Street
Grand Rapids, Michigan

Dear Professor,

I leave the matter entirely to you, and hope you will be successful in your efforts to secure a place for the paper. Of course I would prefer to see it printed in one piece, but if this should be absolutely impossible, we will have to take it in two installments. I forgot to send the title along. This is "Calvinism and Revision." If you notice any un-English expressions or constructions, please do me the favor of correcting them. I had my doubts about several things and, on the whole, found it hard work to anglicize the style.

Is Dr. Kuyper correct in representing his theory as the proper Calvinistic view of infant baptism? Did the older theologians really mean that baptism in each case presupposes regeneration as an accomplished fact? I have never been able to make up my mind on this point, and still feel the necessity of having a more or less decided opinion in my teaching. There are many among us who hold to a much laxer theory and make baptism little more than a symbolic offer of the covenant on God's side, a presentation of the gospel instead of a seal of the gospel promise. It seems to me that Dr. Kuyper approaches more or less to the Lutheran view of baptismal grace, though of course with the necessary restrictions. I shall be very much obliged, if in a few words, you can let me know your opinion.

I have some books recently published in Holland which I hope to review, as soon as my time will permit. My regular work is so manifold that I can only snatch a few spare moments. I am glad that there is no haste about Dr. Bavinck's paper.

Truly yours,
G. Vos

To Abraham Kuyper

February 21, 1891
Grand Rapids, Michigan

Dear and Highly Esteemed Brother,

You certainly have wondered why you did not receive a notice concerning the condition of your article. The reason was that until now I could not find out anything specific with respect to that. Lack of time caused the translation to make slow progress. When it was finished, I could not come to a decision immediately how and where to have it printed. If it appears here in the west it sort of gets buried. Our Dutch ministers who understand English will read it, but that is where it remains. To find a publisher in the east who can advertise it in large areas is not an easy task. I arrived at the conclusion that the readers who must be reached before all the others, can be reached only by the *Review*, for which the article originally was written. Therefore I still wanted to make a last attempt to prevail upon them to insert it. I have sent it to Professor Warfield with an urgent request to grant it a place as soon as possible. He has answered me that he was greatly pleased with the contents of your article and would use all his influence as *one of the publishers* of the *Review* to get it put in the coming July issue *if possible entirely*. If this is not refused absolutely by the other editors, it will happen. Now I trust that Professor Warfield will do his best to get you an audience with the American Reformed people, and I hope that the Lord exerts an influence with your good words. I cannot have a definite ruling before April 1. Professor Warfield wrote that if the insertion as a whole in the July issue proved to be impossible, he would still try to print the first half then and the second half in October.

So this is the result of my first effort. If it does not succeed, then I will try to comply with your wish in another way by first looking for a publisher in the east. If that cannot be done either, then I will try it here. But I have confidence that that shall be unnecessary.

I notice from *De Heraut* that you have noted the polemic which is pursued here against your baptismal view and supralapsarianism.[1] The motive for that is that I myself have had the audacity to lean to that side in my teaching. Still the supralapsarianism is not that which they focused on. It is thought only that this is confessionally the weakest point. The stumbling blocks are the covenant view and baptismal view, which reckon with election, and are dominated by the Calvinistic principle. They will likely adhere to election, but only as something separate that may not influence and have a lasting effect on any other field. I cannot help but think that this leads to an un-Reformed covenant theory. The covenant is employed to render election harmless.

It is difficult to foresee what results this action will have. In our little church there is very little theological development. If the people are persuaded once for all that supralapsarianism is condemned by Dordt[2] and that the disputed covenant and baptismal view is committed to supralapsarianism, then anything can be expected. But God still rules.

May I take the liberty to ask you some questions in connection with this controversial issue? I hope a short response will not take too much of your time. My questions are: (1) Is it correct that Dordt has considered the difference between infra- and supralapsarianism as more or less a controversial issue? Is it on account of this that Gomarus[3] and others have signed the canons? Can one say in good conscience as a supralapsarian: I agree to all that Dordt says, but maintain that there is still something to the other view? (2) Is the peculiarity of supralapsarianism to seek therein that the conclusion to admission of the fall was in order subordinate to that of predestination? And if that is right are there not many infralapsarians, who, by teaching at least the partial subordination, in principle have switched over on supralapsarian ground? In that sense is not the Leiden Synopsis XXIV, 23[4] already supralapsarian? (3) Is there historical proof, beyond the claims of the Remonstrants,[5] that at the Synod of Dordt there were more supralapsarians beside Gomarus? I think Schweizer[6] says somewhere: "Many delegates were from Gelderland[7] and South Holland": was Bogermann[8] supralapsarian? And Festus Hommius,[9] Lydius,[10] Voetius[11] at that time? (4) Can it be proved that Calvin[12] also has expressed himself definitely as a supralapsarian, though the issue itself was not yet strongly formulated? (5) Is not Romans 9:19–23 supralapsarian? From the explanation that the parables contain things hidden from the foundation of the world, does it draw a conclusion for supralapsarianism? (6) Is it true that Professor Maccovius[13] at Dordt was also accused of his supralapsarianism and acquitted there? (7) Is it possible for you to tell me the numbers of the issues of *De Heraut* in which previously this issue dogmatically and historically (against Mr. De Cock[14])is discussed by you?

I am afraid that I cause you much trouble. But it is so difficult here to get access to the sources. If that were not so, then I should be ashamed to ask something from you that I can do myself.

I would still like to congratulate you kindly both with the promotion and the marriage of your son, Dr. H. H. Kuyper.[15] Kindly convey my congratulations also to your wife.[16] May the Lord allow you to behold his goodness and his church for many years. I'll note his thesis[17] with interest as soon as it is possible for me.

If I receive the *Review* in which your article is published, I will send you the issue immediately.

With good wishes and greetings.

                Your servant and brother in Christ,
                Geerhardus Vos

---

* This letter has been translated from the original Dutch.

1. Vos may be referring to a series published in the magazine between August 24, 1890, and June 28, 1891. See especially February 1, 1891, p. 3. The series was gathered in 1891 under the title *Voor een distel een mirt. Geestelijke ove rdenkingen bij den heiligen doop, het doen van belijdenis en het toe gaan tot het heilig avondmaal* (Amsterdam: J. A. Wormser, 1891).

2. The Synod of Dordt (Dort) or Dordrecht (1618–19) is famous for the five anti-Remonstrant canons of doctrine now known as the Five Points of Calvinism.

3. Francis Gomar (1563–1614) was a leading supralapsarian.

4. The text reads: "Meanwhile we confess that man was neither created for an uncertain end, nor that the fall of man occurred without the special providence of God, for if not even a sparrow falls to the ground without our heavenly Father, much less the whole human race; rather God first determined to show what free will would be in man, but then what the benefit of his grace would be. Therefore by the infinite splendor of his knowledge, God foreseeing that man with all his posterity would abuse his image established by free will, by which a more evident way would be opened to his wonderful mercy and justice, he rather deemed to extend his most omnipotent kindness, to do good concerning evil, rather than not to permit evil to exist, as Augustine rightly teaches." *Synopsis purioris theologiae* (1881), 226–27.

5. So-called because of the Remonstrance of 1610 presented to the Estates of Holland, specifying five points of anti-Calvinistic doctrine. The dispute eventually led to the Synod of Dort and the so-called Five Points of Calvinism against the Remonstrants.

6. Alexander Schweizer (1808–88), *Die Glaubenslehre der evangelisch-reformierten Kirche* (Zurich: Orell, Füssli und Comp., 1844–47).

7. A province of east-central Netherlands.

8. Jan Bogermann (1576–1637), president of the Synod of Dort.

9. Festus Hommius (1576–1642).

10. Balthasar Lydius (ca. 1577–1629), present at the Synod of Dort.

11. Gisbert Voetius (1588/89–1676).

12. John Calvin (1509–1564).

13. John Maccovius (1588–1644).

14. Helenius de Cock (1824–1894) was professor of dogmatics at Kampen from 1854 to 1882. He preceded Bavinck in that chair.

15. Herman Huber Kuyper (1864–1945) married Cornelia Maria Joanna Heyblom (1861–1939) on January 20, 1891.

16. Abraham Kuyper married Joanna Henricka Schaay on July 1, 1863. She died tragically in Switzerland on August 25, 1899.

17. *De opleiding tot den dienst des woords bij de Gereformeerden* ('s-Gravenhage: M. Nijhoff, 1891).

To B. B. Warfield

March 12, 1891
48 Spring Street
Grand Rapids

Dear Professor,

After I had informed Dr. Kuyper that his paper was too large for publication in the *Review*, he requested me to publish it as best I could *without imposing any financial restrictions.* From this I infer that Dr. Kuyper would not object to your arrangement with the publisher. I have no explicit directions to the same, but think you are safe in giving the article to the printer. As for myself, I am entirely satisfied with your proposal.

I am very much obliged to you for the sending of your notes on Regeneration and Conversion which I have read with a great deal of interest. Receive my thanks also for the statement of your opinion on infant-baptism. I have secured a copy of Witsius's *Miscellaneorum Sacrorum*[1] for perusal and hope to reach a more definite view. It seems to me that the subject is beset with great difficulties on every side. The Rev. Hulst,[2] to whose remarks against Dr. Kuyper you made reference in your letter, and many others among us, work to cut the doctrine of election love from the covenant. They wish to give baptism a significance altogether independent of the presumption of election. I have never been able to agree with this view. A statement, it seems to me, is more than a symbolic offer of the gospel, combined with the duty of acceptance.

Have you read the articles of Dr. Kuyper on the subject of infant-baptism in *De Heraut*?[3] There he gives quite a lengthy discussion of the matter. If you have not read them, and have time to go over these articles, I should be glad to send you these numbers of *De Heraut* and have your opinion on some of the points involved.

It seems to me that the position taken by Charles Hodge in his *Theology*[4] inclines somewhat to the laxer view of a covenant with obligation to accept, and lays less stress on the unconditional promise and the presumption arising therefrom.

If you will allow me, I shall state my difficulties more fully later on. In the meanwhile, I am with sincere gratitude

Yours truly,
G. Vos

---

1. Herman Witsius, "De efficacia et utilitate baptismi in electis foederatorum infantibus," in *Miscellaneorum sacrorum libri IV* (Leiden: Conradum Meyerum, 1736), 2:480–524.

2. Lammert J. Hulst (1825–1922), editor of *De Wachter* for several years.

3. The editor cannot locate these.
4. Charles Hodge's remarks on baptism are found in his *Systematic Theology* (reprint, Grand Rapids: Wm. B. Eerdmans, 1965), 3:526–611.

To Herman Bavinck

May 13, 1891
Grand Rapids,

Dear and Highly Esteemed Brother,

Your article for the *Presbyterian and Reformed Review* has arrived safely. I shall do my best to translate it into decent American language. I cannot say with certainty when it will be published. Dr. Kuyper had sent a large paper about "Calvinism and Revision."[1] In order that this could be published in the forthcoming issue (July), other pieces had to be omitted. These omitted articles will be next, so that perhaps more than one issue will appear before your contribution is published. In any case, I will finish the translation as soon as possible and send it to Professor Warfield.

For a long time already I had planned to write you in connection with different aspects of my studies. I have to do much and produce much on which I cannot bestow much care and of which therefore it is hard to pass an independent judgment. In these circumstances I feel a great need for the exchange of views with persons with more study and experience. Allow me to write about certain things which perhaps are not interesting to you, and in which you can serve me with advice and information.

My principle difficulty lies in the doctrine of the covenant of grace. The dualistic belief is prevalent among many here which places covenant and election next to each other without inner connection. The covenant becomes a *strengthened* gospel offer and election comes almost last as a second Amyraldian conclusion. Certainly this observation is known to you, so that I do not have to go into more details. As I suppose this theory also has its supporters in the Netherlands, my objection is not so much against the element of truth which lies therein, but against the one-sided presentation of this line of thought as the one and only Reformed view. When speaking about the covenant, people are embarrassed to take the word election on their lips. Actually, I fear that there is here an unconscious effort to brush aside the principle of the sovereign grace of God, that still is so plain to see in the covenant. This whole idea as developed among others in the writings of Pieters[2] and Kreulen[3] is offensive to me. However there are many here who recommend it as specifically Reformed and everyone who does not agree is suspected of narrow-mindedness, or worse of being under the influence of *philosophy*.

I always thought that the issue was as follows: the connection between covenant and election rests on this, that God in the offer of sanctifying grace generally follows the line of descent. That therefore being in the covenant still means more than living under an extraordinary solemn gospel offer or to carrying within one's self a covenant offer. That this greater value exists is the presumption that one finds oneself within the circle or on the line of election, a presumption which rests on God's promise, the God of *you and your seed*. That therefore adults, not born within the covenant, are admitted only on a reliable confession of saving faith. In the meantime, I do not want anyone to *Labadistically*[4] set himself up as a judge over someone's (spiritual) state. I object to falsely leading someone to believe that historical faith only can make *him right* in the presence of God in the covenant.

Furthermore I thought that the sacraments not only seal the offer of the covenant from God's side, but make the covenant a *closed covenant*. That the content of the sealing is: *in the presupposition* that you are a true covenant child, the right of all the covenant blessings is sealed to you. I would distinguish between *"on the condition that"* and *"in the supposition that."* The first sounds totally general and applicable anywhere. In this way, anywhere on the mission field the sacraments could accompany the external calling. The other, however, requires a well-founded presumption that one is talking about covenant children.

Applying this to the children of believers, I would say: they receive baptism because there is the presumption that when they grow up they will appear to be true believers, since God has given his sure and certain promises to believers *also for their seed*. Also with the children it is therefore a closed covenant.

Now if a baptized person contradicts this expectation as he grows up, I would not therefore claim that he had nothing to do with the covenant. Certainly I will agree that his responsibility has become greater and that he will be treated and punished by God as a covenant breaker, therefore insofar as he has been in the covenant. But I have objections against the following: (a) that when the belief of the covenant is weakened and stripped because of this type of case in practice, the most beautiful and most comforting of the Reformed view is lost in its application to life. (b) That when the emphasis of the covenant is sought solely in the [?] of the covenant duties and demands of the children, I fear that this has deadly consequences. (c) That the grace of regeneration is left outside the horizon of the covenant and the covenant is made into a formula for the conscious relation between God and men only.

According to me baptism has to be viewed more pertinently, as including a positive promise that God from the seed of the faithful will beget a seed. Certainly I feel the difficulty that this cannot be easily individualized, and that on the other side the sacrament has to maintain an individual side.

Only in this way am I able to find a logical ground for the thesis that children of believers dying in infancy will be saved. With the other view, which for convenience sake I name that of *Pieters* and *Kreulen*, such a basis is totally lacking as far as I can judge.

It is very well possible that I misjudge these things. So far as I could consult the *old writers*, they all teach this way up to Dordt. For the other view, I find very little support. Or is also this historical judgment wrong?

With great interest, I have followed the discussion of the doctrine of the sacraments by Dr. Kuyper in *De Heraut*. It occurs to me that there are two elements in his observations: one in which he is only repeating and one in which he provides something peculiar and new. With the first, I mean his thesis that baptized children must be presumed to be already regenerated. That is found by many *old writers*, is it not? It seems to me that Dr. Kuyper goes too far when he recommends this as *the accepted doctrine* of the fathers. Were the fathers in fact so united on that point? Good for the fathers, if that was the case! But I cannot believe it. I really wished that he could summon those fathers of Dordt.

The second and new aspect in Dr. Kuyper's baptismal observation is his doctrine of the specific baptismal grace. I object to that. He so stresses it that one can hardly say no to this point of view. Scripture and sacrament bring the same grace. Still I believe that exegetically there is much to say for expounding his view. Doesn't Paul in fact ascribe such a meaning to baptism for the mystical union with Christ?

I thought that with the Reformed, the working of baptism as a means of grace was always in close connection with its working as a seal for the religious life. Dr. Kuyper separates seal and means of grace very strongly. And then his thesis of a spiritual life that can slumber for a long time seems also a little unnatural to me.

Is there a connection in Dr. Kuyper's view between his doctrine of the specific baptismal grace and his supposition that the children are already regenerated? Sometimes it seems to me as if the latter is a consequence to which the former has driven him.

How is it with our baptismal form? Does this, in fact, rest on the position, as Witsius and others claim, that the blessing of baptism is imparted to the children also? I have to admit that the expressions which are found there sound very crass to me and I always feel a protest come up in me against the strange explanations because of which they try to emphatically remove that extreme view, as for instance the sanctified *in Christ*. Do we not find the presumption of election in this? But if I see then how everyone who has a peculiar baptismal view inserts it into the formulary, then I start to despair of a solution of the problem with the help of the Confessions.

Write me what you think on this matter, and what your position is in it.

Yet another question: is it feasible to disengage the covenant of grace and the church from each other as for instance Ten Hoor[5] and my uncle (Rev.) Beuker[6] want to do? Does not the visible church, however pure or impure, have to be present everywhere the covenant of grace is? Is not this distinction one of the aids through which they seek to reconcile the catholic covenant of grace with a sectarian view of the church?

You see I am not being stingy with my questions. If I could talk with you more often, I would not come up with so many questions at once. I hope that it will not burden you too much to answer me. By that I will be obliged to you with much thankfulness.

I too have had my doubts concerning the manner in which the Reformed movement is returning to the absolute inerrancy of Scripture. But every time I have to come back with the conviction that there is no other point of view for a Reformed person. And not even in general. If I had to let go of Scripture, I fear I would be reduced to theological scepticism. For someone who loves to study slowly and calmly there is great fascination in scepticism.

Receive my best wishes for your coming wedding.

I have the dissertation of Dr. H. H. Kuyper.[7] Be so kind as to send me the above mentioned work of Dr. Kuyper.

Forgive me for this time. The kindest regards from my parents and myself to your [family].

> Your brother,
> G. Vos
> 48 Spring Street

P.S. I hope to take care of the correction of your article.

---

* This letter has been translated from the original Dutch.

1. *Presbyterian and Reformed Review* 2 (1891): 369–99.

2. K. J. Pieters (1821–79) was pastor of Franeker Christian Reformed Church (Seceder) from 1851 to 1874, when he was deposed. With J. R. Kreulen, he coauthored *De kinderdoop volgens*

de begins elen der Gereformeerde Kerk, in hare gonden, toediening en praktijk op nieuw onderzocht, beoordeeld en van vele schijnbare zwarigheden ontheven (Franeker: Telenga, 1861). Pieters also published *Het baptisme bij het licht der H. Schrift en der geschiedenis beoordeeld en in 't licht gesteld* (Franeker: Telenga, 1866).

3. J. R. Kreulen (1820–1904) was pastor of Christian Reformed churches at Workum (1843), Spijk (1846), Wildervank (1849), Hallum (1853), Utrecht (1868), Giessendam (1872), Leek (1874), and Suawoude (1882).

4. Jean de Labadie (1610–74) was a Jesuit who converted to the Reformed Church at Montauban, France. He moved to Middelburg in Holland (1666) and became the leader of an extreme Pietist group.

5. Foppe Martin Ten Hoor (1855–1934).
6. Hendericus Beuker.
7. See p. 151 n. 17, above.

To Herman Bavinck

June 30, 1891
Grand Rapids, Michigan

Dear Friend and Brother,

Before anything else I want to congratulate you with your wedding[1] which will be celebrated the day after tomorrow. Receive for yourself and for your wife all the blessings of my heart that God can bestow on you.

Thanks for the immediate response to the questions which I asked in my last letter. I am glad to hear how you think about these matters. Also about the impossibility of bringing them to a solution, I agree with what you wrote. But it is of no use here to have such an irenic attitude. More and more I come to understand that a lack of historical sense and historical denial can lead to dangerous things. Those who have thrown this matter of discord into our small church are as absolutistic as possible. There is only one Reformed opinion and that is theirs. They push the matter through and seem to have in mind that our church will put an end to the issue.

In this matter, my position is not pleasant. I am not a fanatic, and will gladly concede as much as I can, but here I surely cannot. As I wrote you, I cannot agree with Dr. Kuyper in everything. But it seems to me that he is criticized for the good Reformed views in his presentation and his new idea of the law is overlooked in which he deviates from the Reformed types.

I will honestly answer your question concerning the vacancy of Noordtzij.[2] I am well acquainted with the civic and social life in America. I cannot say that of the ecclesiastical and religious life. Lately, I have more and more come to the conclusion that in the long run I do not want to stay in my present position. Then the question arises: what then? More than once I have been approached concerning how I feel about accepting a chair in a seminary of the Presbyterian Church. Lately I like the idea more than before. However there is much in those churches that I am uncomfortable with. Looking at the matter from a *theological* point of view, I would say: I would rather work in the Christian Reformed Church than in a Presbyterian church here. There are two more considerations: (1) my parents are here; (2) there is a certain charm in the American life from which it is hard to withdraw after first having been under the influence of it. It is impossible for me to say to which side the scale would turn, if I had to make a decision. But you did not ask me for that. Your question was: if I would decline *a priori* a possible call. To this I have to answer: No.

For the rest I recommend this matter prayerfully to the Lord.

We were told that we would have the pleasure of seeing you here this summer. I understand however that you have to stay in the Netherlands on account of the coming Synod.

Greetings to your parents from mine and be all kindly greeted by your friend and brother

G. Vos
48 Spring Street

---

* This letter has been translated from the original Dutch.
1. The marriage of Herman Bavinck and Johanna Adriana Shippers occurred on July 2, 1891.

2. Maarten Noordtzij (1840–1915) became professor of Old Testament at Kampen in 1875. He was faced with a choice: accept appointment as a member of Parliament or continue in the chair of Old Testament. He chose to remain at Kampen.

To B. B. Warfield

July 7, 1891
Grand Rapids, Michigan

Dear Professor,
Perhaps you have taken some account of the attack made in *De Wachter*[1] on the conception of an eternal covenant of grace. During my first year's teaching here, I had made a rough sketch of the doctrine of the covenants, and, following the Westminster Catechism, Mastricht,[2] I had viewed the matter under the aspect first mentioned. In doing so I was not conscious of any *material* difference between my view and the more common one which speaks of a covenant of redemption as eternal as a covenant of grace in time, founded on the former (Hodge II, 357[3]). At any rate I thought the doctrine of an eternal covenant between the persons of the Trinity to be beyond all suspicion of heterodoxy. Now, as you will have observed, the idea of an eternal covenant of grace is objected to on grounds which leave no room for a covenant of redemption either, which with equal force will bear against the covenant of works, and which substitutes for the common conception a radically different one. As I understand it, the form of the covenant of grace is sought by the critics in the conditional offer of the gospel: "*If* you believe, etc." Then the sacraments are made to seal this conditional offer. In consequence the covenant is represented as being of much wider extent than election, not only in its human administration (for *that* everybody admits) *but by its very nature* as a mutual contract dependent on the fidelity of both God and man. Taking this view of the matter, they must of course object to every repre-

sentation whereby the close connection between election and the covenant is emphasized. It seems to me therefore that the attack is not so much directed against the *eternal covenant as such*, but rather against the covenant *as presumably coextensive with election*.

My objections to the scheme just stated are as follows:

1.) It would extend the covenant to all whom the eternal call of the gospel reaches. But external vocation and the covenant are not coextensive. The former is merely an offer of the latter. Even to offer with the obligation to accept does not yet constitute the acceptance.

2.) It would entail the necessity of administering the sacraments indiscriminately wherever the gospel is brought. This again is unscriptural and un-Calvinistic. The sacraments presuppose the acceptance of the covenant by faith, either as already existing in the present, or as confidently to be expected in the future (in the case of infants of believers).

3.) This deprives the sacraments of all value and significance. The "*if*" paralyses the "*that*" of God's promises. So far as I can see the Reformed Confessions and Liturgies do not speak of anything to be performed on man's part as an antecedent condition, but only of a duty proceeding from the grace of God previously given.

4.) It takes away the basis of our belief in the salvation of children of believers dying in infancy. If only a conditional offer be sealed to them, there is no valid inference that the same has been accepted and hence they are saved.

5.) It confounds the covenant of works and the covenant of grace. The former *was* dependent on both God *and man*, whereas the latter is of such a nature that God in Christ vouches for man's part also.

For myself I would not insist upon making the covenant of grace eternal *as long as only the form of my statement is objected to*. I believe that the scheme of an eternal covenant is more systematic and find not a little to support it in Scripture. But in order to show that I did not intend anything new or uncommon, I have of late returned to the other way of assuming two covenants. I fear however that this will not satisfy those critics whose idea of the covenant *materially* differs from mine.

Unfortunately I happen to be a supralapsarian in the matter of predestination, though in a very moderate sense, and not so much on logical grounds as for exegetical reasons (Romans 9; Ephesians 1, 3). In some way the idea has been started that the doctrine of an eternal covenant and supralapsarianism are inseparable. I have never been able to discover an *objective nexus causalis*[4] between the two. There may be some affinity however between the subjective tendencies that underly both views.

It occurred to me that it would be a useful thing to describe the historical development of the covenant idea in Reformed theology, and to show how intimately it has been connected from the outset with the practical side of the dogma of predestination. If this could be done, there would be no longer any dispute about the historical right to make Christ the head of the covenant. I have resolved to make an attempt in this direction. In order to succeed, I shall have to familiarize myself with the contributions made by English theologians to the doctrine of the covenants before the time of the Westminster Assembly. Am I right in surmising that the idea of an eternal covenant is specifically English in its origin? Could you oblige me by mentioning the authors in which it successively appeared up to the date of the Westminster Catechisms? I have written to Rev. Dulles for the use of some books from the library.[5] If he should grant my request and you could mention the titles of the English books to him, it would be possible to send them along with the others.

I make use of this opportunity to add a few remarks about Dr. Kuyper's theory of the sacrament, which by this time you will have fully learned from *De Heraut*. My doubts do not relate so much to his view that the child offered for baptism must be *presumed* to belong to the number of the elect. It has become more and more clear to me that this really is universal Calvinism as you stated in a previous letter. But I cannot agree with the Professor on two other points:

1.) That all infants to be baptized must be presumed to be *regenerate*. This is found to be the view of some of the *older* but not nearly of *all* Calvinists. Dr. Kuyper lays it down as *the* Calvinistic view. Not a few (Heidegger[6]) argue that God's ordinary way of regenerating his elect is under the hearing of the word, and that those of the children of believers destined to grow up and to hear the word are not as a rule regenerated until then (Heppe, *Die Dogmatik der evangelisch-reformirten Kirche*, p. 453[7]). Dr. Kuyper wishes to have us consider *and treat* all baptized children as regenerate. This tenet is far-reaching in its practical effects and I feel a great hesitancy about adopting it.

2.) That the sacraments convey a specific sacramental grace not conveyed by the word. Dr. Kuyper says there is grace of the root, grace of the branches, grace of the fruit, but sacramental grace belongs to none of these. It is a thing altogether by itself. Its specific character consists in its effect upon faith. Faith at the beginning has an individual nature, but by this sacramental grace it receives a social character as it qualifies for being the instrument of the communion of saints in the mystical body of Christ. Thus baptism is not the means of the first ingrafting into Christ, but still the means of effecting a closer union with the body of Christ. So at least I understand Dr. Kuyper. He is very positive but not very lucid on this point. But supposing my interpretation of his view to be correct, I would ask: is it consistent with the Reformed principle that the grace offered by the word and the sacraments is specifically the same? Do not all the Reformed theologians agree in this, that the sacraments are *means of grace because and in so far as they are seals*? Dr. Kuyper separates these two things. The sealing efficacy of the sacraments and their mystical operation as means of grace are with him distinct. This seems to approach the Lutheran view. To be sure there is an immense difference between Dr. Kuyper's theory of baptism and the Lutheran doctrine for: (a) according to the Lutheran, baptism is the instrument of regeneration, according to Dr. Kuyper it is the instrument of a grace following regeneration; (b) according to the Lutherans, this grace is communicated to *all* baptized children, whereas, Dr. Kuyper limits it to the elect; (c) according to the Lutherans, it works through the water in the word, according to Dr. Kuyper by an immediate act of the Holy Spirit operating within. Notwithstanding these points of difference however, there is agreement in the assumption of a specific sacramental grace.

I have written more already than I intended. In conclusion, I will say that I am very anxious to have your opinion on these matters. Notwithstanding all trouble and friction, I hope that in this way new and clearer light may be shed on several points.

Yours very truly,
G. Vos
48 Spring Street

---

1. *De Wachter*, Dutch newspaper published from 1877 to 1945.
2. Peter van Mastricht (1630–1706); see "De sacramentis regenerationis," in *Theoretico-practica theologia* (Utrecht, 1699), 815–28.
3. Charles Hodge, *Systematic Theology* (reprint, Grand Rapids: Wm. B. Eerdmans, 1965), 2:357.
4. I.e., "causal connection."
5. Joseph Heatly Dulles (1853–1937) was librarian at Princeton Theological Seminary from 1886 to 1931.
6. Johann Heinrich Heidegger (1633–98).
7. See Heinrich Heppe, *Reformed Dogmatics Set Out and Illustrated from the Sources*, trans. G. T. Thomson (Grand Rapids: Baker, 1978), 622–23.

To Abraham Kuyper

July 30, 1891
48 Spring Street
Grand Rapids, Michigan

Dear and Highly Esteemed brother,

Together with this letter, I am sending you the July issue of the *Presbyterian and Reformed Review*. You will notice that I finally succeeded in getting the piece published in its entirety in this issue.[1] It seemed very undesirable to me to split it in two. I was afraid that the intensity of your argument would be broken by doing so. I am very sorry that to achieve my goal I had to place the financial part in the background. Through Professor Warfield, the publishers let me know that if your article would be published in its entirety, sixteen pages would have to be added to that general issue. The costs of that amounted to $64.00, a little more than your fee and my translation fee together. If I would decide to hand over the article without fee and to take nothing for my translation, they would proceed with the insertion. I have agreed to this. At any cost, I must bring your article to readers of the *Review*. I am not totally convinced of the fairness of this offer, especially towards you, but because of the cause, I thought it better not to force this point. Now I only hope that I have not abused the freedom which you had given me in this case. I hope this case will not restrain you from letting your voice be heard among us again soon.

Professor Warfield has done all that was in his power to insert your article in its entirety. Repeatedly he has expressed to me his high sympathy with what you wrote.

As you will see some little changes were made in your article, which became necessary by the translation. On the whole I set myself to reflect your thoughts as accurately as possible. It was pleasant work to me. I hope now that the outward appearance will not be completely unworthy.

I have noted a few misprints, which I still noticed in the Dutch proof, on the enclosed leaflet.

Without doubt you have taken note of the report submitted by the committee concerning the Revision at the most recent General Assembly of the Presbyterian Church. The changes were not as big as I had feared but are still very radical. This report goes now to the presbyteries for review. I sent you a copy of the *Independent* in which it is inserted in full.[2]

Through the movement against Professor Briggs,[3] the Revision case has fallen temporarily somewhat into the background.

Friendly thanks for your explanation about supralapsarianism. Also be so kind as to express my thanks to Professor Geesink[4] for the drawing up of his instructive memorial. I have decided not to concern myself with a crusade about this point. The polemic of the other side is still going on. They are so ignorant of what historical Reformed is, that all things are possible.

To my joy Professor Steffens[5] stays in his field of activity in Holland. As soon as possible, I hope to send you a few separate copies of your article—which I had asked for, but which I have not yet received.

Greetings and good wishes,
Your brother,
Geerhardus Vos

---

* This letter has been translated from the original Dutch.
1. "Calvinism and Confessional Revision," *Presbyterian and Reformed Review* 2 (1891): 369–99.
2. *The Independent* was a religious weekly published from 1848 to 1928. Henry Ward Beecher was the editor from 1861 to 1863. The report on confessional revision was printed in vol. 43, no. 2217 (May 28, 1891): 16–18. Cf. *Minutes of the General Assembly of the PCUSA* (1891), 22–34.
3. Charles Augustus Briggs (1841–1913) delivered his inaugural address as professor of biblical theology at Union Theological Seminary, New York, on January 20, 1891. Entitled "The Authority of Holy Scripture," the address unleashed a firestorm of overtures from sixty-three presbyteries of the PCUSA, demanding action against Dr. Briggs. By a vote of 449 to 60, Briggs was refused confirmation as professor of biblical theology. Cf. *Minutes of the General Assembly of the PCUSA* (1891), 94–105.
4. Gerhard Herman Johannes Wilhelm Jacobus Geesink (1855–1929) was a professor at the Free University of Amsterdam from 1890 onward.
5. Nicolas M. Steffens.

To B. B. Warfield

August 29, 1891
Grand Rapids, Michigan

Dear Professor,

Many thanks for your instructive report on the contents of *De Heraut*. The papers have arrived in good order. I am also much obliged for your letter of some weeks ago on the covenants. About my study in this direction I hope to write you later on. Our school opens next week already and I am busy with preparations. The numbers of the *Review* you sent for transmission have been forwarded to Dr. Kuyper.[1]

        Yours very truly,
        G. Vos

---
1. Vos refers to the July 1891 issue of the *Presbyterian and Reformed Review*.

TO B. B. WARFIELD

September 8, 1891
Grand Rapids, Michigan

Prof. B. B. Warfield, D.D.
Princeton, N.J.

Dear Professor,

Allow me to introduce to you Mr. Jacob Poppen, formerly a student of Hope College, Holland, Michigan, for the last year a member of the Junior Class of our Seminary.[1] Mr. Poppen wished to avail himself of more ample opportunities for study than we are able to offer here, and I advised him to visit Princeton. He will no doubt prove himself to you as he has done with us, a faithful and able student. Having taught for some time himself, he knows how to appreciate the instruction of others. I shall feel personally obliged to you for any advice or assistance you can render him. Of course we are sorry to see a good student leave, but on the other hand, I know of no place whither I would rather have him go than Princeton where he will enjoy the same sound and thorough teaching of which we ourselves retain such pleasant recollections.

> Yours very truly,
> G. Vos

---

1. Jacob Poppen (1858–1920) attended Calvin Theological Seminary from 1890 to 1891. He received his A.B. degree from Hope College, Holland, Michigan, in 1892. He attended Princeton Theological Seminary in 1893 and received his Ph.D. from the Seminary in 1896. He went on to become a pastor in the Reformed Church of America.

TO B. B. WARFIELD

September 28, 1891
48 Spring Street
Grand Rapids, Michigan

Dear Prof. Warfield,

Enclosed I send you the translation of two articles by Dr. Kuyper on the Revision of the Westminster Confession. They were published in *De Heraut* of September 6 and 13.[1] It occurred to me that the publication of these remarks in some paper might not be out of place. If you think that it would do some good, I could request *The Independent* or the *New-York Observer*[2] to print them. The former has perhaps the larger circulation, but I do not know whether it would find the spirit of Dr. Kuyper's criticism sympathetic enough to give it a place in its columns. Apart from this, the papers will probably hesitate to accept something from one that is unknown to them. If you could assist me in this matter and support my request, it might be done more easily. I leave the matter to you. For the case that you should find it possible to transmit the MS. to some papers directly, I enclose a stamped envelope. If, on the other hand, you think it less advisable to do this, please return the M.S. to me with your kind suggestions.

My paper on the doctrine of the covenants, I intend to publish in Dutch first and afterwards to send you an English translation, somewhat condensed, for the *Review*.[3] First of all however I should wish to insert something on the history of the covenant-idea in English theology. May I remind you of your kind offer to mention the English authors on the covenant (before the Westminster Assembly) to Dr. Dulles? I shall write to him and return some books today or tomorrow.

The translation of Dr. Bavinck's paper will be ready in a couple of weeks.[4]

We have commenced work with about 40 students. I saw with pleasure that the attendance at Princeton shows such a large increase. With kindest greetings,

                Yours very truly,
                G. Vos

---

1. The articles appeared under the title "De revise der Westminster Confessie" (articles 715 and 716 for Sept. 6 and Sept. 13, 1891, on pp. 2–3 and p. 2, respectively).

2. The *New-York Observer* was a religious weekly (1823–1912) featuring news on American Reformed denominations. Kuyper's articles were translated and published in neither of these. Instead they appeared under the title "Calvinism and Confessional Revision" in *Presbyterian and Reformed Review* 2 (1891): 369–99. They were reprinted in *Presbyterian Quarterly* 5/4 (October 1891): 479–516.

3. *De verbondsleer in de Gereformeerde theologie* (Grand Rapids: "Democrat" Drukpers, 1891). Translated as "The Doctrine of the Covenant in Reformed Theology," in *Redemptive History and Biblical Interpretation*, ed. Richard B. Gaffin Jr. (Phillipsburg, NJ: Presbyterian and Reformed Publishing Co., 1980), 234–67. The revised translation of Vos's pamphlet was prepared by Dr. Gaffin.

4. "Recent Dogmatic Thought in the Netherlands," *Presbyterian and Reformed Review* 3 (April 1892): 209–28.

To B. B. Warfield

March 18, 1892
Grand Rapids, Michigan

Dear Prof.,

Before receiving these lines, you will no doubt have heard the results of my deliberations in regard to your call. It is a matter of sincere regret to me not to have found myself able to accept. Personally I look upon it as a self-sacrifice. But the situation here does not allow of any other decision. Were I to leave, the little good that has been accomplished during the last four years, and which gives fair promise for the future, would soon disappear. The better part of our people would lose courage, our seminary would receive a blow that might prove fatal. I cannot but consider it of great importance to preserve our Dutch people for the old Calvinistic faith. If this is to be done, it must be done from within and not from without. Though shrinking from the many unpleasant features of this work, I do not feel at liberty before God to abandon it. Before I received the call, I was also fully aware of this, but it is sometimes necessary to be placed before a definite choice in order to see one's duty clearly pointed out. Though feeling sad, I know that I could not act otherwise. I hope that the necessity in which I am of disappointing you will not make me lose to any extent your brotherly love and counsel, the reliance on which has been a great comfort to me in the past. I do believe, if we are found faithful, that better days are still in store for the Calvinism, which you and we love, and which, each in our own sphere, we try to uphold and restore.

I owe you an apology for not having acknowledged in due time the receipt of the books you sent some weeks ago. In sending them back to Rev. Dulles, I hope to remind him that they were taken out in your name.

It was impossible for me to study much of late, owing to the suspense in which I have been living. It will be better now I hope. Van Leeuwen's *Prolegomena of Biblical Theology* is in my possession and I can let you have a notice of it before long.[1]

In regard to the review of Kuenen's work, I hardly know what to advise.[2] The views for which he stands as a representative are still so much under discussion that it would be hard to assign them their definite place and to estimate their permanent significance for the history of Rationalistic criticism. Sometimes a comparison is made between the views of the school led by Kuenen and the old Tübingen school, and the inference drawn that the former will have as short a time as the latter. It seems to me that the cases are not parallel. The evolutionistic philosophy which underlies this newest phase of Old Testament Criticism is much more exponential of the spirit of our age than the Hegelian philosophy was of the spirit of the times that gave birth to the Tübingen views. A sudden collapse of the hypothesis is not to be looked for. For this reason it is difficult to discuss it, the process having run only half its course.

I know of nobody in the old country to whom the task of writing the article in question could be committed, and who would treat it from our point of view. There as here Old Testament scholars, who have made no concessions to the prevailing tendencies, are rare.

<blockquote>
With kindest regards,
Yours very truly,
G. Vos
</blockquote>

---

1. Vos provided a review of van Leeuwen's *Prolegomena van bijbelsche godgeleerdheid* in *Presbyterian and Reformed Review* 4/1 (January 1893): 143–45.

2. Warfield apparently was asking Vos for a discussion of Kuenen's views. He may have been stimulated to this by Vos's review of *Historisch-critisch onderzoek naar het ontstaan en de verzameling van de boeken des Ouden Verbonds: De profetische boeken des Ouden Verbonds*, by A. Kuenen, in *Presbyterian and Reformed Review* 2 (1891): 139–40.

To Abraham Kuyper

May 11, 1893
48 Spring Street
Grand Rapids

Dear and Highly Esteemed Brother,

I am pleased to hear that before long you intend to publish your *Encyclopedia*. Here we are also in great need of such a work, and we rejoice that you are able to finish it.

I would be pleased, according to my earlier promise, to take charge of the translation. However, you understand that such a quick translation, as would be required by the publication of both editions at the same time, is impossible for me in my busy position. That would be the case even if I stayed here. But the difficulty is still greater because I shall enter a new field of activity at Princeton this coming fall. With such a change, there is always extra pressure. Of my own accord, I should have asked you to release me from my promise.

Until now and as far as I am concerned, the matter is therefore totally in order. Concerning your correspondence with Mr. de Vries,[1] I would hesitatingly like to point out the following: I doubt if de Vries is really the most capable person for that job. I do not know him personally. However, I read his translation of "Calvinism and Art."[2] As a whole, it is not too bad and in some places even good, but there are also passages where it is very poor. It seems to me this is partially due to the less philosophical training of the translator, and this lack would make itself felt certainly not less but rather more with the translating of your *Encyclopedia* into English. The translation which I saw suffers also from a too literal rendering of your words, through which of course the idioms get lost. As far as the latter concerns, I would hardly dare to go by my own impression. Others, however, whose judgment is more qualified, have also made the same comments.

I would feel sorry if a work of such great importance would be introduced in imperfect form. That is why I am taking the liberty to write this to you. Would it not be possible that Mr. Griffith recommend to you either another translator or at least someone who would look at the translation of Mr. de Vries and if need be correct it before it is published?

As for what people know about the "Lodge question,"[3] there is as much confusion here as there is in Holland. The fact is that Americans for a great part do not see much evil in it. This is linked up with their lack of fundamental views in general, perhaps also their moralizing trend, which the Lodge meets. You have explained the antipathy of the Dutch Americans in part exactly from the result of Dutch views. Still, it is true on the other side that many American churches (the [Dutch] Reformed Church included) avoid every conflict with the Lodge for opportunist motives. Whereas not only many members, but also many office bearers in her midst, belong to it.

May we not look forward to seeing you here soon? It is a disappointment that you are not coming this year.

              Yours in Christ,
              G. Vos

---

* This letter has been translated from the original Dutch.
1. John Hendrik de Vries, M.A. (1859–1920).
2. The article appeared in *Christian Thought: Lectures and Papers on Philosophy, Christian Evidence, Biblical Elucidation* 9 (1891–92): 259–82, 447–59.
3. I.e., Freemasonry.

To Herman Bavinck

July 3, 1893
48 Spring Street
Grand Rapids, Michigan

Dear Friend,
I believe that I have to answer two of your letters. First of all the letter, with which you sent me your article for the *Review*,[1] and then also the postcard, in which you recently congratulated me on my appointment to Princeton.

Your article has been translated and is in the hands of Warfield, who certainly will publish it as soon as possible. I think it will be published in the October issue or in the next issue. I have made little use of the freedom you gave me to condense or to make minor changes here and there. As you will see, there is only one abridgment of little significance and the changes are confined to what was required by the translation. The article is perhaps longer than the *Review* usually publishes. To prevent a repetition of what happened with Kuyper's article,[2] I have first written to Warfield about the length. He answered that the *Review*, if the article is useful, would even publish thirty pages, but that in the present circumstances they could only pay for twenty and then still at one dollar a printed page—so half the former fee. The last time I only received two dollars for my review of Kuyper's *De verflauwing der grenzen*[3] (The Fading of the Borders), although that was two pages. I do not know what the reason is for this reduction. So we will for the two of us therefore count on not more than twenty dollars, of which of course you receive three-quarters, while one-quarter is for me for translation wages.

For sometime now my brother and I have been keeping house alone.[4] My parents and sister are en route to the Netherlands.[5] Father is a delegate of the church here to your Synod.[6] The Reformed Church also sends delegates, namely Prof. Steffens[7] and a Mr. Joldersma,[8] whom you perhaps do not know.

I think I will depart for Princeton in the middle of September. I am naturally sorry to leave my present field of activity. At the same time, the appeal of the work here would not have been enough to keep me here in the long run. The young people who study are so poorly educated that despite the diligence of instructors the results that they accomplish are so small that you have to lose heart. Again this year the examination was exceedingly poor. If I take that into consideration, I am glad that I am going.

The trustees have appointed my uncle, Dr. Beuker,[9] as a temporary teacher in theology for one year until the session of the next synod. The intention is to release him from his congregation only after definite appointment by Synod. The ministers of the three Classes in Michigan will look after the service in his congregation. I do not know if my uncle will accept it. He has hardly been in his congregation for a month. Also the work will carry great difficulties for him. Still in the circumstances the trustees have done the best they could. I fear that the school here would have to become radically Reformed before there can come any improvement. The two other instructors are not doing much solid work and yet make it impossible for the church to appoint two or three better ones.[10] Then there is the difficulty that these have to be taught in two languages.

Concerning the work of teaching, I will have an easier job in Princeton. Next year I do not think I will teach more than two hours a week. That will leave enough time for study. I am free to use a textbook, but I think I will lecture. I have reflected long on the question of how to deal with the subject, so that justice will be done to both the demand of the unity and the historical development and to both the theoretical and practical character of revelation, while at the same time deducing the principle of how to deal with the subject from the Scriptures.

I have come to the conclusion that the covenant idea fulfills the requirements the best of all and so I think I will start from that. At the same time I remain grounded on Reformed theology. When Dr. Kuyper says that Cocceius,[11] by bringing the covenant idea itself into prominence, already inflicted losses on the claims of Reformed principles, I cannot go along with that view. Please write me what you think about that. It seems to me that when the covenant represents an *archetypical* covenant in eternity the *absolute* and *unchangeable*, that then also the different covenant gifts as they historically follow each other can represent the *development* of revelation. Moreover the covenant idea is neither purely theoretical, nor purely practical, so that it contains in itself word as well as deed revelation. Finally it presents this benefit that each following covenant development revolves organically from the preceding, while in Scripture the new covenant every time occurs as a benefit in a former covenant.

You can sense how I think about all this in rough outline. Therefore I would greatly appreciate your opinion. The circumstances have just inspired my interest in the covenant idea. I would like to view it, as earlier dogmatic, now also historical.

I observe from *Bazuin* and *De Heraut* how there is no end of troubles where you are. I hope wholeheartedly that they will not make the theology all too ecclesiastical. I do not like an excessive *churchism*, although I myself did that before.

Write me back as soon as possible. My greetings to your wife and parents[12] and God be with you.

From your friend and brother,
G. Vos

As soon as I have read the proof, you will receive the MS. back.

---

* This letter has been translated from the original Dutch.
1. "The Future of Calvinism," *Presbyterian and Reformed Review* 5 (1894): 1–24.
2. "Calvin and Calvinism," *Presbyterian and Reformed Review* 2 (1891): 369–99.
3. *De verflauwing der grenzen: Rede bij de overdracht van het rectoraat aan de Vrije Universiteit, oktober 1892* was published in Amsterdam in 1892. The English translation by J. H.

de Vries appeared as "Pantheism's Destruction of Boundaries," *Methodist Review* 75 (1893): 520–37, 762–78. These segments in the July and September *Review* were also published later in a single pamphlet. Vos's review of the title appeared in *Presbyterian and Reformed Review* 4 (1893): 330–32.

4. Vos had one brother: Bert John.

5. Vos had two sisters: Anna (Mrs. Marinus Van Vessem) (1864–1955) and Gertrude (1870–1962), who never married.

6. The Synod met in Dordrecht, where Vos's father made some controversial remarks; see Peter De Klerk and Richard R. De Ridder, eds., *Perspectives on the Christian Reformed Church: Studies in Its History, Theology, and Ecumenicity* (Grand Rapids: Baker Book House, 1983), 299–300; see also *De Wachter*, September 24, 1893, p. 3.

7. Nicholas M. Steffens.

8. Rense Henry Joldersma (1854–1913) was at the time superintendent of the Western Mission (1889–1894).

9. Hendericus Beuker (1834–1900). He accepted a call to Third Christian Reformed Church (Allen Avenue), Muskegon, Michigan, in 1893.

10. The other instructors were Geert Egbrets Boer (1932–1904), professor of theology (1876–1902), and Gerrit Klaas Hemkes (1838–1920), lecturer in theology (1883–84) and professor of historical theology (1884–1908).

11. Johannes Cocceius (1603–69).

12. Rev. Jan Bavinck (1826–1909) and Gesina Magdalena Holland Bavinck (1827–1900).

To Abraham Kuyper

July 3, 1893
Grand Rapids

Professor Dr. A. Kuyper
Amsterdam

Dear Brother,

Dr. Huizinga[1] from New Platz, New York has generally declared himself willing to try the translation of your *Encyclopedia* into English. Therefore I have the pleasure of introducing him to you by this letter so that he may agree with you about further details. As I wrote Dr. Huizinga, I am willing to help (as much as my time allows) with difficulties occurring in the translation. Hoping that the translation of your work, of which I read the first page with great interest, may make good progress.

> I remain after kind regards,
> Your brother in Christ,
> G. Vos

---

* This letter has been translated from the original Dutch.
1. Abel Henry Huizinga (1859–1905) was pastor of the Reformed Church of America in New Platz, New York, from 1886 to 1894. He was a professor at McCormick Theological Seminary, Chicago, Illinois, from 1894 to 1896.

To Herman Bavinck

October 20, 1893
Princeton, New Jersey

Dear Friend,

Enclosed I am sending you a draft of your article.[1] It will be published in the next issue of the *Review*. As Dr. Warfield gave me two copies, I have corrected the one and kept the other for you. You do not need to wait now till the first of January, but can already see how your article looks in an English edition. In accordance with the agreement, I am returning your own manuscript at the same time.

Since the end of September, I have been here in my new place of work. Initially the change pleases me. It is much better here for my health, and also the intellectual atmosphere, in which people live, is preferable to the one in my former surroundings. It gave me a great deal of trouble to leave Grand Rapids, and the useless bickering in both *De Hope* and *De Wachter* made it even more painful.

I hope that you will continue to send me everything of interest that is published in the Netherlands in the field of theology. It has been a long time since I received the last one. Or has nothing been published?

It surprised me that I did not hear from you during all the summer months. You have received my letter written in May or June, have you not? In that I reported that the translation of your article was finished, and furthermore something concerning my plans for the future in connection with my work here.

For this year I teach not more than four hours a week. I keep myself busy with the Old Testament exclusively. Probably next year I will have more hours, and will have to start with the New Testament also.

I am sorry that you are not close by so that we could see each other once in a while to talk about our studies. Fortunately there is more opportunity here for conversation and scholarly contact than in Grand Rapids. If they had moved you to Amsterdam, it would have been much better for you too. What a pity that the commotion among the ranks did not allow such a thing!

At the moment there is not much happening here. Because of the condemnation of Briggs, many of his followers and defenders are cooled down in their enthusiasm. Also, the conservatives will be benefited by the natural dislike of many to drag up the matter again once it has been decided. However all of this is not a permanent gain, if we do not succeed in awakening or reviving the love for Calvinism from within. Time will tell how far the efforts were successful. I have to say that the Calvinistic sympathies in Princeton are much stronger than they were during my stay as a student here. Particularly Warfield is very decided but others also feel his influence. On the contrary, Union Seminary recedes further and further. The successor of Prof. Schaff

(McGiffert) began his work a few weeks ago with a speech in which original Christendom was pictured as totally individualistic and set apart from every external authority.[2]

Let me hear from you soon. My address is simple. Princeton, New Jersey, United States; or if you will, you can add to it: 209 Hodge Hall. After friendly greetings to you and yours, I remain your friend and brother,

G. Vos

---

* This letter has been translated from the original Dutch.
1. "The Future of Calvinism," *Presbyterian and Reformed Review* 5 (1894): 1–24.
2. Arthur Cushman McGiffert (1861–1933) delivered his inaugural address on September 28, 1893. It was entitled "Primitive and Catholic Christianity: An Address Delivered upon the Occasion of His Induction into the Washburn Professorship of Church History in Union Theological Seminary, New York."

TO HERMAN BAVINCK

November 21 [1893]
209 Hodge Hall
Princeton, N.J.

Dear Brother,

I received your postcard. The article had already gone to press.[1] The wrong dates were corrected in the second proof. In addition there were some other mistakes. I had only quickly read the first proof. However Jan Trijpsma for Trijpsmaker remained.[2] I do not know whose fault this mistake is. Perhaps it is mine, or perhaps it may be the printer's, or it is also possible that you made a mistake. For the rest you do not need to worry that the article is too strict or in any respect arrogant. It will make a good impression. Here in America they are rather too modest than not modest enough. The expression (*"we* had to reconquer it, etc.") which seems too personal to you, is an English idiom that for English readers by no means has any personal meaning in itself. "We" is very common for the impersonal pronoun *uwer* (yours). Even if the article were not already printed, I would advise you to leave it as it is.

Probably the *Review* will be published in the beginning or middle of December, which is a few weeks earlier than usual.

More about this later. Except I will just add this: naturally it was not my intention to take the covenant idea as a guiding principle in Biblical Theology to the exclusion of *Revelation*. I also give the latter priority. Biblical Theology is for me History of Revelation. But beneath that I place the covenant concept, because God has revealed himself in the covenant. Thanks for sending the books.

>Greeting,
>G. Vos

I will write you officially later concerning the son[3] of Prof. Wielinga.[4] There is however no doubt that he will be received here willingly, and his arrival will provide a welcome opportunity for a closer relationship between you and us. He can count on support, at least on 100 dollars and a free furnished room. Perhaps even on 150 dollars, but I do not know that for sure. If he decides to come, it is necessary to notify us before this May. I will be pleased to take charge of it.

>As above
>t. t.[5]

---

* This letter has been translated from the original Dutch.

1. The Future of Calvinism," *Presbyterian and Reformed Review* 5 (1894): 1–24.

2. Jan Volkertsz, also called Jan Tripmaker, was an Anabaptist figure (d. 1531).

3. Gerrit Wielenga (1872–1924), pastor in the Gereformeerde Kerken: Katwijkaan den Rijn (1895), Delft (1899), Zwolle (1909), Rotterdam (1916).

4. D. K. Wielenga (1841–1902) became professor of church history and church polity at the Kampen Theological School in 1883.

5. t.t. = *totus tuus* (Latin). Literally, it means "wholly yours" and is the equivalent of "yours truly."

To Herman Bavinck

February 1, 1894
209 Hodge Hall
Princeton, N.J.

Very Close Friend,

After waiting a long time, the *Review* has finally paid. As I wrote you before, the present payment is one dollar per printed page, therefore twenty-three dollars for the entire article. Your portion of this is 15.32 dollars, that is two-thirds. The rest is my translation fee.

Since I have to pay a bill to the bookseller Bos, I am taking the liberty to add that amount to what is owed you. It amounts to 22.80 guilders. You would render me a service if you could present that to Mr. Bos for me.

Just let me know with a short note when you receive the money.

Your article has made a good impression everywhere as far as I can tell. I say *everywhere* because you will see from the newspaper I sent you yesterday, this is even the case in Scotland. Also, Dr. Warfield received expressions of thanks from England for the excellent contents of the January issue, and certainly your article has contributed to that impression.

Furthermore I sent you a catalogue for Wielenga and the other students who intend to come here.[1] I have talked with Dr. Green[2] about both. Each can get 100 dollars support plus housing. Maybe they can share a bedroom, or each have a separate room. I will be glad to help as much as possible in everything. Their arrival here can serve to strengthen the communication between you and us.

I do work with joy, although my health still leaves much to be desired. The students show interest. As you will see from the catalogue, I also treat the so-called Biblical Theology as History of Revelation. But I do not start with the Doctrine of God in the Mosaic period, as for instance Oehler does,[3] then go to the Doctrine of Man and come finally in the third place to the covenant. I try to show that the latter is the center of the revelation in this stage. Doctrine and history are also, according to my view, inseparable. Beginning with the covenant emphasizes just that.

I have seen many loose pages of Kuyper's *Encyclopedia* part I, before it was published. For the present you do not have to send it to me.

Hoping to hear from you again, your friend and brother,

G. Vos

Taking the enclosed bill of exchange to the bank here I learned that I have to send English pounds. This makes it necessary for me to add a dollar in order that I do not short-change you. I am sending this dollar by money order. Ask Mr. Bos to consider my bill as paid.

---
* This letter has been translated from the original Dutch.
1. Gerrit Wielenga (1872–1924) took graduate courses at Princeton Theological Seminary from 1894 to 1895.
2. William Henry Green.
3. Gustav Friedrich Oehler (1812–1872) wrote the famous *Theology of the Old Testament* (English translation 1874–75, revised 1883).

To Abraham Kuyper

February 26, 1894
209 Hodge Hall
Princeton, N.J.

Dear Brother,

My kindest thanks for forwarding the first volume of your *Encyclopedia*. The interest I already had in the work from the little that I received earlier has increased greatly since I received more of it. All those who love Reformed theology are greatly obliged to you. I do not doubt that the following volumes will shed light on many points for myself and others.

Now I would be very pleased to see your work published in the English language. I was disappointed to learn that Dr. Huizinga has not yet succeeded in finding a publisher. Dr. Warfield talked to me about it last week. The publishers seem to be afraid that the book is of too pure a scholarly tenor to be in much demand in this practical country. There is some truth in that. The theological world here has no eye for the scholarly value and significance of theology notwithstanding her usefulness in the more everyday sense of the word. But exactly because this is so, we are doubly in need of a book which opens our eyes to it. I hope that Dr. Huizinga will succeed in finding a good publisher. Here we shall do all that lies in our power to assist him.

I have begun my work here with pleasure. In the midst of the general defection, Princeton exerts a good influence. In the last years they have become more firm here as matters unfold. In the churches at large things look miserable. Church discipline is fallen very much into disuse and what is more the realization that it *must* be exerted dutifully has been lost. Even in an extreme case as that of Dr. Briggs, it was very difficult to move into action. They allow opinions to be expressed and spread unhindered. Opinions which, without any doubt, not only assail the Reformed doctrine but also the army of Christianity. And the worst is that through this gradually the concept of discipline itself undergoes a change and falsification. It seems to be the curse of the unsound practice, that at the same time it corrupts the theory and so perpetuates itself.

Warm greetings to you and may God be with you in your many labors.

Your friend and brother,
G. Vos

---

[*] This letter has been translated from the original Dutch.

To Herman Bavinck

March 28, 1894
209 Hodge Hall
Princeton, N.J.

Very Close Friend,
Receive my thanks for taking care of the bill of Mr. Bos and for sending the receipt.

I received a letter from the students Smitt and Wielenga,[1] in which was enclosed a friendly note from Prof. Wielenga[2] himself. I answered the first as soon as was possible for me. I hope they carry out their plan and come here next fall.

You asked me what I think about your move to Amsterdam.[3] It is very difficult for me to give an opinion, since I cannot judge the situation in the Netherlands very well. Also you have already made your decision. I do not doubt that you will do an excellent job in the field of Old Testament studies as well. You are still young enough to get thoroughly acquainted. But would it not be a pity if your position in Kampen were handed over to one of the extreme secessionists? Last week I read the address of your colleague Lindeboom,[4] and the lecture displeased me so much that I said to myself: if the training at Kampen has to be directed totally in this spirit, then it is a sad situation for the scholarly prospects in the Reformed Churches of the Netherlands. It seems to me as if your work is the only counterweight to that direction. On the other side, it is true that the Free University is in urgent need of you. Certainly it needs to have a more solid foundation. If Kuyper would be taken from us, it would be doubtful if the Free University could maintain itself.

We continue to struggle here. I am not sure if we are making much progress. The German theology and criticism is imported with full zeal, and the worst is that the practice of doctrinal discipline in almost all American churches has gotten almost totally lost. Even in an extreme case as that of Briggs, it required the greatest effort to take action. Now that Briggs is suspended, no one wants to do anything else and the accomplices of Briggs are left unhindered. Also it appears that the Reformed Church will not do anything about John De Witt, who fully took sides with Briggs.[5]

I would not be surprised if at the next synod in Grand Rapids, my uncle, Dr. Beuker, is not appointed as my replacement.[6] It occurs to me that in the present situation this would be good. But there are also other candidates.

I think I will write a short review in the *Review* about the lecture of Lindeboom.[7] It was sent to Dr. Warfield for that purpose.

At the moment, there is a sociological trend in this country which is also gaining support in Christian circles. The article of Breed in the April issue of the *Review* tells something about that.[8]

Inform me soon of your plans for the future. My address will be here till the 8th of May. After that date, my address will be 48 Spring Street, Grand Rapids, Michigan. With friendly greetings, also from Dr. Warfield,

Your friend and brother,
G. Vos

---

* This letter has been translated from the original Dutch.

1. Wolter Wagter Smitt (1869–1935) attended Princeton Seminary 1894–95. He was a pastor in the Gereformeerde Kerken at Knijpe (1896), Assen (1899), Dennenoord at Zuidlaren (1911), and Vogelenzang (1928). Gerrit Wielenga (1872–1924) took graduate courses at Princeton Theological Seminary from 1894 to 1895.

2. D. K. Wielenga (1841–1902) became professor of church history and church polity at the Kampen Theological School in 1883.

3. Bavinck did not move to Amsterdam until 1902, when he succeeded Kuyper in the chair of systematic theology at the Free University, following Kuyper's selection as prime minister of Holland.

4. Lucas Lindeboom (1845–1933) was a vigorous opponent of Kuyper who taught at Kampen as professor of New Testament from 1883 onward. Vos appears to be referring to his lecture on the thirty-ninth anniversary of the Theological School at Kampen (December 6, 1893) entitled *Godgeleerden* (Heusden, 1894).

5. John De Witt (1821–1906) was a professor at New Brunswick Theological Seminary, New Jersey (1863–1892), a seminary of the Reformed Church of America. He was an editor of the American Standard Version of the Bible (1901).
6. Beuker was professor of systematic and practical theology (1894–1900).
7. Vos never fulfilled this statement.
8. David R. Breed, "Christian Beneficence and Some New Theories Affecting Property," *Presbyterian and Reformed Review* 5/2 (April 1894): 287–302.

To Herman Bavinck

December 22, 1894
Princeton, N.J.

Dear Friend and Brother,

I definitely should have answered your last letter before I received your postcard with the happy news of the birth of your daughter.[1] But I was so busy and had so many things to take care of in the time right after my wedding and our arrival here,[2] that even the most essential things remained undone. It is a pleasure that I can now respond to your congratulations and congratulate you at the same time. My wife and I offer our cordial best wishes on [the occasion of] this new blessing. May the little one grow up robustly and healthy and bring you much joy. You will now feel that you truly have a home.

This is for the time being more than we can say about ourselves. Our house, that is, the building in which we hope to live, will not be available until April first of next year. Until then we must make do with two rooms and board in the family of the widow of a former professor. We are greatly looking forward to having our own home.

My work is pleasant. This year it is mostly in the area of the New Testament, the doctrine of the Savior according to the Synoptics and the Gospel of John. That is a study that interests me greatly. For the Old Testament I am repeating with little change my work of last year.

Wielenga[3] and Smitt[4] seem to fit in well. They work diligently and make a good impression on everyone. Their stay here will not only be beneficial to them but bring about a mutual bond.

I am looking forward to the publication of your *Dogmatics*. If you send me the first volume, I will take care that it will be announced and reviewed as soon as possible in the *Review*, [either] by me or by Dr. Warfield, who is better qualified to do so.[5] I may have moved too far outside the dogmatic mode of thinking. [On the other hand,] Dr. Warfield reads Dutch very slowly, which is somewhat of a drawback.

I agree to some extent with what you write about Dr. Kuyper's *Encyclopedia*, volume II. His dualism is very pronounced. But the question always comes up again: Isn't this the only logically tenable position? Can the fundamental contrast between modern science and Christianity according to Scripture that is present on so many points, be adequately explained in another way?

I shall be pleased to give you a copy of my inaugural address, given last Spring, when you visit us.[6]

Receive with your family our best wishes for the coming year. May it be for you a year of rich blessing.

Please give my greetings to Prof. Wielenga.[7] Also to your parents.

Your friend and brother,
G. Vos

---

* This letter has been translated from the original Dutch.
1. Johanna Bavinck was born November 25, 1894. She died in 1971.
2. Vos wed Catherine Frances Smith in Grand Rapids, Michigan, on September 7, 1894.
3. Gerrit Wielenga (1872–1924): see p. 181, n. 3, above.
4. Wolter Wagter Smitt (1869–1935): see p. 181, n. 1, above.
5. Vos wrote the review that was published in *Presbyterian and Reformed Review* 7 (1896): 356–63; 10 (1899): 694–700.
6. "The Idea of Biblical Theology as a Science and as a Theological Discipline," delivered May 8, 1894, at First Presbyterian Church, Princeton. It is reprinted in *Redemptive History and Biblical Interpretation*, ed. Richard B. Gaffin Jr. (Phillipsburg, NJ: P&R Publishing Co., 1980), 3–24.
7. D. K. Wielenga (1841–1902): see p. 181, n. 4, above.

To Herman Bavinck

July 6, 1895
52 Mercer Street,
Princeton

Dear Friend,

I thank you very much for sending me the first part of your *Dogmatics*.[1] I appreciate this present, not only as proof of your friendship, but also because of the publication itself, as there is no doubt that I will learn much from it and I will receive a clearer understanding on many points. Even though my work is no longer in the field of Dogmatics anymore, still daily I experience how the earlier work has helped me in my present study and so I hope to profit from your work quite a bit.

As I wrote you before, the task of reviewing the volume would have been in better hands with Dr. Warfield. I have handed him your book and although he was obviously very curious of the contents, the volume seems to deter him for he reads Dutch very slowly and with great difficulty. Therefore I have taken it upon myself.[2] I will fulfill this joyous task as soon as possible. We moved the end of May and have now begun for the first time our own household.[3] There was much to do and for weeks the study had to rest totally. When your book arrived we were still in the middle of the confusion. During the spring more than a dozen books collected on my table, which I would review for the *Review*. Some of them are of lesser importance and I can finish quickly, others as Beyschlag's *New Testament Theology*[4] require more work. It is for this reason that till now I had no time to read your book, except the first thirty pages. If it is somewhat possible I will put the review of it in the October issue, otherwise in the issue following that.

We plan to stay here till the first of August and then go for a visit to Michigan. We will be back here in the middle of September. My brother, at present connected with Johns Hopkins University in Baltimore, is now visiting us.[5] Three weeks ago he shared the same privilege you had, a little daughter was born.[6] He sends his greetings to you.

I am very sorry that I did not see the brothers Wielenga and Smitt at their departure from Princeton. I hope they have arrived safe and sound in the fatherland and remember us with friendship. Greet them from me and greet Prof. Wielinga.

As you have noticed, Dr. Steffens has left Holland and gone to the Presbyterian Seminary in Dubuque.[7] They called Dr. Winter in his place,[8] but I fear no improvement, although it could have been worse.

Cordial greetings to you and your family from your friend and brother,

G. Vos

---

* This letter has been translated from the original Dutch.
1. Bavinck's *Gereformeerde dogmatiek*, vol. 1.
2. Vos's review appeared in *Presbyterian and Reformed Review* 7 (1896): 356–63.
3. Vos married Catherine Frances Smith of Grand Rapids, Michigan, on September 7, 1894. They set up housekeeping at 52 Mercer Street, on the campus of Princeton Theological Seminary, in May 1895.
4. Vos's review appeared in *Presbyterian and Reformed Review* 6 (1895): 756–61.
5. Bert John Vos became associate professor of German at Johns Hopkins University, Baltimore, Maryland, in 1893. In 1908, he became professor of German at Indiana University, Bloomington, Indiana—a position he held until 1937.
6. Maude Alida Vos was born on June 11, 1895.
7. Steffens was a professor at Dubuque Theological Seminary, Dubuque, Iowa, from 1895 to 1898.
8. Egbert Winter (1836–1906) was a professor at Western Theological Seminary, Holland, Michigan, from 1895 to 1904.

To Abraham Kuyper

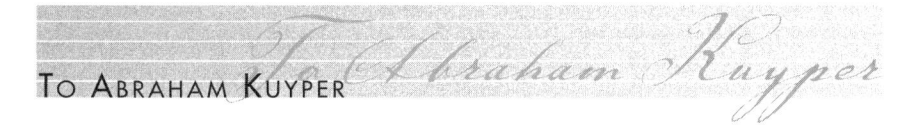

April 30, 1896
52 Mercer Street
Princeton, N.J.

Dear and Highly Esteemed Brother,

Rev. de Vries[1] has asked me to give you information concerning the degrees that will be bestowed by Princeton College this coming fall. I will be pleased to comply with this request and to gain time, especially since I was already planning to write you about this matter, I will send the information you desire directly.

The other theologians besides you who are invited to come here and to receive the degree of D.D. are: Principal Rainy of Free Church College, Edinburgh;[2] Dr. Calderwood of Edinburgh;[3] Dr. Stanley Leathes of King's College, London;[4] and Dr. Henry Wace of King's College, London.[5] It is far from certain that all of these will come. They are, as you see, men of so-called evangelical color, though in our estimation not Calvinists. You are the only theologian from mainland Europe who is invited. I do not know for sure if some are coming from the other faculties in Germany. I hear that Professor Klein, a mathematician (from Göttingen, I think), has promised to come.[6] Also Professor Sohm is invited and may come.[7]

If it is at all possible, I would urgently request you to make the trip to please and honor us with your presence. I say *us* because the faculty of our Seminary has instructed me to press the matter. Your work for the Lord and for Reformed theology and the Reformed churches is cherished by us and with thanksgiving we enjoy the fruit which comes to us most recently in your beautiful *Encyclopedia*. In my conviction, personal acquaintance between Dr. Warfield and others and you can be of significance for the future. Do not let that opportunity pass by.

191

We have learned that the college has invited you to deliver a lecture here during your stay. It is so arranged that theological lectures to be delivered on that occasion will take place for our students, that is in the seminary. The intention was not so much to get a popular, but rather a strictly scholarly, lecture on one or another topic. Naturally the choice remains totally with you. Mrs. Vos has directed me to invite you kindly, if you come, to take up your residence with us. It would be a great joy for us to accommodate you.

A word about the translation of the *Encyclopedia*. I am very sorry that it has been so unfortunate to lose its translator over and over again. It is true, the *Encyclopedia* seems to bring good luck to the translators, for up to three times it has brought an appointment as professor to the translator. I do not envy brother de Vries, but still hope that such an appointment in his case shall stay away long enough to let him complete the work. First, as you know, I had doubts about his competence for the task, but judging from the last proofs, practice in translating has done him very much good. As far as lies in my power I shall do everything to help him.

I rejoiced wholeheartedly about the statement of the brothers Bavinck, Wielenga, etc. May the Lord direct all that friction and unrest for the best.

> With kindest regards,
> Your brother,
> Geerhardus Vos

---

* This letter has been translated from the original Dutch.
1. J. Hendrik de Vries (1859–1920).
2. Robert Rainy (1826–1906) was principal of New College, Edinburgh, from 1874 to 1900.
3. Henry Calderwood (1830–1897) became professor of moral philosophy at Edinburgh University in 1868.
4. Stanley Leathes (1830–1900) was professor of Hebrew and Old Testament exegesis at King's College, London, from 1863 to 1900.
5. Henry Wace was principal of King's College from 1883 to 1903. From 1903 until his death in 1924, he was dean of Canterbury.

6. Felix Klein (1849–1925) was professor of mathematics at the University of Göttingen, Germany.
7. Rudolph Sohm (1841–1917), a jurist and Protestant church historian, was appointed professor at Freiburg (1870), Strassburg (1872), and Leipzig (1887).

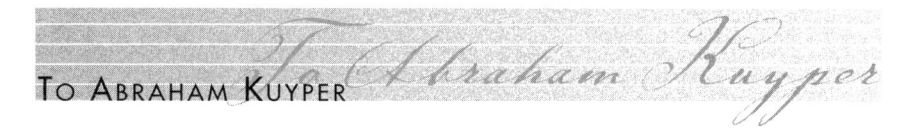

To Abraham Kuyper

June 10, 1896
Princeton

Highly Esteemed Brother,

It has delighted me and all the brethren very much to learn that there are good hopes to see you here next autumn.

So far as Mrs. Vos and I are concerned, we would have loved to lodge you, but respect your rule.

Professor West[1] assures me that if by any chance you should come, a room in one of the hotels here will be reserved for you.

I learn that from the Netherlands only Professor Hubrecht from Utrecht is invited.[2] I could not find out whether or not he will come.

Would it not be possible to let us know shortly here at the seminary, if you could treat us to a lecture?

Do not forget when you come to bring your academic gown.

    With kind regards,
    Your brother in Christ,
    G. Vos

---

* This letter has been translated from the original Dutch.
1. Andrew F. West (1853–1943) became Giger Professor of Latin at Princeton University in 1883. In 1896, he was appointed secretary of the Committee for the Sesquicentennial celebration of Princeton University. In 1900, he became the first dean of the Graduate School of Princeton University, a position from which he retired in 1928.
2. Ambrosius Arnold Willem Hubrecht (1853–1915) was professor of zoology, comparative anatomy, and physiology at Utrecht from 1882 to 1910, and professor of embryology from 1910 to 1915.

To Abraham Kuyper

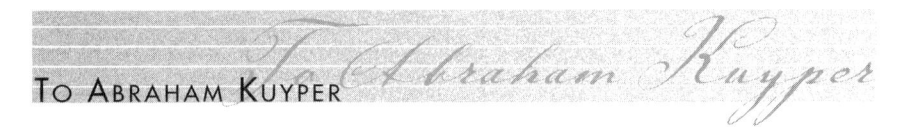

July 11, 1896
Ottawa Beach, Michigan[1]

Beloved Brother,

It pains me very much that circumstances do not permit you to carry out your plan to visit these regions in autumn. We also, the rest of the brethren as well as I, had counted on it and anticipated many good things. Now we are getting used to the idea that you plan to visit us in 1897. In the seminary the classes end about May 8–10 and start again about September 15–20. The college courses at Princeton University end about the middle of June and start about at the same time as ours in the fall. I would like to hear from you as soon as your plans are completed. You must not fail to visit Princeton and make acquaintance with the brothers.

We have certainly followed the events of the problems in the church in your country with interest, but lately also with amazement.[2] You might consider it an honor that you must also bear this defamation for the sake of the cause of God. All those who love the principles you espouse, and many do here, will respect you more because of it and will remember you more earnestly in their prayers.

I have written to Professor West[3] and, as far as there was a need for it, explained the situation to him. Undoubtedly he understands that you could do nothing else than postpone the trip here and that there is no question of either unwillingness or lack of desire.

Meanwhile, remember us and gladden us next year with the news that we can expect you.

With kind regards,
Your brother in Christ,
Geerhardus Vos

---

* This letter has been translated from the original Dutch.
1. Ottawa Beach was a summer resort community on Lake Michigan, consisting of cottages owned by people from Grand Rapids. Construction of the resort began in 1886. The resort was located several miles from Graafschap, Michigan. Catherine and Geerhardus Vos came here to be near his parents (Marianne Radius to the editor, July 30, 1994).
2. Vos is alluding to the so-called Reformation of 1896.
3. Andrew F. West.

To Abraham Kuyper

October 7, 1896
52 Mercer Street
Princeton, N.J.

Dear Brother,

All the brethren here were very disappointed when I informed them that you had to cancel your plans to visit us this autumn. As it appears however from your writing, you have considered coming here next year, and that gives us hope. In view of this, the faculty of the seminary has decided unanimously to invite you to be our Stone Lecturer for the year 1897–1898.[1] We have a fund to pay the costs for a yearly series of six to eight lectures on some theological topic. The proceeds of this fund, paid to the lecturer, is $600. Usually we appoint our lecturer a year or two in advance. For the school year 1897–1898, we had already appointed Professor Jacobus of Hartford Seminary (Congregationalist).[2] Dr. Jacobus however would love to have more time for preparation. This fact, and the prospect of your visit, has compelled us to try to make some change in the order of the lecturers so that you are scheduled in between Professor Moore[3] who comes this year and Professor Jacobus who otherwise should come the next year.

You are totally free in the choice of your topic. Maybe some correspondence would be necessary as not all topics on both sides of the ocean are equally up-to-date. However, this all can be arranged in time, if we at least have your promise. Do you think you can come and do you have one or more topics in mind? In that case it will be a pleasure for us to advise you in this respect. Concerning the time, the lectures will have to be delivered between the end of September 1897 and the end of March 1898. If need be, they could still be delivered in April 1898, but it is more difficult to interest the hearers by the end of our school year.

Usually we urge the authors to allow their lectures to be published at their own expense. However this is not a downright stipulation.

With the invitation on behalf of the faculty, I add my personal wish that God will allow us to see and to hear you this time.

A speedy answer is desired, because your decision will determine when Professor Jacobus will deliver his lectures next year or the year following that.

I use this opportunity to thank you kindly for the forwarding of your speech delivered at the opening of the Synod at Middelburg.[4] I read it with pleasure and rejoice at the favorable result of the meeting which you opened so successfully.

With kind regards,
Your brother in Christ,
Geerhardus Vos

---

* This letter has been translated from the original Dutch.

1. The Stone Lectures were named for Levi Payson Stone (1802–1884), a member of the Board of Trustees at Princeton Theological Seminary. He established the fund for the Lectures in 1871. In 1883, he directed that the lectures deal with "some topic kindred to theological stud-

ies, provided always the lectures shall not contravene the system of doctrine taught in the Standards of the Presbyterian Church."

2. Melanchthon W. Jacobus (1855–1937) became professor of New Testament exegesis and criticism at Hartford Theological Seminary, Hartford, Connecticut, in 1891. His Stone Lectures of 1897–98 were entitled "Present Day Problems in New Testament Criticism." They were published under the title *A Problem in New Testament Criticism* (New York: Scribner's, 1900).

3. Walter W. Moore (1857–1926) became professor of Hebrew language and literature at Union Theological Seminary, Richmond, Virginia, in 1883. His Stone Lectures for 1896–97 were entitled "The Beginning of Hebrew History in the Light of Recent Archeological Research." From 1904 to 1926 he served as President of Union Seminary.

4. "De zegen des Heeren over onze kerken. Rede ter inleiding op het gebed voor het samenkomen der Gereformeerde Kerken in Generale Synode, gehouden in de Noorderkerk te Middelburg, op Augustus 1896."

To Abraham Kuyper

November 11, 1896
October 98, May 99
Princeton

Dear Brother,

Would it be possible for you to deliver the Stone lectures for 1898–1899? Provided that you stay within the bounds of our school year (the first of October through the first of May), you can decide on the time yourself. The topic mentioned by you is excellent. Do not disappoint us this time. A quick reply is desired, so that in case you cannot accept the invitation (which we do not expect) another lecturer can be chosen in enough time.

With kind regards,
Yours in Christ,
Geerhardus Vos

---

* This letter has been translated from the original Dutch.

To Abraham Kuyper

March 6, 1897
Princeton

Dear Brother,

I sent you a copy this morning of Professor Scott's Stone Lectures, which he delivered last year.[1] You can gather from the speech to a certain degree what the lectures usually contain. If I can I will try to obtain a copy of the "deed of gift" under which the lectures are delivered and also forward that to you.[2] Please let us know your topic as soon as you have made a definite choice.

> With kind regards,
> Your brother in Christ,
> G. Vos

---

* This letter has been translated from the original Dutch.

1. Hugh M. Scott (1848–1909) became professor of church history at Chicago Theological Seminary (Divinity School of the University of Chicago), Chicago, Illinois, in 1881. His Stone Lectures of 1895–96 were entitled "Origin and Development of the Nicene Theology; with Some Reference to the Ritschlian View of Theology and History of Doctrine." They were published with that title by the Chicago Theological Seminary Press in 1896.

2. The Minutes of the Board of Trustees for October 31, 1883, contain the following communication: "On the 8th day of May 1871 I gave J. B. Vermilye Esq. Treasurer of your Board Ten Thousand Dollars in 7% Rail Road Bonds to constitute a Lectureship for the Seminary, not directing at the time the character of the lectures to be delivered leaving the matter of detail to a future day. I now direct that the Trustees of the Seminary keep the fund safely invested and that the income be appropriated year by year to the payment of a lecturer chosen by the Faculty of the Seminary who shall deliver a course of lectures upon some topic kindred to theological studies, provided always that the lectures shall not contravene the system of doctrine taught in the Standards of the Presbyterian Church. In case a lecturer should fail to be secured in any given year, I direct that the income of that year be added to the original principal, the income to be expended in like manner to that of the original principal or fund. Should the Trustees at any future day, fail to carry out my directions regarding the character of the lectures to be delivered, I direct that the fund revert to my heirs at law to be shared by them in manners which shall be in accordance with the law of the State of New Jersey."

To Abraham Kuyper

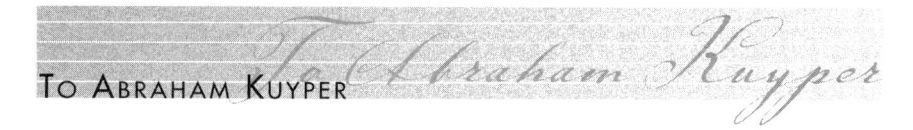

June 15, 1897
Princeton

The Rev. Dr. A. Kuyper in Amsterdam

Highly Esteemed Friend and Brother,

I will be pleased to comply with the request of my friend, Professor Robinson of Toronto, Canada,[1] to introduce him to some of my friends in the Netherlands. Professor Robinson has settled down for some weeks in Leiden. He wants to acquaint himself with the Dutch language and to carry out some work in connection with his profession: the introduction and exegesis of the Old Testament. This requires that for the most part he is in contact with the men of the modern circle and I would be very sorry if he left the Netherlands without having made acquaintance with the Reformed brethren. He is of a strict Calvinistic family, originally a son of the United Presbyterian Church in these regions,[2] though at the moment associated with the Theological School of the Presbyterian Church in Canada.[3]

If you could welcome him and meet with him for a while, though it seems to make great demands with all your pressure, he and I would be very grateful to you.

With kind regards,
Your brother in Christ,
G. Vos

---

* This letter has been translated from the original Dutch.
1. George L. Robinson (1864–1958) was professor of Old Testament exegesis and literature at Knox College, Toronto, Canada, from 1896 to 1898. He then became professor of Old Testament literature at McCormick Seminary, Chicago, Illinois, from 1898 to 1906.
2. The United Presbyterian Church of North America (1858–1958).
3. Knox College, Toronto.

To Abraham Kuyper

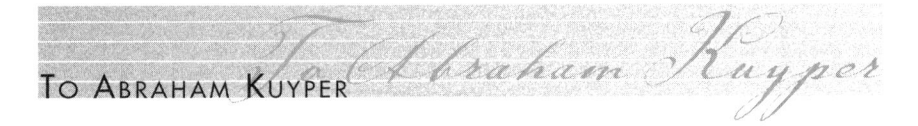

October 11, 1897
The Theological Seminary of the Presbyterian Church
at Princeton, N.J.

Dear Brother,

I have not responded to your letter of last summer because I did not want to disturb you during the well deserved rest of your vacation. We trust that the abundant work of other kinds will not prevent you from writing the promised lectures for us, although we understand very well that sometimes you must feel overburdened with the pressure. Whomever you can make arrangements with concerning the translation should come here if you do not have anyone at your place in mind. Should the time of preparation be too short for you, perhaps the possibility still exists of postponing your coming for a year. It can be attempted if Dr. Foster,[1] who is appointed as Lecturer for 1899–1900, is willing to exchange with you. Naturally I do not know how this fits in with any of your other possible plans or with the course of your official duties. Let me know as soon as possible if you want this, then we can request if it is feasible for Dr. Foster to deliver his lectures a year earlier. The time between now and 1898–99 maybe also short enough for the translation. When would it be possible for you to furnish the Dutch text?

I am happy to have learned that the outlook for publication is good for the translation of the second part of your *Encyclopedia*. So there is a chance to introduce you in the American theological world before your personal appearance in our midst.

With kind regards and good wishes,
Your brother in Christ,
Geerhardus Vos

* This letter has been translated from the original Dutch.
1. Frank H. Foster (1851–1935) served as professor of systematic theology at Pacific Theological Seminary, Berkeley, California, from 1892 to 1902. His Stone Lectures of 1899–1900 were entitled "The Contribution of Christian Experience to the System of Evangelical Doctrine."

To William Elliot Griffis

December 15, 1898
Princeton

Dear Sir,[1]

Dr. A. Kuyper of Amsterdam, doubtless known to you, during his recent visit to this country succeeded in organizing an American branch of the General Dutch Alliance.[2] Other branches exist in Dutch East India, South Africa and [?]. The nature and aims of the association are explained in the constitution of the American branch which I enclose. At a meeting held at the Fifth Avenue Hotel in New York City, Dr. Kuyper, in virtue of the power given him by the central board in The Netherlands, appointed ten gentlemen to serve for the first time as members of the governing board of the eastern section of the branch in this country. Of the ten, you are one, and in compliance with Dr. Kuyper's request I herewith transmit to you a certificate of appointment signed by him. In view of the interest you have shown by your valued writings in matters which will preeminently fall within the sphere of activity of the association, it is very desirable, and will greatly please the other members, I am sure, if you can signify to me your acceptance of the appointment.

Yours truly,
Geerhardus Vos,
First Secretary

1. William Elliot Griffis (1843–1928) was ordained a minister of the Reformed Church of America in 1877. Prior to that, he had established a school in Japan in conjunction with his alma mater, Rutgers University. He authored numerous books on Japan, the most famous of which was *The Mikado's Empire* (New York: Harper, 1876).
2. The Dutch Alliance, established by Kuyper, never really flourished in America after his departure. It was part of a cultural mandate that swept through the Netherlands at the turn of the twentieth century.

To Herman Bavinck

April 29, 1899
Princeton

Very Close Friend,
There is no connection whatsoever between the University established here and our Theological Seminary.[1] Both institutions have totally different origins. The University (formerly a college) is much older. Though it was also established in order to provide solid education in preparation for theological study, this has never been the only purpose. As far as I know establishing a theological faculty with the college was not the plan of the founders. Princeton College has more or less always been under predominantly Presbyterian influence, but there is nothing in the charter that makes this necessary. It was simply the result of the historical development.

Our seminary is established by the church. At first the professors were appointed by the General Assembly. This lasted till the union of Old School and New School.[2] During the split,[3] New School seminaries were established where the appointment of professors was done by a Board of Directors. Then [union] made this applicable to all seminaries connected with the Presbyterian church. These Directors are not chosen by the church. The Board appoints its own members. Besides that there is a Board of Trustees chosen by the Directors. Under the law, the administration of the properties rests in the Directors. They are the official owners. However the church has the right to change this structure under certain restrictions. Changes in the plan have to be adopted unanimously by one Assembly or by two successive Assemblies by a large majority. Besides this the Assembly has the right to once remove one-quarter of the Directors and one-third of the Trustees and to replace them. Finally the Assembly can veto the appointment of professors, but only at the next meeting.

Of the other large universities in the United States only Yale, Harvard, and Chicago, have a theological school.[4] I am not highly informed about Chicago, but I believe the connection is very loose and the administration of the two branches distinguished. At Harvard and Yale, the Board is one and are vested in so-called corporations. Both of these universities have risen out of congregational circles, so that from the outset there was no church body which could control the Theological Department. Harvard is totally free of church administration or church influence. As you know the theology is Unitarian there. At Yale they are under a restriction that a certain number of the members of the corporation has to consist of congregational ministers. This applies to the whole corporation, so that the church influence so carried on concerns the other faculties as well as the theological faculty.

I observe with interest the situation where you are.

I have received Part II and III of the *Dogmatics* and have read it in part.[5] It is a beautiful work. Thus far pressure prevents me from writing the review. It will be the first thing I plan to work on in the vacation.

With friendly greetings,
G. Vos

---

* This letter has been translated from the original Dutch.

1. Princeton University was founded as the College of New Jersey in 1746. Princeton Theological Seminary was established in 1812.

2. The union of the Old School and the New School Presbyterian churches occurred in 1869.

3. The split between the two occurred in 1837.

4. Yale University was established in 1701; Yale Divinity School was founded in 1822. Harvard College (later University) was founded in 1636; Harvard Divinity Hall/School was founded in 1826. The University of Chicago Divinity School was founded in 1892.

5. Part II was published in Kampen in 1897; part III followed in 1898. Vos never completed a review of the 1898 portion.

To William Elliot Griffis

January 13, 1902
Princeton

Rev. and Dear Sir,[1]

Accept my sincere thanks for the copy of your interesting book on Japan and the Japanese, which you so kindly sent to me a few days ago.[2] Both my wife and myself have been reading portions of it with great delight.

Your questions relating to historical subjects I hope to answer at some time in the future, when I shall have a little more leisure to do so carefully.

It is a disappointment to me that you will be unable to attend the meeting in New York next Saturday. Saturday seems to be the day which is most convenient for the majority of the members of the Board, but I fully realize, how for you it makes attendance almost an impossibility.

Your valuable suggestions I shall keep in mind and bring to the attention of the Board.

Your very truly,
Geerhardus Vos

---

1. See p. 202, n. 1, above.
2. Vos probably refers to Griffis's most famous work, *The Mikado's Empire*, which went through twelve editions from 1876 to 1912.

To Herman Bavinck

May 17, 1905
Princeton

Dear Friend and Brother,

My friend Prof. Melanchton W. Jacobus from Hartford's Theological Seminary has asked me to assist him in becoming acquainted with Dutch scholars in the critical field. I am sorry I have to answer him that I cannot help him in this, as I do not have the honor of personally knowing the men of reputation in these circles, and probably my name is not known by any of them personally. As I know that you are on friendly terms with some of them (such as Prof. Wildeboer[1] and Snouck Hurgronje[2]), I am taking the liberty of introducing Prof. Jacobus to you. I will be greatly obliged and thankful for anything you could do to help him in reaching his goal.

Undoubtedly Prof. Jacobus himself will inform you of what he wishes and seeks. In his letter to me he writes as follows: "It is my expectation this summer to spend a month or so in Holland and it is my hope during this time to make more or less of an acquaintance with the university life of that country. I am perfectly aware of the fact that the point of view of Dutch criticism is not the point that either you or I agree with, and yet it is interesting to know as much about the point as is possible through these opportunities of a close contact with the men who represent it."

From this you can already form an idea concerning the plan of my friend.

With friendly greetings and the best wishes for the success of your labor in every way.

I remain your friend and brother,
Geerhardus Vos

---

* This letter has been translated from the original Dutch.
1. Gerrit Wildeboer (1855–1911) was professor of Old Testament at Groningen from 1884 to 1907.
2. Christiaan Snouck Hurgronje (1857–1936), a world-renowned Arabic scholar, became professor of Arabic at Leiden University in 1906.

To Herman Bavinck

February 21, 1906
Princeton

Prof. Dr. H. Bavinck, Amsterdam

Esteemed Friend and Brother,

For my colleagues and not in the least for myself, it was a cause of great joy to learn that you accepted our invitation. The tentative plan projected in your writing meets with our total approval. In my previous letter I forgot to mention that it is expected that the delivered lectures will be printed and published. But without a doubt you counted on that already. How to best achieve this can be looked at later, perhaps upon your arrival here. Naturally the publication of the lectures in English does not stand in the way of the simultaneous publication in Dutch.

I will do my part gladly, if you deem it necessary and prudent, to translate the lectures into English or to get them translated. Your intention to have them ready in 1907 is excellent, since this allows ample time for the translation. Naturally the translation has to be done by myself and also by others, who are familiar with the Dutch. As it is rather difficult to find one person who combines thorough knowledge of the Dutch with total skill in the use of the English idiom (I myself do not lay claim to that), I am in favor of submitting the lectures after the translation to a qualified person, whose native tongue is English, so he can perfect the form in order that what appears in published draft may be totally in harmony with the English idiom. The latter was lacking in the lectures delivered by Dr. Kuyper, and the influence of the otherwise so excellent lectures suffered from it.[1]

As far as the choice of subject is concerned, it is best to follow your own inclination. It is not the immediate impression that is most important, but the lasting effect of the lectures. If you have several topics to that effect and would like help in choosing one, I would be very willing to talk this over with my colleagues.

Undoubtedly you possess the Stone Lectures which Prof. Orr delivered here concerning *The Image of God*, etc.[2] This year we have a series of lectures about "Anthropomorphism in Scripture and Theology."[3] Next year we will have a series about hymnology.[4] The lectures for 1907–08 and thus also the subject are still uncertain.[5] Then it will be your turn in autumn 1908.[6]

Hoping that nothing might come in the way of carrying out our plan to which you agreed so kindly, and hoping that the blessing of the Lord may be on all of your developments, I remain with friendly greetings,

Yours in Christ,
Geerhardus Vos

P.S. I add to the above still this: there is no objection to the rendering of the same lectures in other places in this country or elsewhere, after they are delivered here, on the understanding that clearly then is mentioned, that they were originally delivered as Stone Lectures in Princeton. I mention this because eventually it can be of influence on your travel plans.

---

* This letter has been translated from the original Dutch.

1. Abraham Kuyper's famous Stone Lectures of 1898 were published as *Calvinism: Six Lectures Delivered in the Theological Seminary at Princeton* (New York: F. H. Revell, 1899) and later as *Lectures on Calvinism* (Grand Rapids: Eerdmans, 1931).

2. James Orr (1844–1913) gave the Stone Lectures for 1903–04, which were published as *God's Image in Man and Its Defacement in the Light of Modern Denials* (London: Hodder and Stoughton, 1905).

3. Daniel E. Jenkins, "The Function and Right of Anthropomorphism in Religious Thought."

4. Louis F. Benson (1855–1930), "The Psalmody of the Reformed Churches."
5. David Hay Fleming (1849–1931), *The Reformation in Scotland: Causes, Characteristics, Consequences* (London: Hodder and Stoughton, 1910).
6. Bavinck's lectures were entitled "The Philosophy of Revelation."
They were published as *Wijsbegeerte der openbaring* (Kampen: Kok, 1908) and under the above English title by Longmans, Green, and Company in 1909.

To Herman Bavinck

January 7, 1909
Princeton

Dear Brother,

I was very glad to hear that you and your wife have arrived safely in the Netherlands and found your relatives in good health.

I was very shocked to learn what you wrote about the serious condition of Biesterveld.[1] I gathered from your letter that there was little or no hope for recovery. Still the announcement of his death came as a new shock. It is a great loss for his wife and daughter, for your circles, and also in wider circles for many here. He could have been of much good and done fine work with the talents entrusted to him. It is a mystery. Be so kind to deliver the enclosed letter to the widow Mrs. Biesterveld. I send it to you because I do not know her address.

Your book has not yet been published.[2] It was already long before New Year that we forwarded the most recently read proofs. I do not know what the cause is of this delay. If it does not come soon, I will make inquiries. Perhaps the pressure of Christmas and New Year is to blame.

Recently Dr. de Witt asked me to inquire into the place in the Netherlands from which his ancestors emigrated to this country.[3] I planned to ask Biesterveld for that because I did not want to trouble you since you are very busy due to having arrived home recently. The herewith enclosed letter states what he wishes.[4] Besides that, he spoke with me about a town called "Grooteholt" in "Gelderland" as a town from which his forefather had moved to that place in Friesland or the reverse. He would like to have some information concerning "Grooteholt." I only have a little atlas of the Netherlands here and no geographic dictionary. If it does not cause you too much trouble and you can locate these two towns, he and I would be greatly obliged to you. As far as I can conclude from our conversation, Grooteholt must be somewhere in German territory in the vicinity of the Eastern border of Gelderland or somewhere in that part of Gelderland. We all send you and your wife our best wishes for the New Year.[5]

As always,
Geerhardus Vos

---

* This letter has been translated from the original Dutch.

1. Petrus Biesterveld (1863–1908), professor of homiletics and a colleague of Bavinck at the Free University of Amsterdam, died December 14, 1908. His first wife, Bregtje Nomes, died July 11, 1888. She was the mother of his only child, Anna, born April 10, 1886. His second wife (to whom Vos refers) was Martje Visser (1867–1909).

2. The book was published in 1909 by Longmans, Green of New York.

3. John De Witt (1842–1923) was professor of church history at Princeton Theological Seminary from 1892 to 1912.

4. The letter reads: My Dear Dr. Vos, On the 9th day of June 1661, my ancestor Tierek Claaszen de Witt appeared before a Notary Public in Beaverwyck (Albany, New York) and granted a power of Attorney to his (T.C. de Witt's) brother-in-law Jan Albertz "for the purpose of getting demanding and receiving either amicably or else by means and ways of the law" of his (T.C. deWitt's) brother-in-law, Pieter Jansz, such rents as the aforesaid Pieter Jansz owes him for the use of a farm with a house on it. This piece of land or farm is said to be at *Oosterbemus* or *Oosterbinus* in East Friesland. The gentleman who examined the document at Albany wrote that in his judgment East Friesland does not mean the present East Friesland in Germany, but Friesland the capital of which is Leeuwarden. Have you a map of the Netherlands sufficiently large to enable me to ascertain whether a place with this name exists now—or a map of the Netherlands in the 17th century which would show a small place, like this existing at that date? I have the impression that this is my ancestor's birthplace; and that he left there for Westphalia where it borders on the Netherlands and where the people were Dutch, and that from the latter place emigrated to America. This gentleman, you see, thinks Friesland was called East Friesland in the documents to distinguish it from West Friesland (West of the Zuiderzee) which is not a part of Friesland but belongs to the province of Holland. Now if you can help me to find where *Oosterbemus* or *Oosterbinus* is or was, I shall be greatly obliged. Very sincerely yours, John De Witt, [November 9, 1907, Theological Seminary, Princeton, N.J.]

5. Bavinck married Johanna Adriana Schippers (1868–1942) on July 2, 1892.

To J. Gresham Machen

January 26, 1909
My dear Mr. Machen,
I see that the Septuagint renders Psalm 109:3 at the close:

εκ γαστροσ προ εωσμορον εγεννησα[1]

which the Vulgate renders:

ex utero ante Luciferum genui te[2]

It occurs to me that this passage, if it did not give rise to the view that heretofore Lucifer-Satan was originally (before he fell) the head of *all* the angels, may at least have served as a *locus probans*[3] in support of that view. The passage is Messianic and (as rendered above) implies that the Messiah was begotten before even the *first* creature was created. It would be, therefore, understood as making Lucifer the first *in order of creation*. From there to the view that Lucifer is the *highest* of all creatures, the head of the angels is but one step.

I do not think that the view in question sprang from any single passage like this. It is more natural to assume that Lucifer became the head of the angels in general after and because he had first been regarded as the head of the *fallen* angels.

Duhm in his commentary on Isaiah and chap. 14:12[4] credits Tertullian[5] and Gregory the Great[6] with having first applied the name Lucifer to Satan on the basis of this passage and of Luke 10:18 and Rev. 12:7ff., but he gives no references either for Tertullian or for Gregory.

Yours sincerely,
Geerhardus Vos

---

1. "I have begotten you from the womb before the morning."
2. "I have begotten you from the womb before Lucifer."
3. I.e., "convincing place."
4. Bernhard Duhm (1847–1928), *Das Buch Jesaia* (Göttingen: Vandenhoeck & Ruprecht, 1892).

5. For Tertullian's use of this text and the name Lucifer/Satan, see *Against Marcion*, 2.10, 5.2, 5.9, 5.17 (*Ante-Nicene Fathers* 3:305–6, 448, 454, 466).
6. Gregory I (the Great) (ca. 540–604). The citation cannot be located.

To Henry Beets

March 16, 1912
Princeton

My dear Dr. Beets,[1]
I am much indebted to you for the brochure commemorating the twenty-fifth anniversary of the founding of your church. I have perused it with great interest and extend to yourself and the church my best wishes for all future prosperity.

Let me also thank you for your kind reference in the last *Banner* number to our own anniversary.[2] It is a great pleasure to me to think that Princeton Seminary has been able to do something for the Dutch character in this country. We have this year quite a contingent of Dutch-speaking students, no less than 17. Seven of them are from the Cape Colony in South Africa. And our Dutch students are always among the best in the institution. The men we have from Grand Rapids have made an excellent record again.

With kindest regards,
Yours sincerely,
Geerhardus Vos

---

1. Henry Beets (1869–1947) was pastor of the LaGrave Avenue CRC, Grand Rapids, Michigan, 1899–1915, and Burton Heights CRC, Grand Rapids, Michigan, 1915–1920. He received his diploma from Calvin Theological Seminary in 1895 and thus was a student of Vos's prior to 1893.
2. The centennial celebration of Princeton Theological Seminary took place May 5–7, 1912. See *The Centennial Celebration of the Theological Seminary of the Presbyterian Church in the United States of America at Princeton, New Jersey* (Princeton: Theological Seminary, 1912).

To Henry Beets

October 4, 1915
Princeton

My dear Dr. Beets,

I am much indebted to you for the copy of *"The Compendium Explained"*[1] and still more grateful for the kind remembrance of me that inspired the dedication. It is pleasant to know that I have not been entirely forgotten by some of my pupils of old. My memory still frequently turns back to the hours we spent together in the up-stairs of the Williams Street School.[2] The character of the work you have done on this Explanation of the Compendium shows that the poor teaching given with so few facilities in those days has nevertheless under the blessing of God borne its fruit. That is what should give and does give me even more joy in this dedication than the personal feature of it.

I will ask one of my colleagues to review the book for our periodical.[3] It would give me pleasure to do it myself, but people might think that the nice things that I should like to say about it were due to its having been dedicated to the reviewer.

As we are woefully behind with our budget of books to be noticed it may take some time before the review can get in. I hope, however, we can bring it out early in the new year.

With kindest regards and best wishes for the success of your labors in every sphere.

Sincerely yours,
Geerhardus Vos

---

1. *The Compendium Explained: A Popular Explanation of the Abridgement of the Heidelberg Catechism, Known as "Compendium of the Christian Religion," of the Reformed Churches of Holland, and of Holland Origin* (Grand Rapids: Eerdmans-Sevensma Co., 1915). Beets dedicated the book to his former professor.

2. Calvin Theological Seminary (Theologische School) was located here from 1876 to 1892, when a new building was erected at the corner of Madison Avenue and Franklin Street. Vos's reference to the "upstairs" is the famous "Upper Room" of this Christian school, where the Seminary held classes.
3. The review, by B. B. Warfield, appeared in *Princeton Theological Review* 15 (1917): 183–85.

To Cornelis van Felderen

September 5, 1921
Roaring Branch
Lycoming Co. Pennsylvania

Dear Brother,[1]

Your pleasant letter has, via many detours, finally reached me here, where it is our custom to spend the summer. Hence the delay in responding.

We will greatly welcome your visit. As for the time, it would be best for us if you could make it the last week of your stay here. The seminary opens September 30, and we do not return *en famille* to Princeton until near that date. Then there is much to take care of: opening up the house, cleaning, dealing with the children's resumption of their schoolwork, etc. If you come after these things have been taken care of, there will be more time to become acquainted and to show you various things in which you may be interested.

If, however, this time is not convenient for you, we can also make arrangements for a week earlier. Let us know how this fits in your plans, when you think you will arrive, and by which train. It is easy to reach Princeton from New York, and [there are trains] at least a dozen times a day from Pennsylvania Station, 7th Ave. and 32nd Street.

We expect that you will not make it merely a one-day visit but that you will stay with us a few days.

> With friendly greetings,
> Yours truly,
> Geerhardus Vos
> At the above address until Sept. 15.

---

* This letter has been translated from the original Dutch.

1. Cornelis Van Felderen (1872–1945) was professor of Semitic languages at the Free University from 1905 and professor of Old Testament from 1906 until his death. He was a delegate to the meeting of the Presbyterian Alliance in Pittsburgh, Pennsylvania, September 16–25, 1921. He left Amsterdam in August and returned in October.

To Directors

August 11, 1926
Roaring Branch
Lycoming Co. Pennsylvania

Directors of the "Vereeniging voor Hooger onderwy op Gereformeerden Grondslag."[1]
Amsterdam

Dear Brethren,

I feel greatly flattered by the kind invitation just received from your "collegium" to deliver some lectures for account of the "Calvyn-fonds."[2] It is with very sincere regret that I feel compelled to decline this kind request. Domestic, professional and ecclesiastical circumstances prevent my undertaking this journey and all that is connected with it.[3] Will you kindly convey to the "Directors" my gratitude for the confidence placed in me, and the reason for my inability to respond to it by acceptance?

> Yours sincerely,
> Geerhardus Vos

---

1. I.e., "Society for Higher Research of the Reformed Foundation."
2. On July 29, 1926, the Directors of the Free University had sent a letter to Vos asking him to provide the Calvynfonds (i.e., Calvin Lectures) in the autumn of the year. The lectures were intended to promote cross-fertilization between Dutch and foreign Calvinists.
3. This appears to be a subtle reference to the controversy surrounding J. Gresham Machen. The result would be Machen's resignation in 1929 and the founding of Westminster Theological Seminary in Philadelphia.

To Sylvester Beach

July 13, 1928
Roaring Branch
Lycoming Co. Pennsylvania

My Dear Dr. Sylvester Beach:[1]

I herewith return to you (signed) the resolution of the Board of Directors. In signing it I took into consideration, that the phrasing of the statement had to be a more or less indefinite one, in order to make it suitable for every part and angle of what has grown to be a complicated case. My difficulty (for I admit there was a little) was not so much a personal, but rather a conscientious one. I am quite willing to confess my faults and mistakes and sins, for I should have told myself from the beginning that it would be difficult for me to live through, and take part, in such a long-drawn out disagreement without falling into many things my conscience would in calmer moments tell me were wrong. But after all such matters are to be settled between God and the conscience first, and it is surely in that relationship that the existence and nature and extent of the wrong should be brought to clearness, and repentance with expression of regret to our fellows be put into effect. It would be quite inconceivable that regret and retraction in the technically religious sense should ever be placed on the basis of what has *seemed* to others to be the wrong in us. This does not alter the fact that perhaps, (materially considered), the things to be repented of or regretted or apologies made for might to a large extent coincide with the feeling of injury caused by them in others; only a true Christian repentance can cover only what the conscience bears witness to as having been wrong. No brother's feeling, if I am right in my interpretation of Protestant ethics, can ever be made to underlie this process between God and the soul. I do not wish you to understand, however, that I sign the document otherwise than *ex animo*.[2] I do not practice any mental reservations.

The statements of yours accompanying the resolution have considerably relieved me in the matter mentioned, and I am grateful to you personally for these.

For the rest, the Directors and my colleagues will, I can assure you, find me most peacefully inclined, forgivingly disposed, and ready to do what I can to render the present action successful.

Yours sincerely,
Geerhardus Vos

---

1. Sylvester Woodridge Beach (1852–1940) was pastor of the church which the Vos family attended in Princeton (First PCUSA) from 1906 to 1922. At the time of this letter, he was pastor emeritus and a member of the Board of Trustees of the seminary.

2. I.e., "from the heart."

To Frank Stevenson

December 19, 1928
Princeton

My Dear Dr. Stevenson,[1]

I herewith return the communication of the Board of Directors sent me under date of December 14. It seems to me that only nos. 1, 2, and 4 are intended, in the form offered, to be signed by members of the Faculty. The others (3 and 5) contain declarations on assurances on behalf of the Board concerning their own attitude and feelings toward the Faculty. Of these I take grateful notice, and desire to reciprocate them in the same spirit on my part.

Perhaps it is not superfluous to say that I consider the items specified as intended to enable the Board "to compose the differences in the Seminary," and therefore applying to the present juncture. I have, according to my best ability, tried to practice since virtually identical promises were made by me in answer to the letter received earlier through Dr. Beach, and were implied in my willingness to agree to two of the formulas laid before the Faculty by the Committee of Six.

Sincerely yours,
Geerhardus Vos

---

1. Frank Herbert Stevenson (1893–1934) was pastor of the Church of the Covenant, PCUSA, Cincinnati, Ohio from 1915 to 1927. He was elected a member of the Board of Trustees of Princeton Theological Seminary in 1927. After the reorganization of the Seminary in 1929, he was instrumental in the formation of Westminster Theological Seminary, Philadelphia, Pennsylvania.

To J. Gresham Machen

[? 1930]

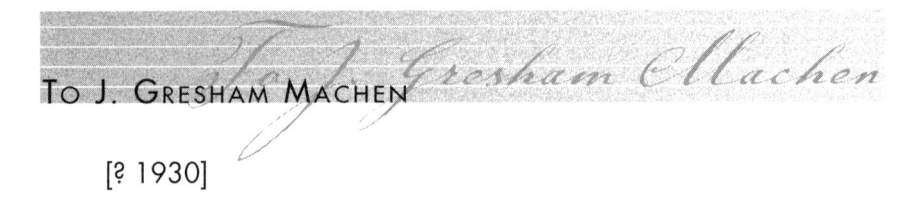

My dear Dr. Machen,

I cannot thank you enough for the copy you sent me of your book.[1] It is a monumental work, and cannot fail to do much good and that for a long time. The completeness and the ἀκριβει,α[2] of it awake my admiration.

With best wishes for success in your new milieu and position.

> Sincerely yours,
> Geerhardus Vos

---

1. *The Virgin Birth of Christ*, published by Harper of New York in 1930.
2. I.e., "exactness."

To J. Gresham Machen

March 31, 1930
Princeton

Dear Dr. Machen,

Just after I had sent my little note of thanks to you, it occurred to me that perhaps one alleged reference to the Virgin Birth in the O.T. had not come to your notice. It concerns the interpretation of "Shiloh" in Gen. 49:10. Reading here for "Shiloh" Shelloh or Shella, and comparing this with a similar word in Deut. 28:57 (or around there) is understood of the placenta or after birth which in the "straightness" of the siege "threatened" the hungry woman will eat and jealously guard from her own family, lest they secure part of it. Now this is curiously connected with the a-paternal birth in this way, that the placenta is that issue of the birth that comes from the mother exclusively and with which the father had nothing to do whatsoever. This is a reading advocated by ancient Jewish exegetes (among others Kimchi[1]), but also by Christian expositors who were not slow to bring it into connection with the virgin birth; so Raymond Martin (in dependence upon Kimchi) +/– 1270;[2] later by Galatinus from Rome (+/– 1500).[3] Still in the 18th century, such men as Simonis[4] and later Ilgen[5] and Botticher[6] defended this rendering of Shllo (or Shella).

I do not want you to understand that I find anything in this for myself. I regard it as no more than an exegetical curiosity. My own preference for the explanation of "Shilo" is to resolve it into "Esher-lo" to whom it (i.e., Jehovah's scepter and ruler's staff) belongs. This (?) is supported by Ezek. 21:27, which passage, it seems to me, is dependent on Gen. 49:10.

All this can be found in detail in the unique work of Dr. A. Posnanski, *Schiloh: ein Beitrag zur Geschichte der Messiaslehre* (Leipzig: J.C. Hinrichs, 1904).

Pardon me for bothering you about this. You are now such a *facile princeps*[7] expert on the subject that even the most remote allusion to the smallest detail must have interest for you. Franz Delitzsch remarks on the proposed reading that it is "too nasty" to deserve consideration.[8] I think that he was too much of an "aesthetic" spirit always to do full justice to the O.T. realism.

With best regards,
Geerhardus Vos

---

1. David Kimchi (ca. 1160–ca. 1235), as cited in Adolf Posnanski, *Schiloh: Ein Beitrag zur Geschichte der Messiaslehre* (Leipzig: J. C. Hinrichs, 1904), 157.
2. Raymundi Martini (1220–1285), as cited in Posnanski, *Schiloh*, 361.
3. Pietro Galatino (fl. 1480–1539), as cited in Posnanski, *Schiloh*, 439.
4. Johann Simonis (1698–1768), *Arcanum formarum nominum hebraeae linguae* (1735), 131.

5. Karl David Ilgen (1763–1834), *Die Urkunden des ersten Buchs von Moses* (1798). Posnanski, *Schiloh*, 70, incorrectly cites Johann David Ilgen. I owe this correction to Grace Mullen.

6. Botticher or Boetticher is Paul Anton Boetticher (1827–1891), who later changed his name to Paul Anton de Lagarde. Vos cites Paulus Boetticher, *Horae Aramicae* (Berlin: C. Grobe, 1847), 25. I owe this identification and citation to Grace Mullen.

7. I.e., "easily first/chief."

8. *A New Commentary on Genesis* (Edinburgh: T & T Clark, 1899), 2:379.

To J. Gresham Machen

May 1, 1930
Princeton

My dear Dr. Machen,

It was my intention from the beginning to present you with a copy of my book, as soon as the first installment came off the press.[1] Unfortunately I discovered so many "fleas" in these first copies, that I was ashamed to send one to you. A further installment is now being prepared and it will give me great pleasure to send you one of these.

Meanwhile I am still more ashamed that you should think it necessary to pay for your own copy. That almost hurt my feelings. Still, I am glad to say, not quite. It requires no apology.

I have sent that separate copy to Mr. Hirzel.[2] The $3.50 for that I will retain.

Together with this I mail the two other copies. Neither of these is intended for you. Please consider them a contribution to the library of Westminster.

My check is enclosed for 7.00. That will straighten things out, I trust.

My boy, Bernardus,[3] Mr. Meeter[4] and some others intend to be present at your commencement next week.[5]

Kindly remember me in faith and affection.

        Sincerely yours,
        Geerhardus Vos

---

1. *The Pauline Eschatology* (1930).
2. Stephen A. Hirzel, president of the University of Pennsylvania chapter of the League of Evangelical Students.
3. Bernardus Vos (1905–1998).
4. Probably John Meeter; see p. 233, n. 3.
5. The first commencement at Westminster Theological Seminary, Philadelphia, was held May 6, 1930.

To F. W. Grosheide

February 19, 1932
52 Mercer St.
Princeton, N.J.
U.S.A.

Dear Brother,[1]

Your letter, which made the journey here once before but did not reach me at the end of its trip, was the second time more successful in reaching me. I feel greatly honored that "The Association of Pastors"[2] has selected me as one of three to judge a possible response to the competition that has been organized. I therefore regret it all the more that circumstances do not allow me to accept the appointment. Having reached the age of 70, I will retire this summer and will consequently move from Princeton, probably to one place or another where I shall not have access to the library here, which in itself will make me less qualified to judge the submission. Please be so kind as to excuse me.

221

In earlier days, when I still taught at Grand Rapids, I found the so-called "covenant of works" very interesting. The documents of the Westminster Confession reflect a concept [of the covenant of works] that, while it does not contradict the earlier concepts, nevertheless goes beyond them in my opinion.

The tendency to equate the covenant with the natural state of revealed religion seems to have been overcome here, since the whole covenant is represented as flowing from God's grace and thus means a *plus* over and above the religion of the beginning. In the period referred to above I published a booklet with the title "*The Covenant in Reformed Theology*,"[3] which deals with those and other issues. If I come across a copy among my books, which are at present in a state of disorganization, I will send it to you.

With high regard,
Your brother in Christ,
Geerhardus Vos

---

* This letter has been translated from the original Dutch.

1. Frederik Willem Grosheide (1881–1972) was professor of New Testament at the Free University of Amsterdam from 1912 to 1953.

2. Vereniging van predikantenvain de Gereformeerde Kerken (Association of Preachers of the Reformed Churches). Their annual meeting was held in Utrecht in the spring.

3. "The Doctrine of the Covenant in Reformed Theology," in *Redemptive History and Biblical Interpretation*, ed. Richard B. Gaffin Jr. (Phillipsburg, NJ: Presbyterian and Reformed Publishing Co., 1980), 234–67.

To J. Gresham Machen

April 28, 1932
52 Mercer St.

My Dear Prof. Machen,

I have been very much touched by your repeated expressions to me of the kindest of feelings and memories living in your heart from the days gone by. Had I not been so preoccupied with the troubles and sorrows of moving these last weeks, I would have replied sooner to what you wrote, for it brought a real refreshment to me. I feel somewhat like Paul, though in a less eschatological state of mind, that the earthly tent-house is broken up and breaking away from me. One's house, though it be "a tent" becomes more a part of one's being. It's in one's routine of years one is accustomed to realize. This is next to the tent of the body in its closeness to our soul, relatives [?] excepted.

Now, as to the reference your note made to books, that reached you through Dr. Van Til and were not paid for.[1] Well, they could have been intended to be paid for. There were some [?] that for one reason or other, I thought you might be interested in. Evidently he misunderstood my intention.

Dr. Van Til, and all your Faculty, have been of invaluable help to me in finding homes or a home for those orphaned children of my [?], especially of that parts of which the Swiss German poet wrote:

"*Streut in der wird, gibt in der Guden Hand.*"

It will be a pleasure for me to see you some time before I leave Princeton. I have the use of the house until August 1st, but will hardly stay till that date. All of May and sometime in June I expect to linger here.

Mrs. Vos intends to go to the Summer home (Roaring Branch, Lycoming Co., PA) earlier. Please come and see me.

With kindest regards,
Yours sincerely,
Geerhardus Vos

---

1. Cornelius Van Til (1895–1987) was professor of apologetics at Westminster Theological Seminary, Philadelphia, Pennsylvania, 1929–1972.

To Paul Woolley

September 9, 1932
Roaring Branch, Pa.

Dear Mr. Woolley,[1]
I send you by Parcel Post a little volume of devotional characters which evidently had become separated from the Parker Society Collection sold to you in the Spring, and which is necessary to complete the latter.[2] I found it among my books here in the country.

This place is an ideal place for convalescence after illness.[3] I can bear witness to that myself.

Wishing Westminster Seminary a good auspicious entrance upon the new academic year.

Yours very sincerely,
Geerhardus Vos

---

1. Paul Woolley (1902–1984) was registrar and assistant professor of church history at Westminster Theological Seminary, Philadelphia, Pennsylvania.

2. Vos is referring to volume 2 of *Select Poetry, Chiefly Devotional, of the Reign of Queen Elizabeth*, collected and edited for the Parker Society by Edward Farr (Cambridge: University Press, 1845), which is volume 22 of the Parker Society Publications. The volume is currently housed in the library at Westminster Theological Seminary, Philadelphia, Pennsylvania.

3. Vos refers to abdominal surgery, as well as the removal of his infected teeth, in the late spring of 1932.

To Albertus Eekhof

October 28, 1932
1212 South Sycamore Street
Santa Ana, California
U.S. of A.

Dear Professor,[1]

You must think that, after your kind letter, I have kept you waiting long (almost to the point of rudeness) for an answer. The reason was the only partial recovery from my illness of this Spring.[2] Although the stay in northern Pennsylvania put me more or less back on my feet because of the cool climate, I nevertheless had to abstain from much work. This was all the more so because the difficult trip from there to here (California) was rapidly approaching. Fortunately it is now behind us. It took about two weeks by car, and traveling 200–300 miles per day in a car is extremely tiring for someone who does not have his normal strength. You know this from your own past experience in this country. Southern California is a lovely land, but I notice that even in an ideal land it is necessary to "acclimatize."

This by way of apology for my slowness in responding to your letter, which greatly appeals to me. Now, as to your concrete proposal concerning *Neerlandia*, allow me to say first of all that my primary purpose in sending my small collections of poems was not publicity.[3] I merely wanted to express my appreciation for your comments in the NRC[4] on the occasion of my retirement—all the more because my brief encounter with you in earlier years gave the comments a somewhat personal character, so that I appreciated the "press clipping" more than I would have the usual, merely factual, newspaper article.

I have always been more averse to rather than a friend of a personal "stepping into the limelight." This is perhaps a residue of the somewhat world-repudiating spirit of the Old Seceder Pietism in which my parents lived and in which I grew up. And you know yourself that the terrible advertising-mania that dominates the "New World" is not conducive to moderating such an inherited aversion. Self-promotion is especially repugnant to me. Two things I would further submit for your consideration. In the first place, I have never had a high opinion of the literary significance of my poetic labors. Had it been my destiny to live my life in the Netherlands, I would have been more successful at doing justice to the Dutch idiom. I know only too well that there are Anglicisms in the poems, and perhaps even more Germanisms. But this realization could not move me to keep inside me that which I felt I had "in my pen." If you think that the product of that urge is not unworthy of mention in *Neerlandia*, then I shall be grateful for your effort.[5]

It is somewhat difficult to oblige you in the matter of the photo. In recent years no portrait has been made of me. I have in my possession a single photo, which is at least twenty years old. My son, who is very handy with the camera, has promised me that he will make a short "film" for me. When that "film" is ready I shall enclose the results with this letter. You can do with it what you may choose; it is not necessary to return it.

I shall try to fulfill your other two requests. I find it difficult to bring myself to writing a formal autobiography, even in concise form. All I can do in this regard is send you a few data concerning the course of my life. I hope you will be so kind as to provide a context for them that will give the data some (small) measure of continuity. You are much more familiar with *Neerlandia* than I, and you can therefore judge better what is suitable or unsuitable in this kind of article.

The most difficult of your four requests is that for a contribution for the magazine. I will have to write from the perspective of those who had their roots in the Netherlands and were nourished by those roots. The truth is that I have spent almost my entire life (at least the "middle portion," 1893–1932) not in Dutch but in English circles. Although I always kept more or less in touch with the Netherlands, this contact was largely in the theological realm through my familiarity with the men from the Free University. Nevertheless, literary sensitivity was not entirely absent. I lived in the Netherlands until my nineteenth year and received many indelible impressions there. It has been a marvel to me how deep such impressions from one's youth take root in the soul, and how they surface involuntarily as soon as more than ordinary effort is made to give expression to the inner life. Although I moved in [an] English-speaking [environment] year after year, nevertheless, as soon as I took up the pen to "weave" a song, the Dutch language surfaced. It was truly something Freudian. To this day, when I have to count, I don't go "one—two—three," etc., but "een—twee—drie": that is at a still deeper level than all literary aspirations in prose or poetry.

I will try to enclose the "small" contribution you request. You must understand that I preferred not to give it a specifically ecclesiastical coloring. Some more general comments on the realm where the American and "Dutch" worlds touch will perhaps strike you as adequate.

Again, my heartfelt thanks for your kind efforts on my behalf.

I would be pleased to receive a few issues of *Neerlandia*. Even here, in an entirely American environment in Southern California, one encounters elderly Dutchmen. Yesterday, I met a merchant, in his seventies, who speaks perfect Dutch and told me that he had come here at the age of three. In the large city of Los Angeles is a Christian Reformed Church with a pastor who received his training in Grand Rapids and Princeton.[6] And there are at least half a dozen places in California where such congregations can be found. But the complete Americanization is unavoidable, and all too often it is accompanied by a loss of all familiarity with and interest in the mother country. But why do I have to write to you about these matters? You are undoubtedly sufficiently familiar with these developments.

With kind greetings I remain,
Yours in Christ,
Geerhardus Vos

P.S. I became, of course, acquainted with your interesting work on Dutch church life in its first beginnings (under the classis "Amsterdam").[7] Yesterday I saw the announcement for a book by (Prof. [?] Plooi)[8] that describes the stay of the Puritans in the Netherlands at the beginning of the seventeenth century. I was glad to be able to order a copy. Among the books I had to leave behind out East was also the work of Mrs. Cockshut[9] on the same topic.

G. V.

---

* This letter has been translated from the original Dutch.

1. Dr. Albertus Eekhof (1884–1933) was professor of Reformed Protestantism (1914–33) and the history of Christianity (1924–33) at the University of Leiden.

2. Vos was hospitalized for bleeding "piles" and infected teeth.

3. Vos's poems are contained in eight small books: *Spiegel der genade* (1922), *Spiegel der natuur en lyra Anglica* (1927) (two editions), *Charis, English Verses* (1931), *Spiegel des doods* (1932), *Western Rhymes* (1933), *Zeis en garve* (1934), and *Rhymes Old and New* (n.d.) under the name "Desiderius."

4. *Nieuwe Rotterdamsche Courant*, in which Eekhof wrote an article on Vos's retirement from Princeton.

5. The article appeared in *Neerlandia* for January 1933 under the title "Prof. Dr. Geerhardus Vos," by Dr. A. Eekhof (pp. 9–10). It includes an appendix submitted by Vos himself and thus represents a primary autobiographical reflection from this very private scholar. Cf. "Autobiographical Notes," trans. Ed M. van der Maas, in *Kerux: The Journal of Northwest Theological Seminary* 19/3 (December 2004): 6–10.

6. Rev. Watson Groen (1893–1951), who graduated from Calvin Theological Seminary in 1917 and Princeton Theological Seminary in 1918. He was pastor of the Christian Reformed church in Los Angeles from 1927 to 1934.

7. Vos is referring to Eekhof's *De Hervormde Kerk in Noord-Amerika, 1624–44* ('s-Gravenhage: M. Nijhoff, 1913).

8. Daniel Plooij (1877–1935) wrote *The Pilgrim Fathers from a Dutch Point of View* (New York: New York University Press, 1932).

9. Winnifred Cockshott, *The Pilgrim Fathers: Their Church and Colony* (New York: Putnam, 1909).

To Donald MacKenzie

February 26, 1935
1212 So. Sycamore Street
Santa Ana, California

My Dear Dr. MacKenzie,[1]

I fear you may think I owe you an apology for something done, in which I had neither intentional part nor actual purpose.

The facts are these: the "Notes" on my courses in Old Testament and New Testament Biblical Theology in use by the Middle and Senior Classes during my later years in Princeton were likewise used at that time in the Seminary of the Reformed Presbyterian Church in Philadelphia,[2] and derived by the students there from the source of mimeographic reproduction in Princeton. Whether any use of these "Notes" was made by the Princeton students in the interval between my superannuation and your actual entrance upon the work of the chair I do not know, having neither then nor afterwards received any intimation to that effect. After your inauguration I took for granted, of course, that there would be no further reproduction or circulation of these old tools. In fact I had not a single copy in my own possession in these finishing months. It was with considerable surprise on my part that I learned through a letter from Mr. Rudolph[3] of the Philadelphia Seminary that, their supply having given out, they had of their own initiative prepared a mimeographed edition of Old Testament and New Testament "Notes" bound together, and were sending me in lieu of royalty some forty copies of this work. I received these and acknowledged the receipt with pleasure. With the exception of perhaps a dozen copies given away this stock is still here under my hand. I had made no serious effort to realize any "royalty" on these. It so happened, however, that a publishing house in Grand Rapids offered to print the "Notes" for publication. Nothing came of this, partly because the material, not covering the entire field, was not without much overworking ready or fit for publication, partly because I did not desire to interfere with the disposal of whatever stock the Reformed Presbyterians had on hand. In the course of the correspondence about this plan I suggested to the Grand Rapids dealers that they might relieve me by the sale of the odd forty copies I still possess, *viz.*, through selling these to Dutch students in their neighborhood. To my surprise I received from them the concrete offer to dispose of all the copies I have through a student in Princeton. To this my immediate reply was that I could not consider such a thing, if for no other reason than that it would involve a grave discourtesy to you as my successor in the chair. When still further pressed to accede to their purpose, I replied in the negative again. I have put away the copies for the present to make absolutely sure that they are not made merchandise with in Princeton Seminary. Perhaps I can through some one in Grand Rapids make them serve a useful purpose there. I think I shall also write to Dr. Rudolph in Philadelphia to intimate to them that they should not supply the Princeton students from their stock which was produced without my knowledge, and of which I received the first intimation when they informed what had been done and shipped me the royalty-copies.

It is possible, of course, that some of their stock has reached Princeton students, although I have no reason to think so. If this has actually happened, it was entirely without my cognizance or intention. Perhaps I should have been more careful, when first apprised of the undertaking and receiving the copies following soon after, to stipulate that I could nor would be a partner to having someone deal with the copies among the students in Princeton. If this was a sin it was a sin of omission and not one "with a high hand."[4] I desire, however to apologize for the dereliction in that respect. To interfere with the teaching of the course in the Seminary after it had been entrusted to your good hands lay far form my intention. Believe me in this, as in all things, to be and remain

      Fraternally yours,
      Geerhardus Vos

---

1. Donald MacKenzie (1882–1941) was professor of biblical theology at Princeton Theological Seminary, Princeton, New Jersey, from 1933 until his death.
2. Actually, it was the Reformed Episcopal Seminary.
3. Robert Knight Rudolph (1906–1986) was assistant professor of systematic theology, biblical theology, and English Bible.
4. Cf. Num. 15:30.

To Donald MacKenzie

March 20, 1935
1212 So. Sycamore Street
Santa Ana, California

Dear Dr. McKenzie:

 I shall be very glad indeed to send you a copy of the volume of "Notes on Old Testament and New Testament Theology." The contents are "notes" and not as the title says: "Old and New Testament Theology." Not a few typographical mistakes have crept into the text, but on the whole it is better than what the students produced in my time.

 You are certainly welcome to any use you can make of these relics.

 There is one thing out of the question, that you should pay for the copy sent. Please accept it as a courtesy from my hand.

 With kindest regards and best wishes for all your work.

      Sincerely yours,
      Geerhardus Vos

To Paul Woolley

January 27, 1936
1212 So. Sycamore St.
Santa Ana, California

My Dear Mr. Woolley:

I am in receipt of the lists designating the selections from the catalogue of my books by the various professors and of the checks of yourself ($32.75) and of Prof. R. B. Kuiper ($6.80) in payment.[1] It is very kind of you, indeed, to assist me in this manner, in a matter, which, without your help, would prove very complicated. I have transmitted these lists to my son, Bernardus H. Vos, at Roaring Branch, Lycoming Co., Pa.[2] Your desire that the several orders shall be separately packed, so that you will have no further bother about sorting the books, will, I trust, be complied with by him. As to the manner of transportation, I must needs leave to his judgment, because the weather conditions in your part of the country, are, to judge from the papers, quite extraordinary, prohibitive perhaps of a transportation by auto. But, in whatever way, he judges best to make the delivery, I am sure he will see to it that the transport is safe.

A few of the books are here; these I shall dispatch myself either by freight or by express. The cost of transportation I intend to pay myself, and I have instructed Bernardus to the same effect.

Previously to your people examining the catalogue, a little collection of the books had been sold to Mr. Meeter of Chambersburg, Pa.[3] It is possible that in a few instances there will be a conflict with what appears on your lists and what he received. I will let you know about this in course of time, and return the money for what could not be delivered owing to that cause.

Once more thanking you most heartily for the trouble and interest taken in the matter, I remain,

        Very sincerely yours,
        Geerhardus Vos

---

1. Rienk Bouke Kuiper (1886–1966) was professor of practical theology at Westminster Theological Seminary, Philadelphia, Pennsylvania.
2. Bernardus was born in 1905.
3. John E. Meeter (1901–1993) was professor of Old Testament at Wilson College, Chambersburg, Pennsylvania, from 1934 to 1945.

To Paul Woolley

January 29, 1936
1212 So. Sycamore St.
Santa Ana, California

My Dear Mr. Woolley:

I have shipped to your address today by freight (prepaid) Sante Fe Railroad the items of our catalogue, purchased by your faculty, which were in my possession here, and are to supplement the consignment to be sent by my son from Roaring Branch, Pa (22 pieces). I trust the box will reach you safely. The slips in each book show to which individual purchaser each belongs, and a list will be found inside the box corresponding to these slips. I regret the necessity of my having to request this additional favor from you. Receive my thanks in advance for it and for the previous assistance rendered.

        Very sincerely yours,
        Geerhardus Vos

To Paul Woolley

February 22, 1936
1212 So. Sycamore Street
Santa Ana, California

My Dear Mr. Woolley:

My son informs me that you would like to have an invoice of the books bought for the library for accounting purposes. There was one book on the library list that had been sold previously to someone else, *viz.*, A. A. Hodge's *Outline*. The price for this was 40 cents. You will receive from him the invoice with this item omitted, so that the bill for the library amounts to $6.40 instead of $6.80, *as already paid by you*. There were some other items in the lists of the faculty members which were pre-sold, and for which likewise, since they have already paid for their complete lists, reimbursements must be made. These are as follows:

Mr. Murray:[1]
Davidson, Epistle to the Hebrews.	20
C. W. Hodge, Apostolic History & Literature.	40
Vos, Mosaic Origin of the Pentateuchal Codes.	25
Vos, The Range of the Logos-name in the Fourth Gospel.	10
	.95

Mr. MacRea:[2]
Schürer, History of the Jewish People in the Time of Jesus Christ.	40
Flinders Petrie, A History of Egypt.	25
Vos, Alleged Development in Paul's Teaching on the Resurrection.	10
Sudermann, Der Katzensteg.	20
Tyrrell, The Royal Road to Health.	10
	1.05

Mr. R. B. Kuiper:
Gass, Schleiermacher's Briefwechsel mit Gass.   50
Mr. Allis:[3]
Habberton, *Helen's Babies*.   25

Total   2.75

When to this total of reimbursement from Prof. Murray, Prof. MacRea, Prof. Kuiper and Prof. Allis is added the .40 cents due the Library, it makes altogether $3.15. For this amount I enclose a check. Will you once more do me the favor of mediating this, I hope final, adjustment, by paying the professors named, the amount specified in each case, and returning the 40 cents to your Library account.

There is a possibility of other discrepancies. If after receiving the books, the consignees find such, kindly ask them to let me know, and I will make it right.

           Thanking you again,
           Sincerely yours,
           Geerhardus Vos

---

1. John Murray (1898–1975) was instructor in systematic theology at Westminster Theological Seminary, Philadelphia, Pennsylvania.

2. Allan A. MacRae (1902–1997) was assistant professor of Old Testament at Westminster Theological Seminary, Philadelphia, Pennsylvania.

3. Oswald Thompson Allis (1880–1973) was professor of Old Testament at Westminster Theological Seminary, Philadelphia, Pennsylvania.

To J. Gresham Machen

May 7, 1936
1212 So. Sycamore Street,
Santa Ana, California.

My Dear Dr. Machen:

I was very agreeably surprised by your letter and the arrival of the present of your book.[1] It is a fine book indeed, but its fine character even is surpassed by its timeliness. It ought to do much good, if the ears of the people were not "stopped," as the prophets would have put it, by so many pleasant messages, which crowd out the substance of the gospel from the pulpit and even the Sunday School. The first Easter I spent here, I attended a church in which the preacher had for his text the passage on the institution of the Lord's Supper. For this he chose the theme: "Victory after Defeat," as though it was a fit subject for a moralizing essay. Not a word was said in the so-called "Easter Sermon" concerning the "soteric" significance of the event and its practical bearing on the sinner's soul. It is sad beyond description. And that happened on "the green tree"; what happens on the dry kind I can hardly imagine.[2]

There are a few students around here you will perhaps remember from your Princeton days. There is Brahams,[3] who ministers to a "community church" at Laguna Beach, where there is an artist's colony. Then there is Prichard[4] near Los Angeles, who left his last church in that city because of the ceaseless inculcation by the people of (and insistence on) Premillenarianism. This doctrine has spread to such an extent here and so overlaid the essence of the gospel, nay of the very core of religion, that it seems hard to speak or argue about it. The sentiment is so strong and so absolutely focused in that one matter of eschatological chronology, that I sometimes am made to feel that the

"Millennium" has become a god, crowding out even the true God in the imagination and religious interest of the people. If you tell them that you have your doubts about the Millennium they ask very naively whether you do not believe in the second coming of the Lord.

Many thanks for the kind words in your letter about Johannes.[5] He is doing a good work in Manchuria. But, since he lays the foundation deep, and does not indulge in any "bally ho" concerning the "thousands" that are waiting to stream in, I am afraid that he might be suspected by some of a lack of missionary enthusiasm in the conventional sense of that phrase.

Kagawa[6] has been here and carried not a few off their feet. He was also in Michigan. My daughter[7] and some other folks from Calvin went to hear him. He professed to be doctrinally sound, but said that he believed in giving the people the meat and not the bones from underneath. My daughter remarked that that gave people no chance of judging how crooked the bones were.

With kind regards to yourself and the other members of your faculty and the assurance that you always have my deep interest and my prayers I remain

Sincerely yours,
Geerhardus Vos

---

1. *The Christian Faith in the Modern World* (New York: Macmillan, 1936).

2. Vos frequently alludes in this manner to Luke 23:31.

3. Raymond Irving Brahams (1899–1976) graduated from Princeton Theological Seminary in 1925. He served as pastor of the Community Church in Laguna Beach, California, from 1925 to 1949.

4. Paul Prichard (1893–1981) was pastor of Grace PCUSA, Los Angeles, California, from 1931 to 1934 and St. Andrews PCUSA, Strathmore, California, from 1935 to 1947.

5. Johannes Geerhardus Vos (1903–1983) was Vos's firstborn child. He was ordained by the Presbytery of Pittsburgh, RPCNA, on March 25, 1929. He served as a missionary in Manchuria for that denomination from 1930 to 1941. From 1954 to 1983 he was professor of Bible at Geneva College, Beaver Falls, Pennsylvania.

6. Toyohiko Kagawa (1888–1960) graduated from Princeton Theological Seminary in 1916. He was a famous modernist.

7. Marianne (Mrs. Williams) Radius (1906–2000).

To Arthur Machen

January 5, 1937
1212 So. Sycamore Street,
Santa Ana, California.

Arthur Machen
Ruxton, Maryland

My Dear Sir:

The announcement of the sudden death of your brother in a newspaper item, came to me as a great shock and filled me with deep sorrow. Since your name was mentioned in the paper, I address this expression of my sympathy to you with a request that you will convey it to the mourning relatives.

Dr. Machen for a short while was my pupil in Princeton Seminary.[1] Afterwards for many years we were associated as members of the faculty.[2] And the time came soon that I learned more from him than it had ever been my privilege to impart to him as a teacher. He was, indeed, a profound scholar, but what counts for more than that, a great man of God and a true defender of our Christian faith in its Presbyterian form. His name will not be easily forgotten, for the impression he made on the religious and theological mind of the church was too deep for that.

Together with the Rev. Craighead,[3] a retired Presbyterian minister here, I sent him a card for a Christmas remembrance. Alas, it probably never reached him.

Once more, may I ask you to convey to his remaining kin, whom I never had the privilege of meeting, and to receive for yourself, these few words of my great sorrow in the loss of such a friend and fellow-brother in the Lord.

>Very sincerely yours,
>Geerhardus Vos

---

1. 1902–1905.
2. 1906–1929.
3. David E. Craighead (1861–1943) was a graduate of Western Theological Seminary in Allegheny/Pittsburgh, PA (1891). He was ordained by Redstone Presbytery of the PCUSA in 1893 and served pastorates in Somerset, PA (1893), Curwansville, PA (1894), Emlenton, PA (1900), Second Church, Mercer, PA (1902), Waverly PCUSA in Baltimore, MD (1906), Worthington, OH (1917), and Strasburg, PA (1919). He retired in 1931 following a massive heart attack, and settled in Santa Ana, CA.

To Ned Stonehouse

December 15, 1938
1212 South Sycamore Street
Santa Ana, California

My dear Prof. Stonehouse,

I owe you much thanks for the Inaugural Address which occupied so large a space in the new *Westminster Theological Journal*.[1] It is a fine piece of work: I read it through at one sitting, and that means much with my weakened eye-sight, and generally declining health. You have made me acquainted with Bultmann, far more than I was before. In fact I had not much proceeded beyond Barth and the ilk of him. It is a pity that I cannot make it a Quarterly. Perhaps it is not worthwhile with my approaching so close to the "city that has the foundation," still I think for good number's sake, and the good cause's sake, I may send you a subscriber's dollar. Some correspondents ask me what the conditions of religion are in California; I used to answer with the title of Eugene O'Neill's play: "Ah Wilderness."[2] Please keep these words of appreciation in confidence.

Yours faithfully,
Geerhardus Vos

---

1. "Jesus in the Hands of a Barthian: Rudolf Bultmann's Jesus in the Perspective of a Century of Criticism," *Westminster Theological Journal* 1/1 (November 1938): 1–42. This was Stonehouse's inaugural address as professor of New Testament at Westminster Theological Seminary, April 14, 1938.
2. The comedy *Ah Wilderness*, by Eugene O'Neill (1888–1953), hit Broadway in 1933.

To Ned Stonehouse

May 18, 1940
1341 Colorado St.
Grand Rapids, S.E.

My dear Dr. Stonehouse,

I am much indebted to you for your kindness in sending me the May issue of the *Westminster Theological Journal*. More than in aught else of the contents, I was interested in your contribution on the views of Dibelius[1] on the Messianic consciousness of Jesus, and the seeming contradiction between the affirmation of this consciousness and the general scepticism of this writer in regard to the historicity of the gospel-narrative as a whole.[2]

Should you happen to come to or [be] anywhere near Grand Rapids during the summer season, do not fail to call on me.

Sincerely yours,
Geerhardus Vos

---

1. Martin F. Dibelius (1883–1947) was professor of New Testament at the University of Heidelberg from 1915 to 1947; there he developed the method of form criticism.
2. N. B. Stonehouse, "Martin Dibelius and the Relation of History and Faith," *Westminster Theological Journal* 2/2 (May 1940): 105–39.

To Henry Beets

October 16, 1940
1341 Colorado Ave. S.E.
Grand Rapids, Mich.

My dear Dr. Beets,

I herewith send back, with thanks, Verkoullie's "Etymologisch Woordenboek,"[1] which you kindly let me have for a while. The perusal of it has proved very interesting and instructive.

The author's name has intrigued me. It seems to be a Flemish form for the Hollandish "Verkoolje". Accidentally I came across the name of Johannes Verkoolje. The date I could gather about this Dutch printer of the 17th century I have noted down on the slip enclosed. The two may be ancestor and offspring of the same family.

Let me also thank you again for your "Toiling and Trusting,"[2] which I have read through with much pleasure. I am sure you have in this work of love saved many facts and features concerning the Indian mission from ultimate oblivion.

I hope you will some time feel inclined to call on me again.

Yours sincerely,
Geerhardus Vos

---

1. Jozef Vercoullie, *Beknopt etymologisch woordenboek der Nederlandsche taal*, 3d ed. ('s-Gravenhage: M. Nijhoff, 1925).
2. Henry Beets, *Toiling and Trusting: Fifty Years of Mission Work of the Christian Reformed Church among Indians and Chinese with Chapters on Nigeria and South America* (Grand Rapids: Grand Rapids Printing Co., 1940).

To Henry Beets

January 1941
1341 Colorado, S.E.

My dear Dr. Beets:
I feel much indebted to you for loaning me the Kennemer Balladen.[1] The perusal of them brought most kindly to mind the old days in Amsterdam when Hofdijk stood before the class reciting some of his own compositions, or left us to our work of drudgery, whilst he himself sat aloof wrapped up in reading delicious things, forgetful of his duties as a teacher. There was a great deal of that method in the old "gym"; I can remember some other professors indulging in the same habit. If home-study had been discountenanced, as it sometimes is in our days, there might have been justification derived from the fact that the students after all had to be given time for writing out their themes, etc. But we had plenty of homework given to us. Well, to return to Hofdijk, when he did occupy himself with the class, he was much outspoken and blunt in his censorship of our mistakes. One of his favorite means of address was on such occasions: "Driedubbel overgehaald uilskuiken."[2] What "overgehaald" exactly meant in such connections, none of us knew.

But his "Ballads" are fine. How steeped in the spirit of Romanticism they were after the type of Uhland and Geibel![3] I was reading the other day in Jonkbloed's *Gescheidenis* etc. a critique upon his style, charging him with "Germanisms" in vocabulary and construction.[4] At one time I could have thought the introduction of "Germanisms" or "Anglicisms" into the Dutch language an unpardonable sin. But after all, both languages are so nearly akin to the Dutch that I do not see what objection there can be to the transposing of an idiom from them into the mother-speech. E.g. in the Dedication to the Queen, which opens the "Balladen" there occurs this line: "Opdat zij in uw schants zich van haar leed herhale." This "herhale" is equivalent to "herstelle," i.e., "to recover" and obviously is the German "sich erholen". But what a little blemish this is, if it is one at all, in view of the fine spirit and delicacy of expression of the "Dedication" as a whole. It is better than any of the ballads.—Well thanks again!

You intimate in the slip in the wrapper of your package that you might print my "Kerstfest-Bede"[5] and thus make it public property. Honestly I would rather have it remain private; it was intended as such and sent only to a few of my friends beside you. Especially in the case of a prayer, there is something less suitable to public inspection than what might find utterance in ordinary composition. But you will do as you feel about this.

I have shipped to me here, a consignment of books from the remainder of my library which enjoys its *otium cum dignitate*[6] in the backwoods of Pennsylvania. There are a couple of items in which I think you will [be] interested and which I shall take pleasure in showing you, should you favor me with another visit. May I keep the Balladen a little longer?

With best wishes to you and yours for the new year just begun, I remain

Sincerely yours,
Geerhardus Vos[7]

---

1. W. J. Hofdijk's poems published 1850–1852.
2. An idiomatic expression that means something like "Complete numbskull that you are."
3. Perhaps the poets Ludwig Uhland (1787–1862) and Franz Emanuel August von Geibel (1815–1884).
4. W. J. A. Jonckbloet, *Geschiedenis der Nederlandsche letterkunde*, 6 vols., 3d ed. (Groningen: J. B. Wolters, 1886).
5. Perhaps a reference to the poem by this name printed in *Heiden Wereld: Missionary Monthly* 49 (1944): 375.
6. I.e., "leisure/rest with dignity."
7. The editor acknowledges the assistance of Ed van der Maas on this letter, especially in deciphering the Dutch and German phrases and for some of the footnotes.

To Henry Beets

January 9, 1941
1341 Colorado Ave., S.E.

Dear Dr. Beets,

I notice that in the yearbook for 1940, the necrology gives as my father's first pastorate "Velzen," which is coordinated with his other pastorates in the Netherlands. This perhaps originated in a misprint. The name of the place is Ulzen, and it is a town in Graafschap, Bentheim, not in the Netherlands. Since there is a town Velzen in Holland, it creates the impression that my father once was pastor there.

I hope that it is not too late for making the correction in the new yearbook.

Yours sincerely,
Geerhardus Vos

To Henry Beets

February 12, 1941
1341 Colorado Ave. S.E.
Grand Rapids, Mich.

My dear Dr. Beets,

Under separate cover I herewith return to you the "Kennemer Balladen" of Hofdijk. Many thanks again for the long loan you have let me have of them. I hasten to send it back since an attack of the influenza through which I have just passed has reminded me of the uncertainties of life in an old man whom anything unusual, though not in itself fatal, befalls. In case I had suddenly been called hence, I should not have wanted you to go to any extra trouble in order to recover the book.

Thanks also for the exchange of Uelzen for Velzen in the recent edition of the yearbook. I feel somehow that the substitution of the real name of his first charge in the necrological report is a last act of "piety" (in the Latin sense of the word) performed in his memory.

I hope the epidemic has left you and yours unscathed. Here we have all been affected from the oldest to the youngest.

                With kindest greetings,
                Sincerely yours,
                Geerhardus Vos

To Ned Stonehouse

July 21, 1944
1341 Colorado Ave. S.E.
Grand Rapids, Mich.

Dear Dr. Stonehouse,

Many thanks for the book on Matthew's and Mark's Witness to Christ you so kindly sent me.[1] I have not quite finished the reading of it, but from what I have read feel sure you have made a real contribution to the subject at issue. I can appreciate this all the more, since in my treatment of the Messianic-consciousness and disclosure question,[2] I have always felt a lack of expert information along the very line you are dealing with.

I trust that, in case you come to Grand Rapids in the future, while I am still on this side of the great divide, you will not fail to call on me, as you so kindly did the other day.

With kindest regards and best wishes for the blessing of the Lord on all your labors in him, I remain

> Gratefully yours,
> Geerhardus Vos

---

1. Ned B. Stonehouse, *The Witness of Matthew and Mark to Christ* (Philadelphia: Presbyterian Guardian, 1944).
2. Geerhardus Vos, *The Self-Disclosure of Jesus: The Modern Debate about the Messianic Consciousness* (New York: George H. Doran Company, 1926).

To Ned Stonehouse

January 11, 1945
1341 Colorado Ave. S.E.
Grand Rapids, Mich.

My dear Dr. Stonehouse,

I appreciate very highly the kind remembrance of me you have cherished for so long a time full of changes and vicissitudes, and which finds new expression in the wish to have a photographic likeness of me. I am sure the desire is not of a "materialistic" nature. To my regret we have no framed photo here that would suit the purpose. It occurs to me that one Jack Turner, the Princeton photographer[1] may have on file an old picture, of which he could sell you [a] copy or even let you have one gratis. See what you can accomplish in that way, should it be unsuccessful, then apply to me again. We will then try to deframe the picture that they have here of the late Mrs. Vos and myself and have a copy made of that for you after which it can be reframed to its original condition.

I often take up your recent book on *The Witness of Matthew and Mark*[2] with profit and pleasure.

Once more a happy new year to yourself and group.

In case you visit these parts, do not fail to pay me a visit.

Cordially yours,
Geerhardus Vos

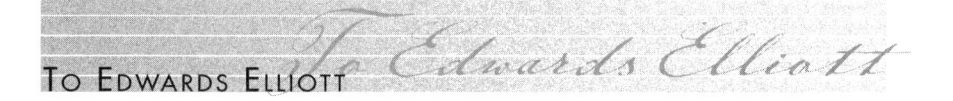

---

1. Orrin Jack Turner (1889–1968).
2. Ned B. Stonehouse, *The Witness of Matthew and Mark to Christ* (Philadelphia: Presbyterian Guardian, 1944).

To Edwards Elliott

January 25, 1946
Grand Rapids, Michigan

To the Reverend Edwards E. Elliott[1]
Baltimore, Maryland

Dear Brother,

I highly appreciate your kind offer to prepare a bibliography of the several books and articles the Lord enabled me to contribute to the progress of his cause. Most gladly would I accede to this and cooperate to the best of my ability, but for a couple of reasons. On the one hand, I never prepared a list of this nature during the years in which the several pieces were actually written. Of course, the books and the articles were in my actual possession for the time. When, however, at my becoming "emeritus," the contents of my library were scattered. I could now, of course, except from my sale of them, the parts with articles and reviews of my own, because that would have made the series incomplete.

As to preparing a list now by research through the institutional libraries, the present state of my health renders this impossible. I am very much troubled with insomnia. My nights are almost a nightmare. Every unusual effort in the daytime would aggravate this trouble at night because by mere effort of will the concerns of the preceding day cannot be dismissed from thought.

I have actually less library collection within my reach where I am living now than you have in the East, at Baltimore and other places.

Why not take your time for the task and postpone the issue of such a bibliography till after my death? It would make one out of two similar memorials.[2]

Should you happen to be in the neighborhood while I am still in the land of the living, do not fail to call on me at the address here, 1341 Colorado, S.E.[3] I retain the most pleasant memory of your visit five years ago.[4]

>Yours in the Lord,
>Geerhardus Vos

---

1. Edwards E. Elliott (1914–1979) graduated from Westminster Theological Seminary, Philadelphia, Pennsylvania, in 1942. He was ordained by the Presbytery of Philadelphia of the Orthodox Presbyterian Church on January 18, 1943. He served as pastor of St. Andrews Orthodox Presbyterian Church (now First OPC), Baltimore, Maryland, from 1943 to 1950.

2. A revised and updated bibliography appears at the end of the biographical sketch printed in this volume.

3. This address is the home of Vos's daughter, Marianne Radius.

4. Elliott's visit of about 1941 ("five years ago") occurred while he was a student at Westminster Seminary, where he evidently gained an interest in Vos from his professors (i.e., John Murray, Ned Stonehouse, and Cornelius Van Til).

POETRY OF GEERHARDUS VOS

The Sword[1]

Should one, for wonted sharing
In Christmas cheer preparing,
Regard that side alone,
This were for transient pleasure
To miss the eternal treasure,
The feast would make us own.
Old Simeon, from his station,
Who Israel's consolation,
Approaching saw the goal;
At the same vision's center,
A sword saw, need must enter
And pierce the Mother's soul.
The child was set a token,
Through words against it spoken,
Sharp cleavage to compel,
Appealing, or appalling,
Rising the cause and falling
Of many in Israel.
Mary, when he did tell her,
This, with what strange befell her,
Hid, pondering, in her heart,
Until the Crucifixion,
The clear-recalled prediction,
Drove home with poignant smart.
Should we, saved by its merit,
Not deepest sense inherit,

Of what the cross implied;
When, by some anguish shaken,
As if of God forsaken,
On it the Savior died?
If, when the scene comes near us,
God makes, like Mary, hear us
Its strains of litany;
Us, too, the second morrow,
Shall change the plaint of sorrow,
To Easter-Jubilee.

---

1. From a letter to Dr. Ned Stonehouse at Westminster Theological Seminary, Philadelphia, Pennsylvania, December 15, 1944, from Grand Rapids, Michigan.

A Song of the Nativity[1]

Ye pilgrims, in the tale retold
What do your wondering eyes behold?
A babe which, scarcely given, gives,
Its every breath a grace that lives;
God turned to his own sacrament,
Spending his all, yet never spent;
Entering our kind and ours alone,
Flesh of our flesh, bone of our bone;
The uncreated Light of Light,
Heaven's noonday, swallowed by our night;
Guileless, incapable of wrong,
More than the lambs he lay among;
His smallness laden with our sin;
Born that his birth-cries might begin
Full thirty years of tragedy,
Each step a step towards Calvary.
And this is the high-holy spot,
Angels are sad to visit not!

Here undergird God's cords of gold
Our earth, and it from falling hold
Into the desperate abyss,
Where love not even a memory is.
This is the blest alighting-ground
Of grace, whence it shall circle round
With one wide-flung redeeming span
All sin and sorrow and pain of man,
And make new paradise streams flow,
That from God's throne through Eden go;
Yea cause all things now mute and dim
Again to shine and sing in Him.
If this ye in the manger see,
A promise and a potency
Of what was for the future willed,
Observe a thing even now fulfilled,
Well worth to open wide your eyes;
Close to the babe, transfigured, lies
She through whom God the Christ-gift gave
The world both and herself to save.
Lest thou the full-orbed glory miss,
Note well the mother's part in this.
The greatest masters of the brush
Put more here than the solemn blush
Of just awakened motherhood,
Trembling at its beatitude;
They tried to limn a mystery
Of God-encompassed ecstasy.
But God, who first the image drew,
Knows more than ever artist knew.
His work is the Madonna-face
With its uncopyable grace,
Where, as in a pellucid stream,
To Him his own eyes mirrored seem.

The light God saw in Mary shine,
The inmost shrine within her shrine,
The whitest flame within the flame,
Religion is its holy name.
From it proceeded the ground-swell,
Upheaved in her high canticle;
The feeling of unworthiness,
Not loath, but eager to confess
Itself but chosen instrument,
A chord through which God's music went,
Like pulses throbbing through the frame
Each to the heart-pulse whence they came;
A hymn unaging, ever new,
An organ-peal the ages through,
Chanting: "The handmaid of the Lord;
Me be according to thy word;"
Made through a fine simplicity
Mindless of its own melody,
Anxious alone that God should hear
A virgin strain pleasing his ear,
Sensing as from within God's mind,
Why He exalts the humble kind,
Puts down the mighty from their seats,
The hungry with his fulness meets;
And, rising high above the thought
Of aught could in return be brought,
Perceives how all the blessed live
Only that God may give and give.
So Mary, with naught else to bring,
Made her sweet psalm an offering,
Wherein the Lord such pleasure found,
He let it through the world resound,
To bless our ears each Christmas night
With notes like drops of liquid light,

So clear, we mean to hear in them
The very voice of Bethlehem,
As had by Mary's side we sat,
And drunk of her "Magnificat."

---

1. This poem was Vos's Christmas message to students and friends in 1924. A revised version appears in Vos's *Western Rhymes* (1933), 1–5.

Kerstfeest-Gebed[1]

Jezus, voor 't vrome Kerstfeest-vieren
Kom Gij ons hart en huis versieren,
Recht Gij ons Zelf het feestmaal aan;
Leer ons van wenschen en gebeden,
Van al de zoete aanminnigheden,
Den zin door U begeerd verstaan.
Geef ons een indruk van uw liefde,
Dat, wijl U onze ellende griefde,
Gij hebt U glans en eere ontzeid,
Om onzentwille neergekomen,
Dienstknechts-gestalte hebt aangenomen,
Als kindeke in een krib geleid.
Buig door uw nederigheen ons neder,
Opdat boetvaardiglijk en teeder
Wij mogen tot die kribbe treen,
Erin de zelfverloochening speuren,
Die door al 't heilige gebeuren
Vandaar tot Golgotha loopt heen.
Verwek in ons een klaar beseffen,
Dat, om ons uit den dood te heffen,
Gij zijt de doods-sfeer ingedaald,
Hebt haar verschrikking niet gemeden,
Met bloed-zweet en verlatenheden
Ons uit de diepten opgehaald;

Dat 't uitzicht in den val verloren
Gij hebt ons, rijker dan tevoren,
Thans onverliesbaar, nieuw bereid,
Doordien, U weigerend den Booze,
Gij God U gaaft in 't weergalooze
Reukoffer der gehoorzaamheid.
Dies, nevens 't lijden, op uw werken
Doe ons dankbaar aanbiddend merken
En achten leed noch last te zwaar,
Die 't U belieft ons op te dragen;
Heer, heilig door uw God-behagen
De poovere gave op ons altaar.
Help ons geduldig 't uur verbeiden,
Dat van de vreemdelingschap ons scheiden
En stillen zal de pelgrims-pijn.
Zoo uwe Bruigoms-min ons open,
Dat heel het op uw toekomst hopen
Zal bruilofts-voorverblijding zijn.
Kerstfeest, 1942

---

1. From a letter to Dr. Ned Stonehouse at Westminster Theological Seminary, Philadelphia, Pennsylvania, from Grand Rapids, December 18, 1942.

The Magnificat[1]

Spirit of God, sing through me,
Thine humblest notes bring to me,
I will exalt the Lord.
With rarest grace He met me,
Above all women set me,
As promised me his word.
I was his handmaid lowly,
And his possession wholly,
In me was nothing great.

Yet has He by sure token
To me of high things spoken,
Despite my low estate.
He singles out my smallness,
And joins it to his allness,
Me to a point to raise,
Higher than which no station,
That every generation
May me most blessed praise.
What foes would fain distress us,
What mighty ones oppress us,
He puts down from their seats.
Rich sustenance bestowing,
With bounty overflowing
The hungering poor He meets.
He scatters the defiant;
The rich, the self-reliant,
He empty sends away.
But those who humbly fear Him,
And seek their refuge near Him,
He rescues when they pray.
O joy, that He will choose me,
And through this wonder use me
For of the oath, He swore
To Abraham, our father,
The ripened fruit to gather,
His handmaid evermore.
Christmas, 1943[2]

---

1. Luke 1:46–55.
2. From a letter to Dr. Ned Stonehouse at Westminster Theological Seminary, Philadelphia, Pennsylvania, from Grand Rapids, Michigan, December 10, 1943.

Index of Scripture

Genesis
3:15—39
6:18—39
12:1-3—39
17:1-8—39
49:10—218, 219

Exodus
19:5—39
24:7—39

Numbers
15:30—230, 231n.4

Deuteronomy
28:57—218

2 Samuel
7:14—39

Psalms
109:3—210, 210n.1, 210n.2

Isaiah
14:12—210, 210n.4
53—57
57:15—63n.176

Ezekiel
21:27—219

Matthew
6:6—74

Luke
1:46-55—256-57
10:18—210
23:31—236, 237n.2

Romans
8:28—79
8:38—79
8:39—79
9—162
9:11-24—28n.63
9:19-23—150

2 Corinthians
5:1—62, 62n.172

Ephesians
1—162
1:4—63n.176
2:4-5—63n.176
2:6—52
3—162

Philippians
2:7—73

Colossians
3:3—52

1 Timothy
3:16—53

2 Timothy
2:15—25

Hebrews
11:6—28

Revelation
12:7ff.—210

259

Index of Subjects and Names

Aalders, G. Ch., 101
Adam, 50–51, 141–42
Adams, Jay, 81n.209
Adams, John, 98
Adams Oscar F., 110
Adickes, E., 127n.19
Afscheiding, 15, 127n.11
Al-Maqrizi, Taqi ad-Din Ahmad, 24n.46, 89, 125, 127n.10
Albertz, Jan, 209n.4
Alexander, Archibald A., 34
Allis, O. T., 36n.83, 70n.190, 235, 235n.3
American Society of Church History, 130, 130n.3
American Standard Version (Bible), 187n.5
amillennialism, 59n.164, 236–37. *See also* eschatology
Amsterdam, 16n.13, 125, 179
    gymnasium, 16, 122
    Vrije Universiteit, 16n.13, 22, 22n.34, 23, 116–18, 118n.1, 118–19, 119–20, 120nn.1,2, 120–121, 121n.2, 166n.4, 185, 186n.3, 208n.1, 213n.1, 214–15, 215n.2, 222n.1, 227
    letter to directors, 214–15(8/11/26)
Amyraldianism, 141–42, 153
Andel, J. van, 127n.15
Andover Review, 137, 138n.7
angels, 210
anthropocentrism, 57–58, 68, 83
Antwerp, 17
Arminianism, 28, 65, 83n.212, 132, 135. *See also* Remonstrants
Armstrong, William P., 36, 36n.83, 97
Auburn Affirmation, 69
Auerbach, Eric, 84n.215
Augustine, 39

Baljon, J. M. S., 94
Baltimore, MD, 248, 248n.1
The Banner, 211
Barth, Jacob, 127n.5
Barth, Karl, 61, 65, 239
Baudissin, W. W. G., 101
Bavinck, Bereneinus J. F., 127n.2
Bavinck, Coenraad Bernardus, 127n.2
Bavinck, Gesina M. H. (Mrs. Jan), 177n.12
Bavinck, Herman, 16n.13, 22n.36, 23n.41, 24n.43, 27n.54, 28nn.61,63, 29n.68, 33, 33n.75,

261

Index of Subjects and Names

36n.84, 37, 37n.87, 38, 39nn.93,94, 41, 42nn.109,110, 44, 44n.119, 64, 83n.212, 91, 92, 93, 97, 139, 139n.2, 140, 143, 143n.1, 146, 148, 151n.14, 158, 169, 169n.4, 185, 186n.3, 192, 208n.6
Dogmatics, 188, 188n.5, 189, 190n.1, 203, 203n.5
letters to, 122–27(6/16/87), 131–33(2/1/90), 136–38(3/4/90), 153–58(5/13/91), 158–60(6/30/91), 174–77(7/3/93), 178–80(10/20/93), 180–81(11/21/93), 182–83(2/1/94), 185–87(3/28/94), 187–88(12/22/94), 189–90(7/6/95), 202–3(4/29/99), 205–6(5/17/05), 206–8(2/21/06), 208–9(1/7/09)
Bavinck, Mrs. Herman (Johanna A. Schippers), 48, 158, 159n.1, 209, 209n.5
Bavinck, Jan, 177n.12
Bavinck, Johanna, 187, 188n.1
Beach, Sylvester, 71, 71nn.193,194, 75, 216n.1, 217
letter to, 215–16(7/13/28)
Beck, David R., 24n.42
Beecher, Henry Ward, 166n.2
Beets, Henry, 14n.7, 15nn.11,12, 22n.36, 29n.67, 66n.183, 109n.4, 110, 110n.4, 211, 211n.1, 212n.1, 213n.3, 241, 241n.2
letters to, 211(3/16/12), 212–13(10/4/15), 241(10/16/40), 242–43(1/41), 244(1/9/41), 244–45 (2/12/41)
Behm, Johannes, 99
Bennett, W. H., 97

Benson, Louis F., 207, 208n.4
Bentheim (Germany), 14, 15, 17nn.16,17, 18n.18, 244
Berkhof, Louis, 14n.6, 36n.83, 79n.203
Berlin, 116, 122, 124
Humbolt-Universität, 22n.33, 127n.5
University of, 22, 23, 125n.5
Bestmann, H. J., 94
Beuker, Gerrit Jan, 15n.10, 17n.16, 18n.18
Beuker, Hendericus, 16, 16n.13, 33n.78, 126, 127nn.15,17, 157, 158n.6, 175, 177n.9, 186, 187n.6
Beyschlag, Willibald, 92, 189, 190n.4
biblical theology, 30, 32, 34, 36–41, 38n.90, 49–59, 67–68, 75, 81n.209, 171, 171n.1, 176, 179, 181, 182–83, 187
and systematic theology, 49, 187
Biesterveld, Petrius, 208, 209n.1
Bilderdijk, Willem, 17
Bismarck, Otto von, 17, 17n.6
Bismark, North Dakota, 82n.210
Black, David A., 24n.42
Blake, Buchanan, 56n.154, 95
Boehmer, Julius, 56n.155, 95, 98
Boer, Geert Egbert, 18, 18n.21, 177n.10
Boetticher, Paul Anton, 219, 220n.6
Bogermann, Jan, 150, 151n.8
Bohn, Friedrich, 96
Bolan, Katherine, 48
Bos, Mr. (bookseller), 182, 183, 185
Bouma, Clarence, 13, 13n.1, 110
Bousset, Wilhelm, 27, 27n.58, 83, 91, 95, 100
Box, G. H., 97
Boyd, James Oscar, 67
Brahams, Raymond I., 236, 237n.3
Bratt, James D., 43n.116, 44n.118
Breed, David R., 186, 187n.8

Index of Subjects and Names

Bremmer, R. H., 36n.85
Briggs, Charles Augustis, 26n.54, 33–34, 34nn.79,80, 35, 36n.83, 40, 41, 44, 67, 92, 133n.1, 137, 138n.5, 165, 166n.3, 179, 184, 186
Brink, J. W., 15n.11, 33n.78
Brinks, Herbert, 110
Brouwer, Wayne, 15n.10
Bruce, A. B., 92
Brückner, Martin, 95
Bruijn, Jan de, 18n.20
Bruins, Elton J., 22n.36
Brunner, Emil, 65n.181
Buck, Pearl, 69
Bultmann, Rudolf, 61–62, 65, 239, 240n.1
Büschel, F., 99

Calderwood, Henry, 191, 192n.3
Calhoun, David, 35n.82, 49n.143, 65n.181
Calvin, John, 150, 151n.12
Calvinism, 28, 39, 40, 141–42, 145n.1, 147, 153, 162–63, 170, 176nn.1,2, 179. *See also* Reformed theology
Carré, Henry B., 102
Caspari, Wilhelm, 98
Charles, R. H., 100
Chicago, IL
  McCormick Theological Seminary, 178n.1
  University of Chicago Divinity School, 203, 203n.4
chiliasm. *See* premillennialism
Christian Reformed Church (CRC), 14, 41, 65, 67, 67n.184, 72, 121n.1, 159, 227
Christian schools, 42n.105, 47n.133
Christocentrism, 39, 51–59, 68, 73–79, 82
Church, 52–54, 58

Civil War, 69
Clemen, Carl, 55n.153, 99, 100
Cocceius, Joannes, 176, 177n.11
Cockshott, Winnifred, 228, 228n.9
Cole, Charles, 48, 48nn.134,135,136, 62n.174
conversion, 152
Costa, Isaac de, 17
Couard, Ludwig, 97
Covenant Theology, 28, 39, 39n.93, 53, 147, 149, 152, 153–57, 160–64, 166, 169, 169n.3, 176, 181, 183, 222
Craighead, David E., 72, 72n.199, 73, 238, 239n.3

D'Orleans, J., 23n.40
Dalmer, Johannes, 57n.158, 93
Darwin, Charles, 21
Davidson, A. B., 37n.89, 96, 234
De Bazuin, 132, 133n.7, 136, 176
De Cock, Helenius, 150, 151n.14
De Groot, William, 110
De Hartog, Arnold H., 121n.2
De Heraut, 81n.206, 136, 137n.1, 141, 149, 150, 152, 156, 162, 166, 168, 169n.1, 176
De Hope, 179
De Jong, Peter, 13, 13n.1, 110
De Klerk, Peter, 89n.1, 177n.6
De Lagarde, Paul Anton. *See* Boetticher
De Ridder, Richard R., 177n.6
De Roeper, 142, 143n.4
De Vries, John Hendrik, 172, 173, 173n.1, 176n.3, 191, 192, 192n.1
De Vrije Kerk, 126, 127n.15, 136
De Wachter, 29, 29n.67, 152n.2, 160, 164n.1, 177n.6, 179
De Witt, John (New Brunswick, NJ), 186, 187n.5
De Witt, John (Princeton, NJ), 208, 209nn.3,4

263

De Witt, T. C., 209n.4
Delitzsch, Franz, 219, 220n.8
Denney, James, 98
Dennison, Charles G., 80n.204
Dennison, James T., Jr., 36n.86, 63n.178, 84nn.213,214, 110–11
Dennison, William D., 62n.175
DeWaard, Hattie, 62nn.174,175
DeWaard, John, 62, 62n.175, 67, 81n.207
Dibelius, Martin, 61–62, 240nn.1,2
Diessner, Kurt, 99
Dieterici, Friedrich H., 127n.5
Dillmann, Christian F. A., 22, 127n.5
Dilloo, F. W. J., 22n.34, 121n.2
Documentary Hypothesis, 21n.30
Doleantie, 125, 127n.11
Dort, Synod of, 29, 29n.65, 149–50, 151n.2–13, 155, 156
Drummond, Robert J., 94
Dubuque, IA
  German Theological Seminary, 138n.2, 190, 190n.7
Duhm, Bernhard, 210, 210n.4
Duker, A. C., 92
Dulles, Joseph H., 162, 164n.5, 169, 170
Dutch theology, 131–32, 145–46

Easter, 236
Edgar, Sam, 60
Edict of Nantes, 14n.10
Eekhof, Albertus, 18n.19, 20n.28, 59nn.162,163, 228nn.1,7
  letter to, 225–28(10/28/32)
Eickenberger, Jos., 95
Elliott, Edwards E., 61n.170, 248nn.1,4
  letter to, 247–48(1/25/46)
Elwell, Walter A., 50n.146
Emerson, Ralph Waldo, 17
Emmet, Cyril W., 98
Engelbrecht, C. J. I., 15
Enlightenment, 26n.54, 27, 34, 38n.92

Erdman, C. R., 20n.27, 71n.192, 82
Eschatology, 27–28, 27n.59, 37, 38, 50–59, 68, 74–79, 82n.210, 85, 223, 236–37
evolution, 37n.88, 38n.92

Faber, Georg, 101
Fabius, Damme P. D., 121n.2
Fairweather, William, 98
Faith, 21n.32
Farmer, William, 24n.42
Farr, Edward, 224n.2
Felix, J. W., 23, 23n.39, 120nn.1,2
  letter to, 119–20(9/4/86)
Fleming, David Hay, 207, 208n.5
Focke, Friedrich, 101
Foster, Frank H., 200, 201n.1
free will, 126
Freemasons, 22n.36, 142, 173, 173n.3
Frei, Hans, 34n.81
Freud, Sigmund, 18, 67, 227
Friedländer, M., 95
Friesland, 13, 14, 74, 209, 209n.4
fundamentalist, 21, 27, 27n.56, 35, 36n.83, 38n.92, 40n.98, 41, 59n.164, 65, 68, 72–74, 79, 80n.204, 83–84
Funk and Wagnalls, 146

Gaffin, Richard B., Jr., 32n.71, 36n.85, 57, 57n.157, 81, 81n.208, 111, 169n.3
Galatino, Pietro, 219, 219n.3
Gardner, Percy, 99
Gass, Wilhelm, 235
Geesink, Gerhard H. J. W., 165, 166n.4
Geibel, F. E. A. von, 242, 243n.3
Gelderland, 150, 151n.7, 209
General Dutch Alliance, 43–44, 44n.117, 201, 202n.2, 204
Gereformeerde Kerken Nederlands, 127n.11

German Old Reformed, 15, 15n.10, 17n.16, 18n.18, 74
Gomarus, Francis, 149, 150, 151n.3
Gooszen, Maurits A., 137, 137n.4, 138
Göttsberger, Joh., 95, 96
Graafschap, MI, 14n.9, 18n.18, 195n.1
Grand Rapids, MI, 15, 16, 17n.16, 41, 46n.128, 47, 61–62, 61n.171, 82, 85, 125, 186, 245
   Calvin Theological Seminary, 16n.13, 17n.17, 18, 18n.21, 19, 22n.36, 23, 24, 25, 25nn.49,50,51,52, 26, 28, 29, 29n.65, 32n.92, 33, 33n.78, 39, 40, 42, 64, 64n.179, 80, 81n.208, 82, 116n.2, 121n.1, 128n.1, 169, 170–71, 178–79, 211, 212, 213n.2, 227
   Grand Rapids Public Library, 42, 42n.106
   Hessel Convalescent Home, 62
   LaGrave Avenue CRC, 211, 211n.1
   Madison Avenue School, 42
   South Congregational Church, 41, 41n.103
   Spring Street CRC, 14n.7, 17, 17n.17, 25
   Williams Street School, 212, 213n.2
   Zaagman Memorial Chapel, 62, 62n.172
Grau, R. F., 93
Gravemeijer, H. E., 26n.54, 90
Green, William Henry, 15n.10, 20, 20n.30, 21, 29, 32n.71, 33, 35, 36, 182, 183n.2
   letters to Geerhardus Vos, 30, 31–32
Gregory I (the Great), 210, 211n.6
Gressmann, Hugo, 83
Griffis, William Elliot, 43n.117, 202n.1, 204n.2
   letters to, 201–2(12/15/98), 204(1/13/02)

Griffiths, H. McAllister, 80, 80n.204, 82n.210
Groen, Watson, 227, 228n.6
Grooteholt, 209
Grosheide, F. W., 36n.83, 72n.198, 222n.1
   letter to, 221–22(2/19/32)
Gunkel, Hermann, 83, 100

Haas, Joh. de, 15n.11, 16n.13
Haberton, John, 235
Hagenbach, Karl Rudolf, 129, 130n.1
Hammerling, Rupert, 17
Hamstra, Alice, 30n.70
Harinck, George, 15n.10, 16n.13, 17n.17, 18n.20, 22n.34, 23n.38, 24n.44, 25n.48, 36n.83, 43n.116, 72n.198, 111
Harms, Richard, 111
Harrisburg, PA, 61n.170
Harvard Divinity School, 203, 203n.4
Hashimites, 24n.46
Hastings, James, 97
Heerenveen, 14, 15
Hegel, G. W. F., 21, 38, 171
Heidegger, Johann Heinrich, 163, 164n.6
Heidelberg Catechism, 137, 137n.4, 138, 212, 212n.1
Heiden Wereld, 243n.5
Hemkes, Gerrit Klaas, 177n.10
Hepp, Valentin, 48
Heppe, Heinrich, 163, 164n.7
Herford, R. Travers, 96
Herringshaw, T. W., 111
Hertlein, Eduard, 50n.149, 99
Heyblom, Cornelia M. J. *See* Mrs. Herman Kuyper
higher criticism, 20n.30, 21, 21n.31, 32, 34, 34n.79, 40, 123, 137, 171, 185–86, 199, 205
Hilgenfeld, Adolf, 97
Hirzel, Stephen A., 220, 221n.2

Index of Subjects and Names

historical Jesus, 54–55, 55n.153
history, 37, 37nn.87,88,89, 38–39, 175–76, 182
history of redemption, 38, 50–59
Hodge, A. A., 20, 26n.54, 133n.1, 234
Hodge, Caspar Wistar, 20, 36, 36n.83, 72, 234
Hodge, Charles, 34, 152, 153n.4, 160, 164n.3
Hoedemaker, Ph. J., 93, 121n.2
Hoekstra, J. B., 25n.52, 109n.4, 110
Hofdijk, W., 17, 242, 242n.1, 244
Holland, MI
  Hope College, 167, 168n.1
  Western Theological Seminary, 138n.2, 190, 190n.8
Holtzmann, H. J., 24, 24n.42, 56
Holy Spirit, 58
Hommius, Festus, 150, 151n.9
Honig, A. G., 28n.63, 91
Hubrecht, Ambrosius A. W., 193, 193n.2
Huguenot, 14n.10
Huizinga, Abel Henry, 177, 178n.1, 184
Hulst, L. J., 22n.36, 29, 29nn.65,67, 32, 79, 152, 152n.2
Hurgronje, Christiaan Snouck, 205, 206n.2

IJselmonde, 15
Ilgen, Karl David, 219, 220n.5
imputation (Adamic guilt), 141–42
incarnation, 73
The Independent, 165, 166n.2, 168
Independent Board for Foreign Missions, 79–80, 80n.205
infant baptism, 147–48, 149, 152, 154–57, 160–64
inspiration (of the Bible), 26n.54, 34, 50, 138n.5
Islam, 24n.46

Jacobus, William Melanchthon, 43n.117, 195–96, 197n.2, 205
Jansen, John, 13, 13n.1, 25n.47, 112
Jansz, Pieter, 209n.4
Japan, 202n.1, 204
Jenkins, Daniel E., 207, 207n.3
Jeremiah (Prophet), 74–81
Joldersma, Rense H., 175, 177n.8
Jonckbloet, W. J. A., 242, 243n.4

Kaftan, Julius, 97
Kagawa, Toyohiko, 237, 237n.6
Kampen, 15, 122, 127n.1, 139, 151n.14, 160n.2, 181n.4, 185, 186nn.2,4
Kant, Immanuel, 38n.92, 50, 50n.148, 124, 126, 127nn.6,7,14,18
Kate, J. L. L. ten, 17
Katwyk an Zee, 15
Keller, Gottfried, 17
Kennedy, H. A. A., 58n.159, 96
Kimchi, David, 219, 219n.1
King, John M., 95
Kingdom of God, 54–55, 54n.151, 56n.155
Kirkpatrick, A. F., 91
Klein, Felix, 191, 193n.6
Knowling, R. J., 97
Kögel, Julius, 95, 96
König, Eduard, 98, 101
Kooi, Cornelis vander, 18n.20
Krabbendam, Hans, 15n.10, 16n.13, 36n.83, 43n.116
Kreulen, J. R., 154, 155, 157nn.2,3
Kuenen, Abraham, 50n.147, 90, 123, 127n.4, 137, 137n.3, 138, 138n.1, 139, 139n.3, 140, 140n.1, 171, 171n.2
Kuiper, Rienk Bouke, 232, 233n.1, 235
Kuyper, Abraham, 16nn.13,22, 22n.35, 23, 28, 28n.64, 29, 36, 36n.85, 40n.96, 43, 44, 44n.120, 50n.148, 64, 81, 90, 91,

118nn.1,2, 121n.2, 127n.11,
  130, 138, 139, 139n.1, 140, 143,
  144, 145n.1, 145–46, 147, 150,
  150n.1, 151, 151n.16, 152, 153,
  156, 159, 162, 167, 168,
  169nn.1,2, 174, 176, 176n.3,
  185, 201, 202n.2, 207, 207n.1
 Encyclopedia of Theology, 129,
  133–35, 141, 172–73, 177,
  178n.1, 183, 183–84, 188, 191,
  192, 200
 letters to, 116–18(5/28/86),
  118–19(6/7/86),
  120–21(10/7/86),
  133–35(2/1/90),
  140–43(7/12/90),
  144–45(10/27/90),
  148–51(2/21/91),
  164–66(7/30/91),
  172–73(5/11/93),
  177–78(7/3/93),
  183–84(2/26/94),
  191–93(4/30/96), 193(6/10/96),
  194–95(7/11/96),
  195–97(10/7/96), 197(11/11/96),
  198(3/16/97), 199(6/15/97), 200-
  201(10/11/97)
Kuyper, Cornelia M. J. (Mrs. Herman H.), 150, 151n.15
Kuyper, Herman Huber, 150,
  151nn.15,17, 157, 158n.7
Kuyper, Joanne H. (Mrs. Abraham),
  150, 151n.16

La Jolla, CA, 47n.133, 59n.161
Laas, Ernst, 124, 127n.8
Labadie, Jean de, 154, 158n.4
Lafayette College (Easton, PA), 64
Laguna Beach, CA, 236
Lawrenceville, NJ, 116, 116n.4
Leathes, Stanley, 191, 192n.4
Leeuwarden, 209n.4

Leeuwen, E. H. van, 37n.88, 91, 102,
  171, 171n.1
Leiden, 24n.44, 125
Leiden Synopsis. *See* Synopsis purioris
Leipzig, 124
Lessing, G. E., 50
Lieb, Theodore H. and Amanda, 45
Lindeboom, Lucas, 143n.4, 185, 186,
  186n.4
Loetscher, Frederick W., 82
Loetscher, Lefferts, 26n.54, 70n.188
Lohman, Jonkheer A. F. de Savornin,
  121n.2
Longfellow, Henry Wadsworth, 17
Longfield, Bradley J., 35n.82
Lord's Supper, 236
Lucifer, 210, 211n.5
Lütgert, W., 54n.151, 55n.152, 93, 96
Lutheran Theology, 147, 163
Lutten, 15
Luyken, Jan, 17
Lydius, Balthasar, 150, 151n.10

Maas, Ed M. vander, 16n.14, 26n.52,
  107, 228n.5, 243n.7
Macartney Clarence E., 82n.210
Maccovius, John, 150, 151n.13
Machen, Arthur, 65n.182, 80n.205
 letter to, 238–39(1/5/37)
Machen, Helen, 80n.205
Machen, J. Gresham, 20n.27, 23n.37,
  36n.83, 47n.131, 49n.144,
  60n.169, 65, 65n.181, 67, 69, 70,
  70n.190, 71, 72, 72n.197, 73, 76,
  79, 80, 80n.204, 82, 82n.210,
  215n.3, 218, 218n.1, 238–39
 letters to, 210–11(1/26/09),
  218(?1930), 218–20(3/31/30),
  220–21(5/1/30),
  223–24(4/28/32), 236–37(5/7/36)
Machen, Mary Gresham, 80n.205
MacKenzie, Donald, 231n.1

267

letters to, 229–31(2/26/35), 231(3/20/35)
MacNeill, Harris L., 101
MacRae, Allen, 36n.83, 82n.210, 234, 235n.2
Maczka, Joyce, 41n.103
Manchuria, 60, 237, 237n.5
Marsden, George M., 80n.204
Marti, Karl, 98
Martineau, James, 56
Martini, Raymundi, 219, 219n.2
Mastricht, Peter van, 160, 164n.2
Matthews, Mark, 82n.210
Matthews, Shailer, 69, 96
McCook, John J., 34n.80
McGiffert, A. C., 40n.97, 180, 180n.2
McIntire, Carl, 40n.98, 79–80, 80n.204, 82n.210
Meeter, H. Henry, 62, 110, 112
Meeter, John, 61n.170, 221, 221n.4, 232, 233n.3
Meier, Conrad F., 17
Meinertz, Max, 97
Meinhold, J., 94
Mercersburg, PA
   German Reformed Seminary, 138n.6
Messiah, 34n.79, 69, 210
Messianic consciousness, 56–57, 240, 245
Methodist Review, 177n.3
Middelburg, Synod of (1896), 196, 197n.4
Mimesis, 84–85
Mira Mesa, CA, 47n.133
modernism, 69–70, 72–73, 80, 80n.204, 83, 237, 237n.7
Moffatt, James, 101
Moore, Walter W., 196, 197n.3
moralism, 58, 236
Muether, John, 32n.71
Muirhead, Lewis A., 27n.59, 96
Mullen, Grace, 219nn.5,6

Murray, John, 36n.83, 48, 65, 234, 235n.1, 248n.4
Muskegeon, MI, 16n.13, 177n.9

The Nation, 137, 138n.8
Neerlandia, 66, 225, 226, 227, 228n.5
New School Presbyterianism, 69, 141, 143n.2, 202, 203nn.2,3
New York, NY, 201, 204
New-York Observer, 168, 169n.2
New York Times, 32
Nicole, Roger, 32n.71, 41n.101
Nieuwe Rotterdamsche Courant, 225, 228n.4
Nöldeke, Theodore, 24, 126, 127nn.5,12
Noll, Mark, 80n.204, 83n.212
Noordtzij, Maarten, 159, 160n.2

Oehler, Gustav, 183, 183n.3
Oesterley, W. O. E., 97, 102
Old School Presbyterianism, 26n.54, 69, 82, 141, 143n.2, 202, 203nn.2,3
Ommen, 15, 16
O'Neill, Eugene, 59n.164, 240, 240n.2
Oosterbemus, 209n.4
Oosterbinus, 209n.4
Organic revelation, 51–54
original sin, 141–42
Orr, James, 207, 207n.2
Orthodox Presbyterian Church, 40n.98, 65, 67, 79, 248n.1
Ottawa Beach. MI, 194, 195n.1

Patton, Frances Landy, 20, 36, 130, 131n.2, 132, 133n.6
Paul (apostle), 24n.42, 53, 57–58, 58n.159, 83, 223
Paulsen, Friedrich, 127n.5
Pella, IA, 25n.52
Pernis, 15
Petrie, Flinders, 234

Index of Subjects and Names

Philadelphia, PA, 17
   Reformed Episcopal Seminary, 61n.170, 229–30, 231nn.1,3
   Wylie Memorial Chapel, PCUSA, 19
philosophy, 21, 23–24, 123, 124–25
Piepenbring, Ch., 21n.32, 92, 154
Pieters, K. J, 154, 155, 157n.2
Pittsburgh, PA
   University of Pittsburgh, 116n.1
Plooij, Daniel, 228, 228n.8
poetry, 16, 16n.15, 66, 67, 76, 79, 242–43
Poppen, Jacob, 167, 168n.1
positivism, 124, 127nn.8,9
Posnanski, Adolf, 219, 219nn.1,2,3
postmillennialism, 57
practical theology, 37n.89, 68, 70, 79, 81
Prat, F., 99
preaching, 55–56, 56n.154, 59n.164, 81–82, 81n.209, 82n.211, 236–37
predestination (see supralapsarianism)
premillennialism, 57, 59n.164, 68, 236–37
Presbyterian Alliance, 214n.1
Presbyterian and Reformed Review, 26n.54, 27, 27n.55, 131, 132, 133n.3, 134, 136, 138nn.1,2, 139, 139n.1, 143, 143n.1, 144–45, 145n.1, 145–46, 146n.1, 148, 150, 151, 153, 157n.1, 164, 165, 166n.1, 167, 167n.1, 169, 169nn.2,4, 171n.2, 174, 176nn.1,2,3, 178, 180n.1, 181, 181n.1, 182, 186, 187n.8, 188, 188n.5, 189, 190nn.2,4
Presbyterian Church, U.S.A., 26n.54, 63, 65, 67, 70n.190, 71, 72, 131, 133n.2, 134, 141–42, 159, 165–66, 202–3
Presbyterian Quarterly, 169n.2
Presbyterian Review, 26, 26n.54, 128n.1, 131, 132, 133n.1, 134

Presbytery of New Brunswick, PCUSA, 20n.27, 41, 60, 71n.192
Presbytery of New York, PCUSA, 35, 40n.97
Prichard, Paul, 236, 237n.4
Princeton, NJ, 46n.128, 47, 48, 48n.142, 213
   College (University), 191, 194, 202–3, 203n.1
   First Presbyterian Church, 41, 42, 43n.115, 71n.193, 216n.1
   Second Presbyterian Church, 41
   Theological Seminary, 13, 14, 19, 19nn.23,24, 20n.27, 29, 31–34, 35, 35n.82, 36n.83, 39, 41, 49, 49nn.143,144,145, 58, 61n.171, 62n.175, 63, 63n.177, 65, 68–73n.190, 70n.190, 72–73, 74, 80, 81n.207, 82, 85, 115–16, 116n.3, 128n.1, 130, 131n.2, 169, 172, 174, 175, 178–80, 184, 187, 194, 202–3, 203n.1, 211, 211n.2, 213, 215–16, 217, 227, 230, 231
   Stone Lectures, 44, 64, 195–96, 196.1, 197, 198, 198nn.1,2, 200, 201n.1, 206–8
Princeton Theological Review, 64, 74, 74n.200, 79, 213n.3
Proctor, Odessa Evans, 62n.174
prophets (OT), 74–79n.202, 92, 93, 138
protology, 50–51
Puritans, 228, 228n.9

Q document, 24, 24n.42

Radius, Marianne, 16n.15, 20, 20nn.26,27, 32n.72, 43, 43n.114, 45n.122, 46, 47, 49, 61, 61n.171, 62, 81n.208, 195n.1, 237, 237n.7, 248n.3
Rainy, Robert, 191, 192n.2
Rationalistic criticism, 171

269

redemptive history. *See* history of redemption
Redlands, CA, 41n.101, 43n.111, 47n.133
Reformed Church of America, 22n.36, 142, 143n.3, 145, 173, 175, 177nn.7,8, 186, 202n.1
Reformed Presbyterian Church of North America, 60, 60n.166, 65, 237n.5
Reformed Theology, 39, 65, 134–35, 141–42, 153–57, 159, 183–84. *See also* Calvinism
regeneration, 28, 147, 152, 155, 162–63
Remonstrants, 150, 151nn.2,5. *See also* Arminianism
Renan, Ernest, 56
revelation, 37–38, 37nn.87,88,89, 50–51, 53, 175–76, 181, 182
Rian, Edwin H., 35n.82
Ridderbos, Herman, 81, 81n.208
Ridderbos, J., 102
Roaring Branch, PA, 29n.68, 45–48nn.121,123,124,126,128,130,131,132, 59, 60, 60n.168, 61n.170, 62, 62nn.174,175, 66, 67, 85, 224, 225, 232, 233, 243
  Griffin Cemetery, 47, 60, 85
  Methodist Church, 45, 46, 62nn.174,175, 66–67
Roberts, William Henry, 19n.23, 20n.29, 116n.1
  letter to, 115–16(8/17/83)
Robinson, George L., 199, 199n.1
Robinson, H. Wheeler, 101
Ropes, James H., 97
Rostron, G. Nowell, 100
Rudolph, Robert K., 61n.170, 229, 231n.3
Rullmann, J. C., 118n.2
Rutgers, Frederick L., 121n.2

S. S. Belgenland I, 17
sacraments, 154–57, 161, 163
salvation, 35, 59n.164, 82n.210, 236
San Diego, CA, 47n.133, 59n.161
Santa Ana, CA, 46n.124, 47, 59–61, 61n.170, 64n.180, 72, 225, 239n.3
Saratoga New York General Assembly (PCUSA, 1890), 141–42
Satan. *See* Lucifer
Schaay, Joanna H. *See* Mrs. Abraham Kuyper
Schader, E., 93
Schaff, Philip, 137, 138n.6, 179
Schiedam, 15
Schlatter, A., 96, 97, 102
Schmidt, Nathaniel, 37n.89, 56, 97
Schnedermann, Georg, 55n.152, 91
Schopenhauer, Arthur, 123, 126, 127n.3
Schrader, Eberhard, 127n.5
Schultz, F. W., 90, 128n.1
Schultz, Hermann, 38n.91, 91
Schultze, Henry, 67, 110
Schürer, Emil, 234
Schweitzer, Albert, 27, 27n.57, 54, 55, 56, 56n.156, 83, 98, 100
Schweizer, Alexander, 150, 151n.6
Scott, Ernest, 97
Scott, Hugh M., 198, 198n.1
Shedd, W. G. T., 132, 133nn.3,5,8
Sheldon, Henry C., 98
Shiloh, 218–19
Shippers, Johanna A. *See* Mrs. Herman Bavinck
Sickenberger, Jos., 96
Sierra Madre, CA, 47n.133
Simonis, Johann, 219, 219n.4
Six, K, 99
Smith, Catherine F. *See* Catherine Vos
Smith, Emily, 41, 41n.101, 48
Smith, Henry, 41, 41n.101
Smith, J. Ritchie, 82

Smith, Lidia, 41, 48
Smith, Mary Ann, 41, 41n.101, 42n.107
Smitt, Wolter Wagter, 185, 186n.1, 188, 188n.4, 190
Social Gospel, 69, 69n.187, 84
Sohm, Rudolph, 191, 193n.7
Sokolowski, Emil, 95
South Africa, 15, 211
Spijknisse, 15
Steffens, Nicholas, 138, 138n.2, 142, 166, 166n.5, 175, 177n.7, 190, 190n.7
Stevens, George B., 38n.90, 94
Stevenson, Frank H., 71, 72, 72n.196, 75, 217n.1
   letter to, 217(12/19/28)
Stevenson, J. Ross, 20n.27, 35, 35n.82, 36n.83, 65, 68, 69, 69n.186, 70, 70n.190, 79, 82
Stone, Levi Payson, 196n.1
Stonehouse, Ned, 14n.6, 35n.82, 36n.83, 59n.164, 61, 65, 70n.189, 71, 240nn.1,2, 245, 246, 246n.1, 247n.2, 248n.4, 252n.1, 256n.1, 257n.2
   letters to, 239–40(12/15/38), 240(5/18/40), 245–46(7/21/44), 246–47(1/11/45)
Strack, Hermann, 22, 90, 127n.5, 128n.1
Strassburg, 23, 24, 42, 89, 124, 125
Strauss, David Friedrich, 56
Sudermann, Herman, 234
Supralapsarianism, 28, 28n.63, 29, 29nn.65,67, 149–51, 162, 165–66
Swart, Jelte, 39n.93, 99
Swete, Henry D., 98
Swierenga, Robert P., 22n.36
Swinburne, Algernon Charles, 17
Synopsis purioris, 150, 151n.4
synoptic question, 24, 24n.42
systematic theology, 49, 81n.209, 189

Ten Hoor, Foppe M., 157, 158n.5
Tennyson, Alfred Lord, 17
Tertullian, 210, 211n.5
Theologisch Tijdschrift, 132, 133n.4, 136
Theologische Studien, 136, 137n.2
Toronto, Canada
   Knox College, 199nn.1,3
Trijpsmaker, Jan, 180, 181n.2
Trinity, 160
Tübingen, 171
Turner, Orrin Jack, 246, 247n.1
Turretin, Francis, 26n.54, 28n.63, 34
two ages, 52–53
typology, 51–52
Tyrell, Charles A., 234

Ubbink, Johan T., 102
Ueltzen. *See* Ulzen
Uhland, Ludwig, 242, 243m.3
Ulzen (Ulsen), 15, 18n.18, 244, 245
Umajads, 24n.46
Union Theological Seminary, New York, NY, 26n.54, 40n.97, 138nn.5,6, 179–80, 180n.2
Union with Christ, 28, 59, 74–79, 156
Unitarian Theology, 203
United Presbyterian Church of North America, 199, 199n.2
Utrecht, 23, 119, 120n.2, 193, 221, 222n.2

Van den Vondel, Joost, 17
Van Felderen, Cornelis, 48, 48n.138, 213, 214n.1
   letter to, 213–14(9/5/21)
Van Til, Cornelius, 13, 36n.83, 61, 61n.170, 62, 62n.175, 64n.180, 65, 70n.190, 85, 223, 224n.1, 248n.4
Van Vessem, Anna (Mrs. Marinus), 14, 14n.7, 177n.5
Van Vessem, Marinus, 14n.7

Van Wyck, Augustus, 43n.117
Vanden Bosch, Jacob G., 14n.5, 24n.44, 33n.78, 112
Veenhof, Jan, 23n.36
Veldhuizen, A. van, 102
Vercouille, Jozef, 241, 241n.1
Verkoolje, Johannes, 241
Vermilye, J. B., 198n.2
virgin birth, 218–19
Voetius, Gisbert, 150, 151n.11
Volkertsz, Jan. See Trijpsmaker, Jan
Volkmar, Gustav, 56
Voorthuizen, Henri du Marchie van, 126, 127n.18
Vos, Aaltje Beuker, 14, 18n.18, 127n.17, 174
Vos, Anna. See Anna Van Vessem
Vos, Bernardus, 32n.71, 41n.101, 42, 42n.108, 43, 43nn.111,113,48, 49nn.143,144, 59n.163, 60, 61nn.170,171, 62, 62n.173, 64n.180, 70n.190, 221, 221n.3, 232, 233, 233n.2, 234
Vos, Bert John, 14, 14n.8, 45, 116, 116n.5, 174, 177n.4, 190, 190n.5
Vos, Brian, 16n.14
Vos, Catherine, 23n.37, 41–43nn.101,102,103,104,105,106,107,110,111, 44, 46, 46nn.124,129, 47, 59–60, 62n.175, 63, 85, 187, 188n.2, 190n.3, 192, 193, 195n.1, 204, 224, 246
  death certificate, 41n.101
  marriage, 42, 42n.107
Vos, Geerhardus
  becomes US citizen, 32n.74
  bibliography, 89–112, 247–48
  call to Princeton, 29–36
  Calvin Theological Seminary, 18–19, 25–36
  filiopiety, 22–23, 32n.72, 33, 245

Germany, 21–25
illness (1932), 23n.37, 59, 59n.162, 224, 224n.3, 225, 228n.2
installation at Calvin Theological Seminary, 25, 25nn.49,52, 126
marriage, 42, 42n.107, 187, 188n.2, 190n.3
poetry, 16, 16n.15, 17, 225, 228n.3, 243, 243n.5, 251–57
Princeton Theological Seminary, 20–21, 30–34, 36–41, 49
works
  Biblical Theology: Old and New Testaments, 51, 66, 104, 105, 229–30, 231
  "The Doctrine of the Covenant in Reformed Theology," 28, 28n.60, 90, 169, 169n.3, 222, 222n.3
  Dogmatiek, 26, 92
  The Eschatology of the Old Testament, 52, 64n.180, 104, 107, 109
  Grace and Glory, 19n.24, 55–56, 63nn.177,178, 71n.193, 73, 82n.209, 103, 107, 108n.3
  "The Idea of Biblical Theology as a Science and as a Theological Discipline," 36, 36n.86, 41, 52, 91, 188, 188n.6
  "Jeremiah's Plaint and Its Answer," 74–81
  Die Kämpfe und Streitigkeiten . . ., 24n.46, 89, 127n.10
  The Kingdom of God and the Church, 54–55, 63n.178, 94–95
  The Letters of Geerhardus Vos, 108
  The Mosaic Origin of the Pentateuchal Codes, 13, 15n.10, 20n.30, 63n.178, 89, 234
  The Pauline Eschatology, 13, 14n.6, 36n.83, 52, 57–58, 63, 64,

Index of Subjects and Names

69n.187, 74, 74n.201, 103, 220, 221n.1
"The Pauline Teaching in Survey," 27n.59
"The Prospects of American Theology," 25, 25n.52, 26, 90
The Self-Disclosure of Jesus, 56–57, 63, 103, 245, 246n.2
The Teaching of the Epistle to the Hebrews, 104, 105
Vos, Geerhardus, Jr. (Jerry), 16n.15, 43, 43n.115, 48, 49n.144, 59, 61n.171, 62
Vos, Gertrude, 14, 14n.9, 177n.5
Vos, Jan Hendrick, 14, 14n.7, 15, 15nn.10,11,12, 17, 17nn.16,17, 18, 18n.18, 25, 33n.78, 42, 174–75, 177n.6, 244, 245
Vos, Johannes Geerhardus, 43, 43n.112, 60, 62, 237, 237n.5
Vos, Marianne. *See* Marianne Radius
Vos, Maude Alida, 190n.6

Wace, Henry, 191, 192n.5
Wagenaar, Larry J., 16n.13
Warfield, B. B., 14, 26, 26n.54, 28, 28n.62, 29, 29n.66, 35, 35n.82, 36, 49, 49nn.143,144, 61n.170, 63n.177, 69, 69n.185, 72, 133nn.1,3, 134, 140, 144, 148, 149, 153, 165, 174, 178, 179, 182, 184, 186, 188, 189, 191, 213n.3
    letters to, 128(2/2/89), 129–31(10/22/89), 138(4/9/90), 139(6/13/90), 140(7/2/90), 143(8/5/90), 145–46(1/31/91), 147–48(2/12/91), 151–53(3/12/91), 160–64(7/7/91), 166–67(8/29/91), 167–68(9/8/91), 168–69(9/28/91), 170–71(3/18/92)
Watkins, Eric, 16n.15
Weaver, J. D., 50n.146
Webster, Ransom L., 112
Weiss, C. P. Bernhard, 22, 127n.5
Weiss, Johannes, 55n.152, 56, 91, 95
Wellhausen, Julius, 21n.30
Wells, H. G., 83n.212
Wernle, Paul, 56n.154, 95
West, Andrew F., 193, 193n.1, 194, 195n.3
Western Theological Seminary, Pittsburgh, PA, 26n.54
Westminster Assembly, 162, 169
Westminster Confession of Faith, 26n.54, 65, 67, 69, 71n.192, 83n.212, 131, 132, 133n.2, 134–35, 141–42, 143n.1, 144, 147, 165, 168, 169nn.1,2, 197n.1, 198n.2, 222
Westminster Shorter Catechism, 160, 162
Westminster Theological Journal, 239, 240, 240nn.1,2
Westminster Theological Seminary (Philadelphia, PA), 35, 36n.83, 47n.131, 60, 60n.169, 61n.170, 65, 68, 70, 70n.190, 71, 71n.191, 79, 80, 82, 215n.3, 217n.1, 220, 221n.5, 223, 224, 224n.2, 232–35, 239, 240n.1, 248n.3
Wielenga, D. K., 181, 181n.4, 185, 186n.2, 188, 188n.7, 190, 192
Wielenga, Gerrit, 181, 181n.3, 182, 183n.1, 185, 186n.1, 188, 188n.7, 190
Wildeboer, Gerrit, 37n.88, 92, 205, 206n.1
Wilson, Robert Dick, 70n.190, 71, 71n.191, 72

273

Wilson, Woodrow, 45n.120
Windelband, Wilhelm, 24, 124, 126, 127n.6, 126
Winstanley, Edward W., 98
Winter, Egbert, 190n.8
Witsius, Herman, 152, 152n.1, 156
Woltjer, Jan, 121n.2
Wood, Irving F., 96
Woods, Laura H., 80n.205
Woolley, Paul, 47n.131, 59n.163, 60n.169, 224n.1

letters to, 224(9/9/32), 232–33(1/27/36), 233(1/29/36), 234–35(2/22/36)
Woudstra, M. H., 112
Wrede, Wilhelm, 56–57

Yale University, 203, 203n.4

Zeller, Eduard G., 127n.5
Zöckler, Otto, 90
Zwaan, J. de, 102
Zwaanstra, Henry, 22n.36